ADVANCING THE LEARNING AGENDA IN JEWISH EDUCATION

ADVANCING THE LEARNING AGENDA IN JEWISH EDUCATION

Edited by
JON A. LEVISOHN
and JEFFREY S. KRESS

Boston
2018

The research for this book and its publication were made possible by the generous support of the Jack, Joseph and Morton Mandel Center for Studies in Jewish Education, a partnership between Brandeis University and the Jack, Joseph and Morton Mandel Foundation of Cleveland, Ohio.

Library of Congress Cataloging-in-Publication Data

Names: Levisohn, Jon A., editor. | Kress, Jeffrey S., editor.

Title: Advancing the learning agenda in Jewish education / Jon A. Levisohn and Jeffrey S. Kress, editors.

Description: Boston: Academic Studies Press, 2018. | Includes bibliographical references.

Identifiers: LCCN 2018023237 (print) | LCCN 2018024454 (ebook) | ISBN 9781618117540 (ebook) | ISBN 9781618117533 (hardcover) | ISBN 9781618118790 (pbk.)

Subjects: LCSH: Jews—Education. | Jewish religious education. | Judaism—Study and teaching.

Classification: LCC LC715 (ebook) | LCC LC715 .A33 2018 (print) | DDC 296.6/8—dc23

LC record available at https://lccn.loc.gov/2018023237

© Academic Studies Press, 2018
ISBN 978-1-618117-53-3 (hardcover)
ISBN 978-1-618117-54-0 (electronic)
ISBN 978-1-618118-79-0 (paperback)

Book design by Kryon Publishing Services (P) Ltd.
www.kryonpublishing.com

Cover design by Ivan Grave

Published by Academic Studies Press
28 Montfern Avenue
Brighton, MA 02135, USA
press@academicstudiespress.com
www.academicstudiespress.com

Table of Contents

Introduction: What the "Learning Agenda" Is and Why It Matters   1
Jon A. Levisohn and Jeffrey S. Kress

PART ONE
Learning from the Learning Sciences   9

Activating Jewish Learners: Positioning Youth for Persistent Success in Jewish Learning and Living   11
Rena Dorph and Christian D. Schunn

Fostering Identity and Disposition Development in Jewish Education: A View from the Learning Sciences   29
Janet L. Kolodner

Learning about Learning in Jewish Education   53
Ari Y. Kelman

Old Traditions, New Practices: A Proposal for a Return to Text Study as a Centerpiece of Jewish Community and Family Life   73
Daniel P. Resnick and Lauren B. Resnick

PART TWO
Learning from Jewish Education   95

Observing *Havruta* Learning from the Perspective of the Learning Sciences   97
Baruch Schwarz

Learning the Whole Game of Shabbat   116
Joseph Reimer

What We Can Learn about Learning from Holocaust Education   133
Simone Schweber

PART THREE
Conceptualizing Learning Outcomes   145

Is this a *Real* Story? Learning Critical History and Learning Its Limits   147
Sam Wineburg

Learning to be Jewish   165
Eli Gottlieb

The Holistic Goals of Jewish Education   183
Gil G. Noam and Jeffrey S. Kress

Subject-Specific Learning Versus Jewish-Developmental Outcomes in Jewish Education: What Should We Aim For?   205
Jeffrey S. Kress and Jon A. Levisohn

Index   221

Introduction: What the "Learning Agenda" Is and Why It Matters

Jon A. Levisohn and Jeffrey S. Kress

The title of this volume declares its aspiration: to advance the learning agenda in Jewish education. What does that mean? Why does something called "the learning agenda" need to be advanced? And how might that happen?

Over the past thirty years, we have seen the growth of familiar forms of Jewish education and the development of new ones. In the former category, we can name day schools, camps, academic Jewish studies, and Israel trips, as well as innovative new forms of supplementary Jewish education and renewed interest in early childhood education. In the latter, we can point to Jewish service learning, Jewish environmental and food programming, Jewish heritage tourism to other countries, online Jewish learning and Jewish gaming, and more. In every sector, talented and creative educators are developing new materials and new pedagogies.

Yet, amid the creativity and growth, we believe that contemporary American Jewish education is not as strong as it could be. And we believe that at least part of the reason for this is that American Jewish education suffers from a lack of clarity about our desired learning outcomes, inconsistent focus on and assessment of those outcomes, and insufficient understanding of the experiences of learners. For example, supplementary school educators have been known to say that their programs should be more like camp. This is undoubtedly an important development, but their focus tends to be on the atmosphere and activities, the things that make camp "fun" rather than clarifying appropriate learning outcomes or documenting impact. The field of Israel education, according to several studies, bounces between uncritical celebrations of Israel and narrowly focused advocacy activities, lacking a coherent framework that describes what can reasonably be called "learning outcomes" in the domain of Israel education. And in higher education, academics in the field of Jewish studies tend to invest their time and energy in crafting the excellent lecture or presentation, or assembling the most important materials into a syllabus, but invest far less time in exploring their students' understanding.

It is a truism in teacher education that novice teachers must overcome a natural tendency to focus on themselves—on saying and doing the right thing in the classroom—in order to focus on the students in front of them. In her work on novices, Sharon Feiman-Nemser calls this the "transition to pedagogical thinking."[1] We can also describe it as a move from thinking about *teaching*, primarily, to thinking about *learning*. At the risk of hyperbole, we believe that this is a move that the field of Jewish education, as a whole, needs to make. The point is not to reach consensus or unanimity about what those desired learning outcomes are. That is unlikely to happen, and our efforts here should certainly not be understood as endorsing one particular set of learning outcomes over others. But we do believe that educational leaders in the various settings in which Jewish education takes place need to focus more attention on learning.

Thus, the "learning agenda" is shorthand for encouraging increased focus on conceptualizing learning outcomes in sophisticated ways, more sustained attention to how learning actually happens and how it sometimes fails to happen, and deeper curiosity about the experience of learners themselves in educational environments. "Advancing the learning agenda" means promoting these ideas among practitioners and researchers alike. We want educators and educational policy makers to be asking more and better questions about what kinds of learning ought to be happening, and what kinds of evidence we might have that they are.

Why? We are scholars, but our interest in advancing the learning agenda is not only a scholarly one. Our interest is also a practical one. We believe that the more we understand about what we want students to learn and how that learning comes about (or does not come about), the more directed and more effective our educational efforts will become. In other words, advancing the learning agenda in the ways we have described is a strategic intervention into the system. We believe that the best way to improve pedagogic practice is by helping educators, of all kinds, to be more reflective about their desired

---

1   Sharon Feiman-Nemser and Margret Buchmann, *The First Year of Teacher Preparation: Transition to Pedagogical Thinking?* (East Lansing, MI: The Institute for Research on Teaching, Michigan State University, 1985), microfilm.

outcomes, more self-critical about the effectiveness of their teaching, and more curious about the learning of their students.

An example may be useful to illustrate what this can look like. Recently, as part of another project, we have had the opportunity to share the results of a pilot study of recent graduates of Jewish day schools—specifically, a study of their thinking about and understanding of rabbinic literature. Setting aside the specific findings of that study, what is relevant here is the reaction of educators when they learn about the findings, or even when they encounter the interview transcripts. In this case, we watched as they responded with energetic and intense curiosity. They eagerly pulled apart the data, interpreting nuances in the students' formulations and raising endless questions about their significance. Unprompted, they turned their analyses back on their own teaching, challenging their prior assumptions, and they expressed excitement about asking similar questions of their own students or even designing their own studies.

We cannot claim that all educators will react in similar ways, of course, nor do we know precisely how these reactions will translate into classroom practices. But we consider these experiences as corroborations of our hypothesis. Professionals in the field of Jewish education have precious few opportunities to dive into the learning of their students, and few structures to support doing so. The cultures of Jewish educational programs and institutions do not emphasize this kind of attention to learning. However, when given the opportunity to do so, educators seize hold of it with enthusiasm. This is what it can look like to advance the learning agenda in Jewish education.

∗∗∗

For the most part, the chapters of this book do not present specific empirical studies of learners and learning (although almost all are based on empirical work by the authors or others). Instead, these chapters and this book strive to advance the learning agenda in different ways—by promoting nuanced ideas about what learning means in Jewish education and by drawing on work outside of Jewish education to propose new models and frameworks. In several instances, authors took the opportunity to think out loud, as it were, about how we might think differently about learning in Jewish education.

The first section of the book, "Learning from the Learning Sciences," does this most explicitly. Two chapters, one by Rena Dorph and Christian Schunn and one by Janet Kolodner, build upon extensive research in science education, the most well-developed area of the learning sciences. Researchers in that field have long understood that they cannot be satisfied with rote learning, that the desired outcomes are more subtle and nuanced (and harder to assess) than that. In Kolodner's chapter, she describes her work in developing a series of science education programs that explicitly focus on cultivating a kind of scientist- or engineer-identity, and draws implications from that work for Jewish education. Dorph and Schunn, on the other hand, delineate an outcome that they call "science learning activation," that is, a set of dispositions, practices, and knowledge that enable success in proximal learning experiences. They propose, in other words, that the goal of science education is to enable further (richer, deeper) science learning, which is enabled by "science learning activation." The analogy to Jewish education, while imperfect, is generative: they propose that in Jewish education, too, the goal is to enable further (richer, deeper) Jewish learning—and not just learning but also living.

In the third chapter in this section, Ari Kelman starts by broadening our purview; he wants us not to focus on learning specific Jewish content, primarily, but rather to think about "learning Jewish," i.e., how people learn the numerous practices, formal and informal, that comprise Jewishness. He then roams widely over the literature on learning in general education in order to chart a number of promising avenues for investigating learning in Jewish education, avenues that are attuned to the situated and social nature of learning in ways that Jewish education rarely is.

Finally, in the last chapter of this section, co-authors Lauren Resnick and Daniel Resnick call our attention to the dramatic shift in the scholarship on general education from didactic pedagogy to dialogic pedagogy—pedagogy that creates an environment for substantive conversation around a text. This paradigm emphasizes inquiry over information transmission. Notably, this kind of dialogic pedagogy has begun to take hold in fields such as science and math, and also, unsurprisingly, in the humanities. The Resnicks celebrate the tradition of text study within Judaism, but call for renewal of that tradition, especially in liberal Jewish settings.

The second section of the book, "Learning from Jewish Education," includes three chapters that focus on specific Jewish educational settings. The authors are each experienced researchers of those settings, but in these chapters, their task is not merely descriptive. Instead, they attend to those settings in order to draw out ideas or implications for learning more generally.

It is commonplace, in the study of contemporary Jews, to separate the orthodox and especially the *haredim*, or ultra-orthodox. Their lives are different, with ritual and cultural practices that seem oriented around an entirely distinct set of norms. It is a culture that, at least for men in *yeshivas*, is intensely focused on *lernen*—a Yiddish term which is typically Anglicized to "learning" but which, unlike the standard usage of the word "learning" as an achievement term, actually signifies the process of reading and discussing classical texts. Baruch Schwarz believes, however, that we have a lot to learn from how *haredim* engage in *lernen* in *yeshivas*, especially in terms of the positive valuation of argumentation and the cultural conditions that support high levels of self-motivation for study.

The contemporary liberal Jewish summer camp is about as far from the traditional *haredi yeshiva* as one can imagine. But just as Schwarz brings the perspective of the learning sciences to bear on the latter, Joseph Reimer brings that perspective to bear on the former. And what he sees, when he does so, is an educational opportunity that is not fully realized—in part because it is not well conceptualized. His particular focus is on Shabbat at camp. Kids learn to do Shabbat, which is unlike anything they know from home, over time, through a process that looks a lot like Jean Lave and Etienne Wenger's "legitimate peripheral participation."[2] But then their learning trajectory flattens out. Reimer argues that David Perkins' concept of "whole game learning"[3] provides a more compelling framework, not just for understanding what *does* happen when kids learn to do Shabbat at camp, but for imagining about what *could* happen if we were to think about this process more ambitiously.

The last chapter in this section turns to Holocaust education as a location for thinking about learning. Simone Schweber begins by admitting that we may be averse to trying to learn from an extreme case like Holocaust education, but persists in her inquiry nonetheless. She avoids the standard approach, which is to emphasize the moral lessons of the Holocaust. Instead, she finds other important lessons about learning—about appreciating the "messiness" of real lives and real moral quandaries, about the ways in which contexts shape our thinking, and most generally, about a desired outcome of Jewish education that she calls "reasonable Jews."

The third and final section of the book, "Conceptualizing Learning Outcomes," includes four chapters that tackle the question of learning outcomes directly. Of course, this distinction is somewhat artificial, because other chapters also propose ways of thinking about what we want students or participants to learn. Dorph and Schunn, for example, proposed "Jewish learning activation" as an outcome. Kolodner focused on fostering a self-conception of

---
2 Jean Lave and Etienne Wenger, *Situated Learning: Legitimate Peripheral Participation* (Cambridge: Cambridge University Press, 1991).
3 David N. Perkins, *Making Learning Whole: How Seven Principles of Teaching Can Transform Education*. 1st ed. (San Francisco: Jossey-Bass, 2009).

oneself as capable within the domain of Jewishness. Schweber, we just noted, identified "reasonable Jews" as her desired outcome. But the three chapters in this section take up the question of outcomes directly, not just identifying them but exploring them and also problematizing them.

For those familiar with Sam Wineburg's research on historical thinking, it should come as no surprise that he is impatient with hagiography or mythologizing. But in his chapter here, he tries to move beyond the poles of uncritical memory and critical history, noting that there is a role that the past does and perhaps should play that is not quite encompassed by—and in fact stands in tension with—the bounds of academic, critical history. "Can there be a course," he asks, "that steers between dogmatic belief and absolutist disbelief?" Lurking beneath the question is a fundamental challenge to our assumptions about why study history, especially Jewish history, at all.

When we ask the question about how Jewish education differs from other kinds of education, we might be tempted to argue that Jewish education is a form of religious education. But it turns out that we're not quite so clear on what that means. Eli Gottlieb has been thinking about and studying the religiosity of religious education for a long time, or more specifically, has been studying how children and others think about God and theology and how they might be encouraged to do so differently. His chapter here surveys what he's learned from this process; perhaps most intriguing is his suggestion that, among our desired Jewish educational outcomes, is the capacity to engage in the kind of "epistemic switching" that he documents among a set of sophisticated Jewish adults.

The third chapter of this section argues for greater attention to social-emotional learning outcomes in Jewish education—and not just greater attention but in fact more rigorous assessment as well. The Resnicks advocated for learning texts. Reimer focused on learning Shabbat. Wineburg explored the learning of history. But for Gil Noam and Jeffrey Kress, all of these subject-specific outcomes are overly narrow, and secondary to our primary desired outcome in Jewish education as in other arenas, namely, the cultivation of healthy, well-adjusted, mature individuals, with all the inter- and intra-personal qualities that those adjectives entail. This is not an add-on to the core educational endeavor, conceived of as learning "content." This *is* the core educational endeavor.

Thus, Noam and Kress, in expanding beyond the cognitive, build on aspects of earlier chapters. Kolodner, for example, emphasized the cultivation of a certain kind of identity. Kelman explored the myriad ways that people learn to be Jewish. Schweber's conception of "reasonable Jews" goes far beyond what those Jews know to a stance they take toward the tradition, the community, and the world in general. Indeed, all of the scholars in this volume would endorse the idea that advancing the learning agenda means, among other things, attending not just to what students know, and not even what they can do or how they feel, but rather, to the kinds of people that they learn to become.

Finally, the last chapter of the section and the book—co-authored by the editors—frames a debate between two different ways of thinking about the desired outcomes of Jewish education. The first way, argued by "Abraham" in the chapter, focuses on the development of the student, the Jewish individual. The second way, argued by "Sarah," focuses on achievement within specific domains. Neither position is entirely satisfactory on its own. But in pursuing the debate, we believe that we can offer some helpful ideas to the field, to think in deeper, more nuanced, and more critical ways about learning in Jewish education. This, in the end, is the "learning agenda" that we want to advance.

**

This volume is a product of a research project at the Jack, Joseph and Morton Mandel Center for Studies in Jewish Education at Brandeis University. The authors presented their ideas initially at a conference in March 2015. We are grateful to the other participants in that conference for their critical and collegial input. We are also grateful to the staff of the Mandel Center for their contributions that have enabled our scholarly activity, including Elizabeth Dinolfo, Pamella Endo, Rebecca Neville, and Susanne Shavelson. Finally, we are grateful to the Jack, Joseph and Morton Mandel Foundation, for their ongoing support of scholarship on Jewish education, in the service of a thriving Jewish future.

Part One

LEARNING FROM THE LEARNING SCIENCES

Activating Jewish Learners: Positioning Youth for Persistent Success in Jewish Learning and Living

Rena Dorph and Christian D. Schunn

What can Jewish education learn from science education? In this chapter, the first of two chapters by learning scientists who focus on science education, Rena Dorph and Christian Schunn draw on their theory of "science learning activation" to make the case for a parallel theory of "Jewish learning activation." According to this theory, successful learning happens when one particular learning experience enables and motivates the learner to undertake and succeed in the next learning experience. What they mean by "science learning activation" is the combination of dispositions, skills, and knowledge that enable learners to be successful in subsequent science learning experiences. It can serve as a goal for Jewish learning experiences over and above the specific knowledge or skills that a participant might acquire.

Introduction

A striking feature of the body of research on the impact of Jewish education is that much of it employs behavioral indicators in adulthood (rather than cognitive or affective indicators) as the outcome measures by which the effectiveness of Jewish learning experiences that occur during youth are judged. For example, Steven Cohen[1] notes that attending day school has a positive

---
* Special thanks to our colleagues Kevin Crowley (The Learning Research and Development

(albeit quite modest) correlation with four indicators that he examined (inmarriage, observance, affiliation, and a feeling of belonging). The same study also notes that some dosages of supplementary school (in particular the once-a-week format) may actually have a negative impact on these indicators. Cohen's most promising finding: participation in three informal educational experiences (including camp, youth group, and visiting Israel) during one's teen years actually surpasses even the impact of day school.

The assumption underlying these claims is that learning experiences influence youth in a way which would manifest in behaviors when they are adults, related to marriage, observance, synagogue affiliation, and belonging. However, there is no clear theory or chain of evidence to help us understand why that assumption is appropriate or what the mechanisms are that connect early learning experiences with complex adult behaviors. While these and other sociological studies' findings offer interesting fodder for consideration, they may have received more attention than they ought to and have been misinterpreted to mean more than they should because there is a paucity of alternatives.

What is missing? The field of Jewish education lacks a body of research that allows us to systematically and empirically examine the causality and underlying mechanisms of relationships between learning experiences, proximal learning outcomes, and more distal impacts. More specifically, the field lacks a learning theory that provides a conceptual framework for describing how Jewish content knowledge, skill sets, and ritual practices are learned through both intentionally designed and naturally occurring experiences; theoretically grounded notions of what "success" looks like and the standards that would embody that vision; agreement on what counts as evidence of learning; rigorous, scalable assessments that can cut across learning experiences; and a research agenda that would enable us to develop the frameworks, tools, and studies that would provide us with anything better.

In the face of the correlational and behaviorally focused existing findings and absent a body of research to help us understand the reasons we found them, this chapter addresses some critical questions:

Center, University of Pittsburgh) and Matthew Cannady (The Lawrence Hall of Science, University of California, Berkeley) who work with us in the Science Learning Activation Lab; they are our co-authors on writing related to this in science. We credit them as co-authors of the aspects of this chapter that relate to science learning activation.

1 Steven M. Cohen, *A Tale of Two Jewries: The "Inconvenient Truth" for American Jews* (Jewish Life Network/ Steinhardt Foundation, 2006).

1. How does/could/should the field of Jewish education conceptualize consequential outcomes for Jewish learning experiences?
   a. What do we mean by persistent engagement Jewish living and learning or positive Jewish identity?
   b. How can we think about the learning that students do and the effects that that learning has on them, on their self-understandings, on their lives?
2. What set of Jewish learning outcomes—dispositions, practices, and knowledge—positions, empowers, and enables young people to engage in Jewish learning and living more frequently, in more settings, and with greater success across their lives?
   a. What enables persistent engagement in Jewish learning and living in the twenty-first century?
   b. What experiences support youth to develop positive Jewish identities?

This chapter responds to these questions by offering a theoretical framework for the substance and function of an outcome construct called *Jewish learning activation* that extrapolates from the work that we have done related to science learning. Analogies and inferences drawn from them are necessarily inductive rather than deductive; however, analogies are often a productive source of inspiration in all areas of academia. First, we provide a brief synopsis of the work-to-date related to *science learning activation*. Next, we consider the *Jewish learning activation* analog and the implications of this framework for designing and evaluating Jewish learning experiences. We conclude the chapter by discussing implications for a Jewish learning research agenda that is grounded in this framework.

The Analogy of Jewish Learning to Science Learning

How is Jewish learning like science learning? Before we delve into the specifics of the construct of Jewish learning activation and its implications, it may be helpful to consider the reasons, possibilities, and limits of the analogy.

- *The enterprises themselves:* Both Jewish tradition and science seek to provide explanations for natural and physical phenomena through a process of examining evidence, argumentation, and meaning making. They both seek to understand the origins and place of human beings in the world. Although the exact phenomena being examined, the typical sources and

types of evidence, and the rules of discourse have differences, there are many parallels across the enterprises.
- *The learning process*: Both Jewish learning and science learning have curiosity, questioning, inquiry, social support, and texts as critical drivers and processes of the overall learning experience.
- *The learning outcomes:* The short-term outcomes we seek to achieve have many parallels and overlaps. That is, we believe that both Jewish and science education seek to develop a combination of dispositions, practices, and knowledge within the learner that drive toward proximal successes. This hypothesis is the crux of the discussion of the remainder of this chapter.
- *The role of identity:* Both science educators/funders and Jewish educators/funders, believe that the development of a (science/Jewish) identity or an identification with a (scientific/Jewish) community is a critical aspect of one's self-concept on the path toward positive and lifelong engagement with the subject.
- *The desired long-term impact:* On the one hand, both the scientific and Jewish communities want to create educational opportunities that enable some individuals to become professionals in the field—professional scientists (science researchers, science teachers) and Jewish leaders (scholars of Jewish studies, teachers of Jewish studies, lay or professional leaders of Jewish institutions). On the other hand, the majority of efforts of both science education and Jewish education is about supporting the development of a (scientifically/Jewishly) literate society or community. Literacy in this context means that every citizen will appreciate that ways of thinking, reasoning, and values of the disciplinary (science/Jewish) community and apply them to their daily lives and communal/societal participation.

The Case of Science Learning Activation

The Science Learning Activation Lab (the Lab) is a multi-institutional research collaborative[2] dedicated to understanding the malleable factors associated with persistent success in science learning and pursuit of STEM[3]

---

2 The Lawrence Hall of Science at the University of California, Berkeley; The Learning Research and Development Center at the University of Pittsburgh, and SRI.
3 STEM is the acronym for science, technology, engineering, and mathematics.

careers and, in turn, supporting learning experience design.[4] The work of the Lab responds to the need to build a theory that explains both short- and long-term effects in science learning. Expanding on recent advances in science education, cognitive and social psychology, and socio-cultural studies, Lab researchers propose a construct called *science learning activation* and a theoretical framework that describes the characteristics, function, and impact of this construct. We hypothesize that a new construct called *science learning activation*[5] is one such critical factor. We define science learning activation as the combination of dispositions, practices, and knowledge that enables success in proximal science learning experiences and are in turn influenced by this success (i.e., participate in a positive feedback loop over time). We refer to the elements of this combination of dispositions, practices, and knowledge as *dimensions* of activation.

Our conceptualization of science learning activation focuses on what the learner consistently carries from one experience to the next (dispositions, practices, and knowledge) as opposed to what is less consistently carried from one experience to the next (e.g., particular physical resources, personal relationships). *Dispositions* refer to attitudes and beliefs about the self vis-à-vis various aspects of learning science content and engaging in science practices. *Practices* refer to skills and abilities that an individual draws upon as resources to solve science-related problems and scenarios in productive ways. *Knowledge* refers to the (explicit, declarative) understanding of science phenomena, concepts, theories, processes, and social resources that are used together with scientific practices to engage in scientific sense making and solve science-related problems and scenarios in productive ways. Further, this conceptualization focuses on *proximal science learning experiences,* that is, the most temporally proximate learning experience an individual has (e.g., their next science class, next visit

---

4 The Science Learning Activation Lab engages in multiple, concurrent lines of research. More information about design and methodology associated of these various studies can be found on the Lab's website, www.activationlab.org.

5 Rena Dorph et al., "How Science Learning Activation Enables Success for Youth in Science Learning," *Electronic Journal of Science Education* 20, no. 8 (2016): 49–85; Rena Dorph et al., "Crumpled Molecules and Edible Plastic: Science Learning Activation in Out-of-School Time," *Afterschool Matters* 25 (Spring 2017): 18–28; Rena Dorph et al., "Science Learning Activation: Positioning Youth for Persistent Success in Science Learning, Literacy, and Careers" (presentation, American Education Research Association Annual Meeting, San Francisco, CA, 2013); Rena Dorph et al., "Activating Young Science Learners: Igniting Persistent Engagement in Science and Inquiry" (structured poster session, American Education Research Association Annual Meeting, Vancouver, BC, Canada, 2012).

to a science center, next time they do a science activity at home, next time they participate in an afterschool science club) as opposed to the current or long-distance experiences.

Extensive literature reviews and empirical research have revealed four dimensions (or aspects) of *science learning activation* each of which constitutes useful set of personal resources that an individual carries from one learning experience to the next:

1. *Fascination* with natural and physical phenomenon (emotional and cognitive attachment/obsession with science topics and tasks);
2. *Valuing* of science (understands various intersections of self with science knowledge and skills and places value on those interactions within their social context);
3. *Competency beliefs* about self in science (perceives one's self as capable of successfully engaging in science activities and practices); and
4. *Scientific sensemaking* (engages with science-related content as a sensemaking activity using methods generally aligned with the practices of science).

These resources impact the chance that an individual will have a successful learning experience. We operationalize "success" as four elements that designers of science learning experiences hope to impact through their interventions *and* that function as we describe further below. These elements of success include: (1) choosing to participate in science learning opportunities; (2) experiencing positive engagement (affective, behavioral, and cognitive) during science learning experiences; (3) perceiving oneself as successful during science learning experiences; and (4) meeting science learning goals during these experiences.

A successful learning experience supports the individual to develop higher levels of the dimensions of science learning activation, which, in turn, will increase the chances of success the next time a learner bumps into a potential science learning experience. This positive feedback loop—from science learning activation to success to science learning activation—is the heart of our framework. Learning experiences that are more likely to lead to positive changes in science learning activation can resonate forward and make it more likely that youth follow pathways to science. Conversely, poor experiences can lead to declines in science learning activation that undermine future success and thus make it more difficult to follow a science pathway.

In order to test the hypotheses embedded in this theory, we have developed measures of each dimension and each success element and then empirically investigated whether the hypothesized dimensions of activation indeed both predict successes and further increase as the result of successes. Thus far, our empirical studies of youth have demonstrated the relationship among the four dimensions of science learning activation and success in science learning experiences.[6] The studies, using complex statistical models that are carefully controlled for learner demographics and prior achievement, found positive connections between each dimension and one or more of the forms of success.

The studies also found that the success variables were also predictive of increases in levels of the dimensions of science learning activation. For example, fascination is strongly correlated with choice preferences while scientific sensemaking is correlated with content learning.[7] These findings help illuminate the mechanism by which science learning activation could have both short and long term predictive power. By supporting success (choice, engagement, and learning) in proximal learning experiences, science learning activation provides momentum—a ramping up effect—that supports persistent engagement and success in science learning over time. It also offers an explanation for the opposite effect of decreased momentum, lack of persistence, and decreased success in science learning over time.

The Jewish Learning Analog

So, what is the analog for Jewish learning? What set of dispositions, practices, and knowledge position a young person for success in Jewish learning and living? What does "success" mean in a Jewish learning framework? Clearly some aspects must be different. While the science learning activation framework we described was built on a wealth of prior empirical studies, researcher insight, and practitioner input, the ideas here are constructed based on our extrapolation of that work to the Jewish learning context. Accordingly, the ideas we present for what must be adapted are a hypothesis rather than a tested theory. Much effort would be required

---

6 Dorph et al., "How Science Learning Activation Enables," 49–85; Dorph et al., "Crumpled Molecules and Edible Plastic," 18–28; Dorph et al., "Science Learning Activation"; Dorph et al., "Activating Young Science Learners."
7 Dorph et al., "How Science Learning Activation Enables," 49–85.

to investigate these assertions further. We describe an approach for such a research agenda later in this chapter.

Analogous to the science learning context, we define *Jewish learning activation* as the combination of dispositions, practices, and knowledge that enables success in proximal Jewish learning and living experiences and are in turn influenced by these successes. We refer to the elements of this combination of dispositions, practices, and knowledge as *dimensions* of activation. Also similar to the science learning context, our conceptualization of Jewish learning activation focuses on what the learner consistently carries from one experience to the next (dispositions, practices, and knowledge) as opposed to what is less consistently carried from one experience to the next (e.g., particular physical resources, personal relationships). *Dispositions* refer to attitudes and beliefs about the self vis-à-vis various aspects of learning Jewish content, engaging in Jewish practices, and belonging to a Jewish community and the Jewish people. *Practices* refer to skills and abilities that an individual draws on as resources to engage in Jewish learning and living in meaningful ways. *Knowledge* refers to the (explicit, declarative) understanding of Jewish concepts, traditions, values, and social resources that are used together with Jewish practices (including but not limited to ritual practices) to engage in Jewish living and community in productive ways.

Like the science learning context, this conceptualization focuses on *proximal Jewish learning experiences*. At the same time, we broaden this idea a bit within the Jewish context to include proximal Jewish living experiences, as well. In particular, in the Jewish context we are looking for both enabling success in temporally proximate learning experiences an individual has (e.g., next Jewish learning opportunity; next time they visit a Jewish museum; next time they participate in Jewish learning at home; next time they participate in school, religious school, or another afterschool program) as well as in temporally proximate Jewish living experiences (e.g. next time they go to synagogue; next time they participate in a Jewish home ritual; next time they go to a lifecycle event). Though these are not primarily learning experiences, these living experiences also involve a reinforcing cycle of activation and proximal success. As in science, proximal experiences are those that are the next one they have, as opposed to the current one they are in or the long-distance ones they will eventually have as successive proximal experiences are the path from the current experience to the long-term.

We have identified six[8] dimensions that we think have high likelihood of functioning the way the dimensions of science learning activation do for science learning within a Jewish learning activation framework:

1. *Fascination* with Jewish culture, tradition, and practice (emotional and cognitive attachment/obsession with Jewish topics and tasks);
2. *Valuing* of Jewish culture, tradition, and practice (understands that Jewish knowledge, practice, community offer meaning, joyful structures, and ways of relating to the divine, to self, and to others);
3. *Competency beliefs* about self as a Jew (perceives one's self as capable of/having the skills to successfully engage in Jewish learning and living);
4. *Interpretive thinking* (understands that there is meaning beyond the literal; knows how to interpret texts and cultural artifacts in order to access deeper meaning);
5. *Sense of belonging* (perceives one's self as belonging to/among the Jewish people).
6. *Spiritual stance* (appreciates the existence of the spirit/soul and its relationship to a Divine or creative source; recognizes ways of connecting with and nurturing the spirit/soul).

According to the activation framework, having high levels of each dimension of Jewish learning activation should enable an individual to generally experience success in proximal Jewish learning and living opportunities. Just as importantly, in order to lead to long-term outcomes, those successes, in turn, should support the individual to develop higher levels of each dimension.

The obvious methodological question here is, how was this list generated? We approached this task through the following thought process. First, we carefully considered the character, role, and function of each of the dimensions of science learning activation within that framework. Next, we engaged in a thought exercise of extrapolating these dimensions to the Jewish context, which led to the first four dimensions listed above.

Once we completed this extrapolation process, we considered the aspects particular to Jewish learning and living that might play an important "activating" role that were not accounted for by this extrapolation process. The fodder

---

8 Note that the evolution of the science learning activation work involved the Lab testing more than the current four dimensions and amassing evidence for those that persisted through these investigations. Hypothesizing and testing more dimensions to test than those that actually stick is a part of the research effort, as the empirical efforts naturally winnow down non-predictive dimensions.

for this thinking emerged from a few sources: (1) literature on Jewish education that we have read in service of the efforts of one of the authors (Dorph) to design Jewish learning experiences; (2) observations of a variety of Jewish learners and learning experiences, some of which we have designed and some in which the children and their friends of one of the authors (Dorph) have participated; and (3) reflection on conversations with Jewish educators and learners in a variety of settings. This process yielded dimensions 5 and 6 listed above. Our thinking about these two dimensions—*sense of belonging* and *spiritual stance*—has also been influenced by work in science learning. More specifically, the dimension of *sense of belonging* is extrapolated from an outcome construct used in environmental education known as "sense of place." The dimension of *spiritual stance* is inspired by a dimension we call "innovation stance" that is a dimension of a construct that casts a slightly wider net—*STEM* (rather than science) *learning activation*.[9]

Through a similar process, we approached another, equally important task: thinking through how success in Jewish learning (and living) could be conceptualized. Extrapolating from the *science learning activation* framework, we propose four elements: (1) choosing to participate in Jewish learning, practice, and/or community; (2) experiencing positive engagement (affective, behavioral, and cognitive) during Jewish learning and living; (3) perceiving oneself as successful within Jewish learning experiences, practice, and/or community and (3) meeting Jewish learning and living goals during these experiences.

In order to bring these dimensions of activation and success elements into sharper focus, consider examples of each that we have observed or extrapolated through interactions with children and their families who participate in the afterschool Jewish learning programs that we have been involved in designing or advising. These examples are intentionally related to children during their elementary school years, as it is often most difficult to identify and capture examples in young children. Subsequent research could involve systematic investigation of these variables across multiple ages and contexts and offer opportunity for thorough analysis and presentation of such exemplars. In this chapter, we have simply provided brief examples in table form below.

---

9 Rena Dorph and Matthew A. Cannady, "*Making the Future*: Promising Evidence of Influence," a report submitted to Cognizant Technologies by The Research Group, The Lawrence Hall of Science, University of California, Berkeley, May 2014.

Table 1 Examples of Dimensions of Jewish Learning Activation

Dimension of Activation	Example
Fascination	A mother takes her kids to a paint your own pottery stores. The kids look around at the options for items to paint and are having a difficult time deciding what to choose, until they see the area with the *kiddush* cups and *mezuzot*. Quickly, one child selects a *kiddush* cup and the other child selects a *mezuzah*. They agree that they will each paint one of the items, but to share them both at home.
Values	A second-grade boy becomes the catalyst for family engagement in Jewish ritual participation in his home. He routinely brings home the Jewish objects (e.g., *tzedakah* box, *hagaddah*, *hanukkiah*) that he has made in his Jewish afterschool program, explains to his family how to use them, and requests that he and his family use them together.
Competency Belief	A first-grade girl asks her mother to come to her public school classroom and tell the kids in her class about Passover. The mother agrees, enthusiastically, and asks the teacher if this would be possible. The teacher immediately agrees and tells the mom that the best time would be Tuesday afternoon. The mother replies, "Unfortunately, I'm not available Tuesday afternoon." The girl's fourth-grade sister immediately says, "Don't worry, *Ima*, I can come into the first-grade class and present *Pesach* to them."
Interpretive Thinking	A group of eight- and nine-year-olds write their own *midrash* (interpretation or commentary on Biblical text) exploring how Queen Esther became an orphan, how she felt about not having parents, and the role that her orphan status played in *Megillat Ester*. The children then work with a drama specialist at their afterschool program to create a *Purim shpiel* (play) based on their *midrash*.
Sense of Belonging	A ten-year-old girl visits Israel for the first time. While she is shopping in a grocery store, she marvels at the amount and variety of kosher meat products available in the grocery store. She excitedly says, "Israel is a place that is made for us." "What do you mean by 'us'?" her mother asks. "*Ima*, you know what I mean, Jewish people," she replies.
Spiritual Stance	On a Jewish family retreat, participants sit around a campfire singing songs with lots of goofing off and rowdy actions. As soon as the song leader begins to play one of the prayers (*U'fros aleinu sukkat shlomecha*) that the kids are used to singing every evening as part of their service at closing circle, the mood changes. The kids settle down, they focus on the words, they sing them sweetly and with intention. The same people, same place, same song leader, same guitar moves from the profane to the sacred, in a split second—the singing becomes a spiritual expression and the connection to the divine, palpable. The kids sing sweetly: "Shelter us, beneath your wings, oh, *Adonai*; guard us from all harmful things, oh, *Adonai*; keep us safe, throughout the night, till we wake with morning light; guard us *eli* wrong from right, oh, *Adonai*; Amen, Amen. . . ."

Table 2 Examples of Elements of Success in Jewish Learning and Living

Success Elements	Example
Choice	A mother comes to pick up her kindergartener at school at the end of the school day during *hol hamoed Pesach*. The mother walks into the classroom during the last few minutes of the day while a birthday celebration is underway for one of her child's classmates. The mother notices that there is a cupcake sitting in front of her child and says, "Before you eat the cupcake I want to remind you that its *Pesach* and the cupcake is *hametz*. It's your choice to decide if you want to eat it or not." The six-year-old thinks about it for a minute and then says, "No, I won't eat the cupcake since we don't eat *hametz* on *Pesach*, but will you get me another cupcake when *Pesach* is over—and can I have a different snack now?"
Engagement	A parent arrives at 5:30 p.m. to pick up her child at her Jewish afterschool program. Her seven-year-old son is sitting at a table playing a Hebrew language card game with other kids in the program. His mother asks him to wrap it up and grab his things so they can go home. "Is it time to go already?" he asks. "I wish I could stay and play longer."
Perceived Success	An eleven-year-old girl participates in *Birkat Hamazon* after Shabbat dinner. After the meal is over and the guests have gone home, the girl says to her mother, "Did you notice that I finally learned *Birkat Hamazon*? I was able to follow along and sing the whole thing tonight!"
Learning	Several fourth graders in the program decided they wanted to learn to chant Torah. One day, after hearing one of the girls chant a *pasuk* (sentence) from the week's Torah portion, the teacher said, "Wow, you guys worked SUPER hard today—you each learned a whole pasuk AND we did a bunch of review." The girl, in turn, responded: "I mean, it was a really easy pasuk though." The teacher replied: "A really easy pasuk! Just being able to say that sentence means that you are comfortable enough with reading Hebrew AND with the trope, that there even exist 'really easy' p'sukim (sentences). Six months ago, I said, you wouldn't have known a thing about 'easy p'sukim' and today you're saying you didn't work that hard?! Clearly, your efforts all year have paid off!"

It is worth noting that some of the examples presented above simultaneously include evidence of more than one dimension of activation and/or success. There are several reasons for this. First, qualitative descriptions of lived experiences are rich with complexity and nuance such that a compelling illustration of a phenomena may necessarily include aspects of other simultaneously occurring phenomena. Second, because these dimensions and elements are conceptually distinct at the same time that they are interactive with one another—influencing and being influenced by each other—their enactment is necessarily overlapping. Finally, theoretically, we would expect co-occurrence of these dimensions and elements, so finding evidence of them within the same example, and/or having the same example provide evidence for multiple aspects is further evidence of the theory as conceptualized.

As we step back and consider the functional theory of activation through the lens of the Jewish learning context, we also realize that a few additional factors must be considered. One factor is how we articulate our distal outcomes—that is the long-term end-game that we are pursuing. We extrapolate from the science learning case and suggest that there are two distal outcomes that are important to pursue: (1) Jewish literacy and (2) persistent engagement in Jewish learning and living. It will be important that we can measure those in ways that are meaningful in the twenty-first century rather than assuming that behavioral proxies like the ones Cohen[10] uses are the right fit for this framework.

A second factor is the ancestral and historical "baggage" that the learner also carries with him/her and plays a significant role in shaping his/her dispositions, practices, and knowledge. While this is also the case in the science context—parental and cultural beliefs about science dramatically influence and shape an individual's attitudes toward science learning—it is even more so in the Jewish context. Attitudes toward being Jewish, toward heritage language learning, and toward religious practice and beliefs about God and Jewish tradition are all contextually complex and emotionally laden, and all play a role in shaping an individual's level of activation across all dimensions. Thus, a theory of Jewish learning must pay close attention to the personal and socio-cultural context in which learning is situated. In this case, the functional theory of Jewish learning activation must account for this "baggage" in order to understand and measure the process by which a learner may develop Jewish learning activation and design learning experiences and environments that are effective at increasing activation.

Implications for Designing Jewish Learning Experiences

Consequential outcomes from early Jewish learning experiences will take place more regularly when we discover which experiences have effects that maintain or grow rather than dissipating. In order to do that, we need to both know what immediate effects are predictive of growing long-term effects, which in turn requires being able to measure them rigorously. The theory described herein suggests that those designing learning experiences could intentionally target Jewish learning activation as an outcome while understanding it as an input as

---

10 Cohen, *A Tale of Two Jewries*.

well. Designing Jewish learning experiences for youth could focus on strategic interventions designed to produce immediate effects on the dimensions of activation, with the idea that such immediate effects could launch the iterative process that produces long-term outcomes. Future design efforts could then focus on understanding the specific features of learning experience interventions that support the development of activation.

So, what kinds of learning experiences support the development of Jewish learning activation? Synthesizing across a wide range of input from research, practice, and original empirical data, Lab researchers have compiled a list of several features of learning experiences that have been suggested by researchers to support changes in the conceptual building blocks (e.g. curiosity, interest, persistence, etc.) that underlie the science learning activation dimensions.[11] Here, we extrapolate from that list to propose a list of features that have high probability to support the dimensions of Jewish learning activation that we hypothesized above:

- *The learning environment:* goals, materials, accessibility, intellectual richness, expertise.
- *The social affordances:* development & demonstration of expertise, sense of belonging, supportive culture, opportunities to engage in collaborative interpretation of Jewish text and artifacts, interaction with accessible role models.
- *The learning experiences:* relevant, authentic, joyful, immersive, engages learners in interpretive text study and meaningful Jewish practice, offers opportunities to enact Jewish values, offers choice/control/autonomy, offers increasing complexity and opportunities for mastery.

While empirical work designed to understand if and how these features support the development of *science learning activation* is currently only in its early stages, preliminary results indicate that we not only have to pay attention to which features support activation, but we also must pay close attention to other related questions. For example, how/when do these features interact with an individual child to support activation? For whom do different combinations of activation dimensions work in what way? And, under what conditions these features will yield activation. We anticipate that similar questions would apply to the case of Jewish learning as well. For instance, we are

---

11 Dorph et al., "Crumpled Molecules," 18–28.

noticing gender effects in science activation and are intrigued about similar effects related to Jewish effects.

Accordingly, the design of Jewish learning experiences must be responsive to a broad range of learners. "Jewish education" is used to refer to a diverse collection of learning content and learning environments. At the same time, Jewish knowledge, Jewish skills, and dispositions toward Jewish learning are developed in diverse contexts that span many learner years and involve many formats. Such formats include books, traditional classrooms, various forms of classroom guided experimentation, afterschool programs, summer camps, museum and science center visits, TV programs, the internet, and home learning experiences. Hence, there is wide diversity in quantity and format of Jewish education within both school and out-of-school settings. As a result, children entering a new Jewish learning environment can differ greatly in prior experiences. Similarly, children exiting any given Jewish learning environment can also differ greatly in what kinds of Jewish learning experiences (especially out-of-school experiences) they will be offered next.

This heterogeneity in incoming and outgoing experiences creates challenges in designing effective Jewish learning opportunities, particularly around the notion of a pathway that resonates and builds on each successive learning experience. Further, these experiences exist within a complex ecosystem of designed, emergent, and accidental Jewish learning opportunities. Some elements of this ecosystem are intentionally designed to enhance connections and coherent pathways across the settings; other elements are not, unintentionally introducing confusion for learners and their families as they seek to make meaning across disparate experiences and options.

Implications for Evaluating Jewish Learning Experiences

This work may also have practical implications for evaluating Jewish learning experiences for several reasons. First, Jewish learning activation is hypothesized to present convenient short-term evaluation targets with meaningful long-term predictiveness. Second, the development of instruments to assess of the dimensions of Jewish learning activation as well as specified success factors would provide scalable measurement tools currently unavailable to evaluators in this field. Further, these efforts offer a framework that is meaningful across learning environments and settings and thus affords the potential for engaging in comparative studies that are impossible in the absence of robust measures of learning. The ability to engage in more systematic and robust evaluation of

Jewish learning experiences would support the improvement of those experiences and enhance the impact that they could make.

The promise of utilizing this framework and measures in support of rigorous evaluation research is underscored by relevant work being done by the Lab team to operationalize the framework and instrumentation that the Lab developed for research in ways that are useful in evaluation contexts. This project will enhance the infrastructure for high-quality evaluation of science learning experiences and expand the capacity of small-scale evaluation efforts to collect, analyze, and interpret data, which, in turn will support program improvement. Given that evaluation efforts related to Jewish learning programs are usually quite small in scope and funding and rarely engage teams with sophisticated methodological expertise related to assessment and psychometrics, an analogous infrastructure for evaluating the impact of Jewish learning experiences across environments would be useful.

Implications for Research on Jewish Learning

Developing a research agenda that explores the applicability of this framework in the Jewish learning context would be a very powerful approach to synthesizing and developing an important perspective for the field. We envision that such an agenda would need to begin with an intentional planning phase and include the following elements (at minimum):

- Synthesis of existing research in Jewish and religious learning.
- Qualitative and phenomenological studies of powerful learning outcomes and experiences for youth across multiple ages and stages.
- Retrospective studies of the life histories of individuals who epitomize the types of adult engagement with Jewish learning and living that we idealize as success.
- Development of deep and scalable measures of Jewish learning activation and success and of an understanding the affordances and limitations of measurement strategies.
- Longitudinal studies of youth engaged in diverse Jewish learning experiences.
- Design-based research studies that support the systematic investigation of learning experiences that support Jewish learning activation.

Before embarking on such a research agenda, it is important to understand that the research agenda underway related to science learning activation has been highly resourced—both intellectually and financially. Intellectually, a multi-disciplinary team of researchers and learning experience designers from three institutions developed and drives this agenda. Financially, the initial investment in these efforts was very well capitalized (approximately $5 million over a three-year period) by a private foundation that launched this work and enabled enough progress to be made so that the agenda is now funded through several more millions of dollars from multiple federal grants and private sources for particular related studies.

No less than such an investment would be required to make significant progress on the comprehensive agenda described above within the Jewish learning context. Although the work done by the Lab related to science could offer a shortcut, it is probable that making progress in the Jewish learning context would require even more extensive financial resources and a longer time horizon given that the field of Jewish learning research provides a far less developed starting point than the field of science learning. That said, it is not necessary to begin with all of these resources in place, and early work can establish the viability of the overall approach that will then increase confidence in the need for a larger investment. The Lab's work began as a one-year planning effort that was funded by a modest grant from a private foundation. Through a planning process that included extensive literature review efforts and multiple convenings of researchers, designers, and educators, we envisioned an agenda and hatched productive collaboration. Since that time, we have garnered additional support that has enabled us to advance the field of science learning research.

The same is possible for research on Jewish learning. Engaging in productive collaboration and the systematic study of Jewish learning is as important to the future of the Jewish people as the study of science learning is to the future of the United States. The United States has invested both public and private funds into the research and development efforts described above because many believe that the future of our country depends on developing a scientifically literate citizenry, broadening participation in STEM learning and careers, and both inspiring and preparing the next generation of scientists and innovators. There is an analogous case to be made for engaging in the systematic study of Jewish learning. Getting from here (the current state of Jewish education) to there (where we need to be in Jewish learning and teaching) in the twenty-first century will require collective and individual investment in rigorous and systematic study as well as expert learning experience design. The future of the Jewish people depends on creating a Jewishly literate citizenry, broadening participation in Jewish learning and living, and both inspiring and preparing the next generation of Jewish leaders and educators.

Bibliography

Cohen, Steven M. *A Tale of Two Jewries: The "Inconvenient Truth" for American Jews.* Jewish Life Network/ Steinhardt Foundation, 2006.

Dorph, Rena, and Matthew A. Cannady. "*Making the Future*: Promising Evidence of Influence." A report submitted to Cognizant Technologies by The Research Group. The Lawrence Hall of Science, University of California, Berkeley, May 2014.

Dorph, Rena, Matthew A. Cannady, and Christian D. Schunn. "How Science Learning Activation Enables Success for Youth in Science Learning." *Electronic Journal of Science Education* 20, no. 8 (2016): 49–85.

Dorph, Rena, Christian D. Schunn, and Kevin Crowley. "Crumpled Molecules and Edible Plastic: Science Learning Activation in Out-of-School Time." *Afterschool Matters* 25 (Spring 2017): 18–28.

Dorph, Rena, Kevin Crowley, Christian D. Schunn, and Patrick Shields. "Activating Young Science Learners: Igniting Persistent Engagement in Science and Inquiry." Structured poster session at the Annual Meeting of the American Education Research Association, Vancouver, BC, Canada, 2012.

Dorph, Rena, Christian D. Schunn, Kevin Crowley, and Patrick Shields. "Science Learning Activation: Positioning Youth for Persistent Success in Science Learning, Literacy, and Careers." Presentation at the Annual Meeting of the American Education Research Association, San Francisco, CA, 2013.

Fostering Identity and Disposition Development in Jewish Education: A View from the Learning Sciences

Janet L. Kolodner

In this second chapter drawn from the area of science education, Janet Kolodner draws insight from her Learning by Design approach, through which learners not only grapple with subject matter but also come to "see themselves as scientists and engineers." Kolodner, like Dorph and Schunn in the preceding chapter, sees an analogy to Jewish education's goals in the area of identity. Knowledge, ability, and identity are inextricably intertwined. The author draws on ideas about learning in communities of practice to emphasize the need to create opportunities for Jewish learners to enact valued, authentic Jewish activities in social contexts. She concludes by using the case of her Kitchen Science Investigator program as a springboard for recommendations for Jewish education.

During the late 1990s and early 2000s, I was involved in designing a new approach to science education for middle school, a project-based approach that used engineering design projects as a context for learning science content, the practices of scientists and engineers, and communication, collaboration, and project practices. The approach, called Learning by Design[1] (LBD) has learners playing the roles of scientists and engineers as they work on achieving design challenges. Acting as civil engineers, they design ways of managing water flow and erosion around a basketball court. Acting as mechanical

---

1 Janet L. Kolodner et al., "Problem-Based Learning Meets Case-Based Reasoning in the Middle-School Science Classroom: Putting Learning by Design into Practice," *Journal of the Learning Sciences* 12, no. 4 (2003): 495–547; "Learning by Design," Georgia Institute of Technology, http://www.cc.gatech.edu/projects/lbd/home.html.

engineers and physicists, they design vehicles and their propulsion systems that can navigate different terrains. Acting as geologists, they give advice to civil engineers about where to take core samples to determine the rock formations across Georgia so that a train tunnel can be planned at the appropriate depths across the state. They plan investigations, carry them out, analyze data, read appropriate resources, make sense of what they are experiencing, explain results, and so on—sometimes in small groups, other times as presenters to the whole class, and other times as advisors to other small groups. They live the lives of scientists and engineers for forty-five minutes a day over a fifteen or twenty-week period.

As we had hoped, students learned science content and scientific practices very well.[2] In addition, something very interesting happened that we had not expected. *Many students came to see themselves as scientists or engineers*—people who investigate to answer questions, take the design of investigations seriously so that they can trust results, attempt to mechanistically explain phenomena, solve problems and make design decisions based on the needs of the context, and so forth. Not only did they report that to us, but they exhibited an array of behaviors that supported their claims. They presented to the class, sought out advice from their peers, and advised each other in "professional" tones and using rigorous scientific language. They did their best to be respectful to each other when countering each other's claims. They interacted with others in ways that showed they assumed others could learn and wanted to learn from them. They asked each other questions, reveled in each other's successes, and did their best to give each other good advice, even when there was a competition involved. When presented with (made up) shoddy or confused work by those who should have known better (e.g., high schoolers or professionals), they expressed disbelief about how confused and unprofessional that work was and what those others were not aware of.

These results were stunning. Without knowing how to foster identity development, we had somehow designed learning experiences that made students into comfortable scientific and technological thinkers and that caused many of them to adopt behaviors and dispositions, and perhaps even the identity of scientists and engineers, in the classroom. Learning by Design was designed to foster science learning; it seemed to result as well in scientist and

---

2 Kolodner et al., "Problem-Based Learning," 495–547; Janet L. Kolodner et al., "Promoting Transfer Through Case-Based Reasoning: Rituals and Practices in Learning by Design Classrooms," *Cognitive Science Quarterly* 3, no. 2 (2003): 183–232.

engineer identities. We sought to find out what was responsible for this identity development.

In this chapter, I present the literature I've used to understand how to foster such identity development—both the theory framing what I've learned and some of the practicalities of implementation I've considered and identified. My hope is that what I've learned will be useful in development of Jewish education approaches that foster Jewish identity development. Such approaches will successfully help youngsters develop and use a Jewish lens as they navigate the world and become people who make "doing and being Jewish" a core part of who they are. I do not, however, make assumptions about what particular core Jewish identity we seek to nurture. We recognize many different flavors of Jewish identity among those we identify as doing and/or being Jewish: some ardently follow *halakhah*, some feel strong affiliation with Jews as a people, some feel strong affiliation with Israel as a homeland, some focus on social justice as the core Jewish identity, and so forth. The suggestions I make are independent of what particular Jewish identity educators are aiming to foster; they will work just as well for whatever Jewish identity one is aiming to promote.

Background

By *identity*, I refer to the feeling of being a certain kind of person and taking on the attitudes, beliefs, and practices of that kind of person. It could be as simple as "I'm a person who likes (or hates) to cook" or as sophisticated as "I'm a Conservative Jew" or "I'm a particular kind of researcher who believes in certain types of methods and the need for certain types of evidence." While people try out and take on temporary or situational identities as they engage in different activities and different groups, they define themselves (consciously or unconsciously) through a "core identity" that embodies the essentials of what they believe in and influences the attitudes and beliefs they bring to new situations and the key practices and behaviors they engage in. In Learning by Design, students developed situational identities as scientists and engineers as they worked toward achieving scientific and engineering challenges in the classroom. They took on scientific and engineering practices, attitudes, and beliefs even when not specifically required, leading us to infer that they were working toward integrating aspects of those situational identities into their core identities. Our goals in Jewish education are not just that our students will know and be able to do things that are identified as "Jewish." Our aim is that our students will make "being and doing Jewish" a part of their core—that they will, over time, integrate beliefs, attitudes, and practices consistent with being some type of Jew into their core identities. Our hope is that this would result in behaving in ways consistent with those beliefs and attitudes even when not in the presence of teachers and parents who expect it in their presence, just as Learning by Design students were doing with the beliefs, attitudes, and practices of scientist and engineers.

By *disposition*, I mean the inclination to take initiative to carry out the practices and play the roles of those one feels like, as the Learning by Design students did when looking at the work of others and critiquing it. Jewish dispositions might mean being observant in some ways, celebrating at certain times and in certain ways, standing up for Israel, and/or considering Jewish values and ways of thinking when making decisions.

Research shows that fostering such identity and disposition development is more complex than many educators have been led to believe. There are several common (mis)understandings of identity that are implicitly (and sometimes explicitly) brought to bear in educating. Some think that if we aim for learners to learn a lot and become competent at what we are hoping for, identity will develop as a natural consequence. The idea here is that identity develops from understanding and capability. Once learners know things and know how to do things, they will have the disposition (take the initiative) to do other related and similar things. Others believe that if we bombard learners with positive emotional experiences and help them understand and feel just how important all of the things they are experiencing are, then they will develop identity and disposition as a result. The idea here is that identity will develop from experiences that help someone know how he/she belongs, and then learners will have the disposition to do things that those with that identity do. The first of these is an assumption that long-term identity follows from learning; the second, that many moments of identifying are enough for fostering and sustaining core long-lasting identity.

The relationships between identity, learning, experience, and emotion, however, are far more complex and nuanced than what either of these conceptions assumes. The literature suggests that for long-term and core identity development, it is essential to begin with activities learners can easily identify with, to use those to help learners develop curiosity and identify personal goals for learning, and to help them develop understanding and capabilities along with new personal goals.[3] The literature tells us that learning and

---

3 Angela Calabrese Barton and Edna Tan, "We Be Burnin'! Agency, Identity, and Science Learning," *Journal of the Learning Sciences* 19, no. 2 (2010): 187–229; Tamara L. Clegg and

identity are intricately intertwined, such that learning, goals, and identity all drive each other's development,[4] and further, that without fostering identification with learning goals and activities, neither targeted identity nor deep learning will systematically develop. Identification with what one is about to learn is required for learning; learning produces new goals; new goals lead to updated identity, and vice versa; they all influence each other. Identity gives rise to goals, which give rise to learning goals and learning activities as a way to achieve goals, which gives rise to identity refinement. Goals are a mediator for learning and identity; they influence each other through generation and attempted achievement of goals.

From this theoretical perspective, development of understanding, capabilities, and identity need to be addressed simultaneously in designing curriculum and learning environments. The big challenges, this theory suggests, are to figure out the kinds of experiences and facilitation of learning from those experiences that will promote both positive feelings and curiosity, and to follow up immediately with new experiences that address the new curiosity and deepen understanding. Further, educators are challenged to help learners identify and appreciate what they are learning, see its usefulness to them, and identity what they still need to learn. Finally, they must continue to strengthen learning (understanding and capabilities), goals (curiosity and want to learn more), and identity (who I am that makes all this important to me) in conjunction with each other.

Theories abound about how identity develops and how to foster positive identity development. A set that seems particularly relevant to educating toward identity development focuses on identity showing itself and developing through group affinity and participation. Erik Erikson[5] posited that one's identity is an interaction between how one perceives oneself and how one

---

Janet L. Kolodner, "Bricoleurs and Planners Engaging in Scientific Reasoning: A Tale of Two Groups in One Learning Community," *Research and Practice in Technology Enhanced Learning* 2, no. 3 (2007): 239–65; Na'ilah Suad Nasir, "Identity, Goals, and Learning: Mathematics in Cultural Practice," *Mathematical Thinking and Learning* 4, no. 2–3 (2002): 213–47; Na'ilah Suad Nasir and Victoria Hand, "From the Court to the Classroom: Opportunities for Engagement, Learning, and Identity in Basketball and Classroom Mathematics," *Journal of the Learning Sciences* 17, no. 2 (2008): 143–79; Joseph L. Polman and Diane Miller, "Changing Stories: Trajectories of Identification Among African American Youth in a Science Outreach Apprenticeship," *American Education Research Journal* 47, no. 4 (2010): 879–918.

4 See, for example, Nasir, "Identity, Goals, and Learning," 213–47.
5 Erik H. Erikson, *Dimensions of a New Identity* (New York: W. W. Norton & Company, 1979).

is seen and treated by others; that such self-concept changes over time and interactions with others; and that its development comes from simultaneous activity, observation, and reflection.

Etienne Wenger[6] took the idea of group membership and its roles in fostering identity several steps further, seeing identity in terms of *membership in Communities of Practice (CoPs)*—a group of people who share beliefs and ways of doing. According to this approach, learning involves acclimating to the norms of the community and becoming more able to carry out its practices. Such acclimation (or enculturation) best begins, Wenger claims, through Legitimate Peripheral Participation (LPP)[7]—when one has a chance to see the whole picture of the community and what its participants do, and one engages at one's level of capability and, with the help of others, develops competence that allows one to gradually become more central to the community. Wenger claims that one develops identity through such participation in each community one is part of, and identity development itself happens through *engagement, imagination,* and *alignment*. In each Community of Practice one belongs to, one engages in the community's activities with others; one notices what others are doing and thinking and imagines one's future self in those situations (or rejects them), and one works toward aligning oneself with one's imagination. Others in the community (and outside) play roles in helping one shape one's imagination and pathways to alignment. I like to add awareness to engagement in Wenger's cycle. The cycle, then, is that awareness and engagement drive imagination, which drives alignment, which results in awareness of new things and engagement in new activities, and so forth.

James Paul Gee[8] adds more specificity to what it means to identify with a group and to the relationship between the kind of person one is within a particular group and one's *core identity*. Core identity is the set of values, beliefs, attitudes, and practices one engages in/with from group to group as one participates. Our core identity, Gee says, comes from our pathways through the many communities we participate in—the views, norms, and ways of being we take from each of those communities and assimilate into our ways of engaging in other communities. Developing core identity, Gee asserts, involves

---

6 Etienne Wenger, *Communities of Practice: Learning, Meaning, and Identity* (Cambridge, UK: Cambridge University Press, 1998).

7 Jean Lave and Etienne Wenger, *Situated Learning: Legitimate Peripheral Participation* (Cambridge, UK: Cambridge University Press, 1991).

8 James Paul Gee, "Identity as an Analytic Lens for Research in Education," *Review of Research in Education* 25 (2000–2001): 99–125.

synthesizing across identity developed in different contexts and communities, choosing those aspects that one values, and bringing them to other contexts and communities one engages with.

A big part of identity development, as stated earlier, is learning how to do the things that are done in a community and learning whatever content one needs to know to do those things. Na'ilah Suad Nasir,[9] recall, articulates relationships between identity, goals, and learning. Other researchers, as well, tell us that identity development rests on development of competence, the motivation to participate, opportunities for showing one's skills and understanding, and recognition by oneself and others of one's capabilities.[10]

Disposition, it follows, develops from practice in using what one is learning across a variety of situations and requires valuing the practices one is learning, developing capabilities of using the content and skills one is learning across a variety of situations, and becoming able to recognize when what one has learned may be appropriately used.[11]

There are several other trends these literatures tell us about the relationship between learning and identity development. From Nasir and others,[12] we learn that when youth can make connections between their personal identities and what they are doing, they engage better and learn more. They do not, however, always recognize the connections between what they are doing and the things we might want them to learn; they need help in doing that.[13] Also, fostering such development requires giving learners *opportunities for agency*[14] (i.e., for taking their own initiative). Angela Calabrese Barton and Edna Tan[15]

---

9 Nasir, "Identity, Goals, and Learning," 213–47.
10 Heidi B. Carlone and Angela Johnson, "Understanding the Science Experiences of Successful Women of Color: Science Identity as an Analytic Lens," *Journal of Research in Science Teaching* 44, no. 8 (2007): 1187–218; Zahra Hazari et al., "Connecting High School Physics Experiences, Outcome Expectations, Physics Identity, and Physics Career Choice: A Gender Study," *Journal of Research in Science Teaching* 47, no. 8 (2010): 978–1003.
11 Carl Bereiter, "A Dispositional View of Transfer," in *Teaching for Transfer: Fostering Generalization in Learning*, ed. Anne McKeough et al. (Mahwah, NJ: Lawrence Erlbaum Associates, Inc., 1995), 21–34; Kolodner et al., "Promoting Transfer," 183–232.
12 Na'ilah Suad Nasir, "But When is an Identity: Challenges and Tensions in Operationalizing Identity in the Study of Learning" (paper presented at the annual meeting for the International Society for Cultural and Activity Research, Seville, Spain, August 2006); Nasir and Hand, "From the Court to the Classroom," 143–79; Stanton Wortham, *Learning Identity: The Joint Emergence of Social Identification and Academic Learning* (New York: Cambridge University Press, 2006).
13 Nasir, "Identity, Goals, and Learning," 213–47.
14 Polman and Miller, "Changing Stories," 879–918.
15 Calabrese Barton and Tan, ""We Be Burnin'!," 187–229.

suggest letting learners choose roles they will play and allowing them to exert themselves as community experts when appropriate, to encourage development of personal expertise, offering of it to others, and celebrating its use.

On the other hand, when youth are asked to engage with each other according to norms that are not connected to those they identify with, they don't know how to engage, learning is difficult, and they fail to develop enough interest, curiosity, or desire to develop targeted skills and understanding.[16] *Because learners come with different capabilities, interests, and identities, fostering capability and identity therefore requires tapping into the identities of all participating learners.* Indeed, one of the key elements in fostering identity and disposition development seems to be balancing the tension between giving learners enough agency that they can choose some of the things they are doing to learn and how to engage in those activities and maintaining enough structure to provide the scaffolding and guidance learners need for success and effective learning.

Joseph Polman[17] has coined the phrase Zone of Proximal Identity Development (ZPID) to refer to just how close connections to one's identity need to be for new activities to foster learning and further identity development. Similar to L. S. Vygotsky's[18] Zone of Proximal Development (ZPD), the ZPID is the zone of identity development a learner is ready for: one cannot identify with something one cannot imagine; having experiences that expose more to be imagined is key to developing imagination.

Implications for Designing Learning Environments and Activities

The recurring claim that participation in a group is key to identity development[19] suggests the importance of helping people *feel* they are part of a group as part

---

16 Bryan A. Brown, "'It Isn't No Slang That Can Be Said about This Stuff': Language, Identity, and Appropriating Science Discourse," *Journal of Research in Science Teaching* 43, no. 1 (2006): 96–126; Signithia Fordham, "Racelessness as a Factor in Black Students' School Success: Pragmatic Strategy or Pyrrhic Victory?," *Harvard Educational Review* 58, no. 1 (1988): 54–85.

17 Joseph L. Polman, "The Zone of Proximal Identity Development in Apprenticeship Learning" ("La Zona de Desarrollo Próximo de la Identidad en Entornos de Aprendizaje de Oficios"), *Revista de Educación* 353 (2010): 129–55; and Polman and Miller, "Changing Stories," 879–918.

18 L. S. Vygotsky, *Mind in Society: The Development of Higher Psychological Processes* (Cambridge, MA: Harvard University Press, 1978), 79–91.

19 Some colleagues have observed that identity development can also happen through the feeling of opposition to a dominant group. I do not disagree, but I am not familiar with scholarly literature on how to orchestrate such development. I suspect that the practice of making group

of fostering identity. To feel part of a group, people usually need to feel comfortable interacting with people in the group and enjoy those interactions, find meaning and personal value in the kinds of activities the group engages in, and know that they are being seen by others as being part of the group.

Wenger's stance tells us about the kinds of activities that foster identity development within a community. He suggests that learners need to engage in authentic ways in the activities of the community others want them to identify with—in ways that allow them to imagine themselves playing roles others are playing. Also required, for those who may not have such imagination themselves, is to help learners imagine what they could be in those groups and to help them align themselves with those roles; this means helping them plan toward playing such roles and helping them learn what they need to learn to play those roles.

Therefore, an important issue in developing such learning experiences in the pursuit of Jewish identity will be to identify the practices, beliefs, and other norms of Jewishness that we want learners to take on and decide what authentic activities we should have them do so that they will come to value those norms and learn to do/use them well. Another important issue will be deciding who we want our learners to be interacting with; those who are teaching or facilitating or otherwise playing leadership roles in a group context need to be welcoming, as do already-more-central members. Additionally, it is difficult to engage in authentic ways in the activities of a CoP without enough more-expert community members available to model ways of learning that learners can imagine and align themselves to. This, in turn, suggests the importance of having the right people modeling and mentoring—those learners can identify with and who are also genuine and authentic practitioners of what we want learners to learn.

But having authentic activities within the context of the community we want learners to identify with is not enough to foster core identity development. From Gee, we learn that fostering core identity requires not simply helping someone learn to do something within a group but also helping learners recognize the *value* of what they are learning to other aspects of their lives, so that they will be prepared to take some of those values and practices with them and use them outside of the community in which they are learned. *The implication is that we should be designing educational systems so that the learners are supported in taking what they are learning in one context into another.*

---

identity explicit would also help those in opposition to that group identity to recognize and articulate their opposition (and thus their identity), but this is, of course, only a conjecture.

Such support will usually need to be in the context of learning activities, as it is hard to provide support in more ad-hoc situations. One can do this by making sure that the educational environment is set up to help learners value what they are learning and learning to do, recognize the applicability of what they are learning and learning to do, and be given opportunities to practice and experience the effects of taking what they are learning into new contexts.

Finally, Polman's work reminds us that when learners imagine who they are and who they might be, they can only identify as far as their imaginations go. I call this the Zone of Proximal Imagination (ZPI). To help develop learners' imaginations, Polman and Dianne Miller[20] suggest leveraging the possibilities of the worlds to which learners are already tightly connected (e.g., school, family) and designing "borderland spaces" to facilitate connections to targeted identities. A borderland space is a kind of "figured world," a world created for educational reasons that is similar enough to the real world to be authentic but that helps a learner focus on those aspects of what they are experiencing in ways that will lead to targeted learning.

Taking all of this into account, we can see that designing environments for identity development requires engaging learners in the authentic activities of those with whom we want them to identify in ways that foster development of masterful capabilities and understanding of important content and that help them come to value what they are practicing and learning. We can then help learners imagine beyond what their experiences have been and feel part of a group they come to value (or if they feel apart from that group, to know enough to know deeply what makes them not part of it).

Kitchen Science Investigators: A Case Study in Design for Identity Development

Armed with the understandings above about identity development and how to foster it and use it to foster learning, two of my students (Tamara Clegg and Christina Gardner McCune) and I set out to design an after-school program to foster scientific identity and disposition development.

Our program was called Kitchen Science Investigators (KSI).[21] Participants took on cooking and baking goals and learned scientific practices

---

20 Polman, "Zone of Proximal Identity Development," 129–55.
21 Tamara, L. Clegg, "Kitchen Science Investigators: Promoting Identity Development as Scientific Reasoners and Thinkers" (PhD diss., Georgia Institute of Technology, 2010);

and science content as they gradually developed expertise in a set of culinary practices. The idea was that cooking and baking would be used to draw them in, and that as they did activities authentic to those of kitchen scientists, they would come to learn and value the practices of scientists that they were enacting (inquiry as well as project practices) and recognize and value the role of the scientific knowledge they were learning in their success.

In early sessions, called *Semi-Structured Days*, the facilitators posed challenges to the participants in the form of letters to an advice column in a cooking magazine (e.g., "All the recipes for brownies I see seem to result in cakey brownies; I want my brownies to be as gooey as the warm ones I get for dessert in restaurants"). In later sessions, called *Choice Days*, they chose their own challenges to achieve, often working on them over a several-week period. In the leavening "curriculum," participants learned about using leaveners (e.g., eggs, baking soda, baking powder, yeast) to make breads, cakes, and cookies rise, and all made pizza dough, cakes, and cookies. In the thickening "curriculum," participants learned how to thicken sauces, gravies, and desserts and made a variety of those kinds of dishes. The dishes of their own choosing each required learning some additional science content, ways ingredients work and how to use them, and/or ways of doing things.

Our design of KSI took from Learning by Design elements that we identified as important to learning and identity development among those who participated in it; we adapted those activity sequences and cycles to work in an after-school environment; and we added new components based on the literature cited earlier that specifically focused on identity and disposition development.

From the Learning by Design approach, we took several components:

- Early activities allow participants to gently make their way into the practices we want them to learn and value and to become curious about targeted content, with later activities helping them further

---

Tamara L. Clegg et al., "Playing with Food: Moving from Interests and Goals into Scientifically Meaningful Experiences," in *Learning in the Disciplines: Proceedings of the 9th International Conference of the Learning Societies*, ed. Kimberly Gomez et al. (Chicago: International Society of the Learning Sciences, 2010), 1135–42; Clegg and Kolodner, "Bricoleurs and Planners," 239–65; Tamara L. Clegg and Janet L. Kolodner, "Scientizing and Cooking: Helping Middle-School Learners Develop Scientific Dispositions," *Science Education* 98, no. 1 (2014): 36–63.

- develop those capabilities, come to value them more, and deepen their understanding of the targeted content.
- Learners engage in sustained inquiry for the purpose of achieving some challenge or mission the curriculum helps them identify with.
- Learners share results, observations, and plans with each other and request advice from their peers.
- Challenges are approached iteratively.

Figure 1 shows how these last three components are integrated and sequenced in Learning by Design units. Investigations are done on a need-to-know basis as learners are attempting to achieve a challenge. Presentations are done regularly as learners are both attempting challenges and investigating. Both cycles are iterative cycles, repeated until a challenge is sufficiently achieved.

In addition, for KSI, we sought to build in components that would influence more of the participants toward development of core identities as student scientists or kitchen scientists. We drew these design principles from the literature cited above.

- Learners progress at least part of the time according to their own needs and interests.
- Deeply embedded into activities of the collective is reflection and sharing with participants that highlights the practices being employed, the beliefs behind those practices and their purposes, and the connections between those practices and the practices of the established communities that use those practices. Such sharing and reflection is meant to help participants see themselves as part of an established community and to prepare them to share what they have done, learned, and produced with others outside of the program who are important to them.
- Facilitators grab all the opportunities they can to help participants recognize the authenticity in what they are doing and their successes in engaging in authentic practice, and help participants figure out how they can improve their practice and what they can learn from their experiences.
- Some facilitators are real practitioners of the authentic practices; others are less masterful practitioners but hungry to learn along with participants.

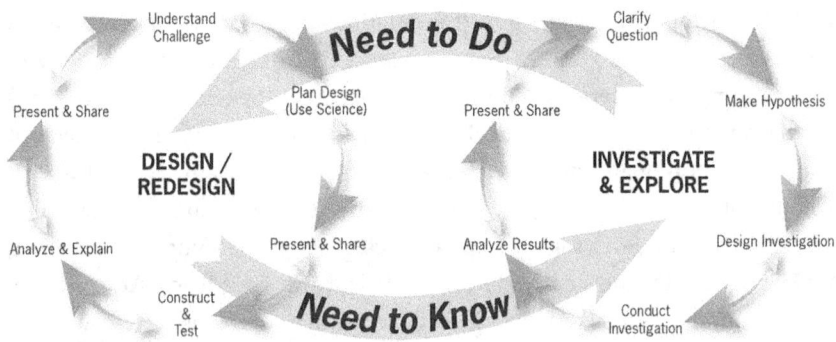

Figure 1: Learning by Design's and PBIS's Cycles. One can think about the left-hand cycle as being one concerned with iteratively addressing goals and challenges and refining one's achievement and solution of those, while the right-hand cycle includes learning activities; originally published in Kolodner, Gray, & Fasse, 2003.

It all fits together like this. Each session begins with about ten minutes of facilitators helping participants review what they had experienced and having the participants share whatever they wanted with others relating to those experiences. Participants often talked about cooking with a parent or explaining something to a friend or sibling. The facilitator helped them reflect on those experiences and articulate practices, beliefs, and purposes and added commentary connecting what they were reporting to the practices of three types of professionals: investigators, scientists, and kitchen scientists. Then the day's challenge was introduced and discussed (on Structured Days) or the logistics of small-group work was worked out (on Choice Days). On some Structured Days, additional planning was done to organize a Class Experiment and the condition each small group of participants would try so that the experiment would produce sound results. Small groups then worked together for a half hour to an hour, planning, cooking, and doing related recordkeeping and writing, and sometimes including a science activity and its related recordkeeping. Facilitators sometimes worked directly with groups and sometimes kept their eyes on several groups at a time, making themselves available to answer questions, show how to do things, and notice opportunities for pointing out connections between what the participants were doing and what investigators, scientists, or kitchen scientists do. Sometimes facilitators acted as scribes, helping a small group with their recordkeeping and inference making. The whole group got together again after the work period to report back for more sharing and reflection. Sometimes participants would ask about some science content, and there would be discussions, presentations, and finding of resources to address learning that content. Sometimes facilitators prepared an activity to help participants experience content (e.g., watching the effects of yeast in different mixtures). On Structured Days, when each small group had carried out some condition of an experiment, time would be spent examining all the data (often that meant measuring, feeling, and tasting the food), making data tables, and drawing inferences together. When each group made something different, time was spent tasting what had been made and giving feedback. And so forth. At the end, the next session was introduced, and discussions were had about the kinds of ingredients facilitators should bring the next time. Sessions lasted an hour and a half to two hours, and participants left with recipes in their hands. The last two sessions were spent preparing for presentations to parents, and parents came for the last hour of the last session to taste their children's creations and hear their stories.

What We Learned

In the final year of our study, my students (Clegg and Gardner McCune) followed four "focal" participants in depth. Clegg's research goal was to understand how identity and disposition develop and what factors were most important to that development.[22] Gardner McCune's goal was to understand how learning happens and what it looks like as it is happening when participants engage through a far more informal project-based learning atmosphere than is usual in a classroom.[23] We collected videos of each small group at work and of the full-group discussions. In addition, Clegg interviewed each of the four focal participants several times during the year and interviewed a parent of each and their science teachers twice.

Each focal participant developed different science-related identities—two as kitchen scientists, one as a scientifically minded pastry chef, another as an accurate measurer and understander of units of measurement, and one as a future research scientist (some developed multiple identities). The scientifically minded pastry chef, for example, told us how proud she was that

---

22 Clegg, "Kitchen Science Investigators"; Clegg et al., "Playing with Food," 1135–42; Clegg and Kolodner, "Bricoleurs and Planners," 239–65; Clegg and Kolodner, "Scientizing and Cooking," 36–63.
23 Christina M. Gardner, "Supporting Cognitive Engagement in a Learning-by-Doing Learning Environment: Case Studies of Participant Engagement and Social Configurations in Kitchen Science Investigators" (PhD diss., Georgia Institute of Technology, 2011).

she was acquiring skills that would allow her to use science and carry out experiments to perfect her techniques and recipes when she joined the profession. She had already identified as a future pastry chef when she joined our program; now she was differentiating herself from the rest of the pack and beginning to understand the special identity she would have within the profession. The accurate measurer showed her identity in science class. The class was engaged in running an experiment that required careful measurement. This young woman took it on herself to help the rest of her group understand the importance of making sure the units of measurement were being followed and showing them how to carefully measure out the correct amounts. When her teacher noticed, she had this young woman help the whole class understand these practices and ideas. This participant reported to us her pride that she was able to teach the others and her feelings of competence and confidence. She felt she was prepared now to participate well in science labs in the future and even to think about such activities as something she could participate in in later life.

Overall, Clegg was able to develop case studies of the identity development of each of the focal participants based on what each shared with her about what she had learned and who she was becoming; what each shared with parents, friends, and/or classmates; and through reports from the participants, their parents, and their teacher about the participant's behaviors and talk, Clegg was able to track how the practices and ways of doing they were learning in KSI were becoming integrated into their everyday activities and core identities and some of what was responsible for that development. Some of what we had built into the program was important to that development (e.g., iteration—the opportunity to fail, getting help with explaining what happened, and having the opportunity to try again; others valuing what participants taught them and giving participants pats on the back), and some things we did not design for were made possible by experiences in KSI (e.g., sibling rivalry in which one of the participants got to teach her older brother something about science, interactions in informal ways with their teachers, getting to know and identifying with the graduate students running the program). These studies thus demonstrated a lot about what makes a difference in fostering identity and disposition development.[24]

---

[24] Clegg, "Kitchen Science Investigators"; Clegg and Kolodner, "Scientizing and Cooking," 36–63.

Our analysis added confirmatory evidence to some of the theory we used to design KSI and helped us learn additional lessons about learning and identity development.

- Learners did indeed sustain their engagement over long periods of time (some as many as twenty weeks, and they wanted to continue) when they were learning science content and practices in the context of doing something interesting, important, and familiar to them.
- Every participant learned content and skills, but, as expected, they did not all learn the same things; nor did they learn at the same pace. Each learned more about what she was interested in than about other things; the will to succeed at goals they were undertaking led each of the participants to focus on learning those things important to achieving her goals. The participant we identified as a measurer, for example, was chagrinned when her group-mates put 1/4 cup of baking soda into a cooking recipe rather than 1/4 teaspoon. She paid special attention to units from then on and made sure she paid attention to units in every recipe, learned how to measure different ingredients, and used different kinds of measuring methods; she later made herself a go-to person for measuring advice in her science classroom. She experienced her success in doing that and that others appreciated her skill. The participant who wanted to be a pastry chef someday was particularly interested in the roles of different thickeners and how they work. Another paid special attention to the scientific practices and used what she was learning to do to make sense of what scientists in the world do; she had always been interested in science but had not had a chance to make sense of what that meant before.
- Because what participants were doing as they designed and ran cooking experiments and applied what they were learning to recipe perfection was authentic to the practices of investigators, scientists, and kitchen scientists in the real world, and because facilitators helped participants recognize that, participants were able to take what they had learned about science practices to other venues in their lives. The participant who learned about measurement took what she learned into science class and helped her classmates learn. The participant who had previously been interested in what scientists do paid new attention in science class and argued with her older brother about what is real science. Some participants began

- looking at ingredients while out food shopping with their moms. All of the participants remade recipes at home, tried out new similar techniques at home, and taught their family and/or friends what they were learning.
- All got pats on the back from their parents, teachers, and friends after sharing what they were learning and/or the dishes they had made; they reported that it made them feel confident, proud, and like scientists and investigators.
- When the room setup allowed and encouraged informal interactions across work groups, there was much informal sharing going on as participants were preparing their foods; they got ideas and became curious when they saw what others were doing.[25]
- It was the first time for many participants that they felt that their ways of thinking were valued, and this made them ready to recognize how they could enhance their capabilities in more scientific ways.
- Participants reported that their interactions with facilitators who are scientists gave them a whole new appreciation of what a scientist is and could be. It is important to mention, here, that the participants were girls of color, and most of our facilitators were also. It was the first time some participants thought about themselves as people who could be scientists, even though most expressed at least some interest in science from the start.
- Since cooking and eating are things that people do in multiple venues and with multiple groups, what the participants were doing in KSI had connections to many different facets of the their lives; this made it easy to have opportunities to share what they were doing and learning with others.
- Two connections between formal and informal education were quite important to the identity development of focal participants. (a) Teachers got to see participants playing roles as student scientists, and participants got to interact with their teachers in a more informal setting than the classroom. Teachers gained an appreciation of what the participants in KSI could do and called on them more and expected more of them in class; participants had a new appreciation for their teachers as people and were more willing to participate. The new dynamic may have been life-changing for

---

25 Gardner, "Supporting Cognitive Engagement."

some of these girls. (b) Participants made friends with students they would not have otherwise become friends with. It was easy to continue these friendships in science class, since they knew things and had experiences that others had not had. In all cases, this led to more attentive and engaged work in science class (though all participants continued to complain that science class was not enough like the science they were doing in KSI).

Jewish Identity and Disposition

So what does any of this have to do with Jewish identity and Jewish dispositions and their development? It has been clear for a long time that only some of our youth benefit from our Hebrew schools. Many more benefit from certain kinds of Jewish summer camp experiences, but fewer of our youth participate in those. Those of us who enjoy being Jewish find it a shame that so many of the Jewish population don't know enough to be able to enjoy being Jewish in the same ways we do. Those of us who hope for a robust Jewish future want more of our population to both identify Jewishly and practice Jewishly (whether as Reform, Conservative, Orthodox, cultural, or post-denominational Jews). Those of us who are Zionist want our children to celebrate the achievement that the State of Israel represents, to identify with Israel as our homeland, and to contribute to the fulfillment of our aspirations for the State. Whatever the goals, the kinds of engagement with Judaism we want our Jewish schools to engender requires that our youth identify themselves as some kind of Jewish, gain understanding of what that means and how to do that kind of Jewish, become knowledgeable about why Jewish people do as they do and about the history of those practices, and take it on themselves to participate in life in Jewish ways. One's sense of oneself as a Jew should coalesce with knowledge and behavior related to this.

Though development of science identity and Jewish identity seem quite different from each other on the surface, I argue that they share the same challenges and that guidelines developed for fostering each can inform fostering of the other. As a beginning to supporting this argument, I point out that the particular foundational approaches to identity development that I focus on in my analysis (those of Erikson, Wenger, Gee) address development of core identity in general rather than on development of specific identities. They all suggest that core identity develops as a process of developing situational identity through engaging with groups and integrating aspects of one's different situational identities into one's core identity through trying them on in other contexts of one's life. Those who build on those theories (Nasir, Polman, Clegg) focus on interactions between those processes and processes involved in gaining understanding, competence, and imagination, adding to those foundations new findings about the cognitive, social, and affective processes that influence situational and core identity development. Though they study identity development in specific contexts, their research focuses on drawing out lessons about identity development that apply more generally across development of different types of identities. When my students and I draw lessons from our work on developing science and engineering identity, we are focusing similarly, analyzing our data from the perspective of these foundational theories so as to be able to add to the understanding of how core identity develops and to make suggestions about fostering core identity development that are applicable beyond the particular contexts in which we do our research. Whatever the core identity development we are seeking to foster, we need to be mindful of these and complexities of influencing that development:

- Core identity development begins in situational settings in the contexts of activities that participants find meaningful and in the contexts of communities that learners enjoy engaging with, that give them opportunities to develop expertise, be recognized for their expertise, and become more central to the operations of the community, and that reward them for their growing capabilities.
- Core identity development takes significant time and happens as learners try out the attitudes and practices of their developing situational identities in new situations and in the contexts of other communities they engage in.
- A requirement for learners to take the initiative to try out those attitudes and practices in new situations is that they know something about when those attitudes and practices apply and feel enough competence and confidence that they think they can be successful and that their attempts will be appreciated in those new situations. Gaining understanding and developing disposition require development of identity and also the converse: as identity is developing, we need to help our youngsters learn practices, gain understanding, and grab opportunities to apply what they are learning.
- Core identity development is strengthened with each attempt to use situationally developed beliefs, attitudes, and practices in a new

context or with a new community, provided learners have a chance to debug their failures and be valued for their attempts.

Identity development, thus, is not something any one educator or educational institution can have complete control over; different participants in the same well-designed environment for fostering learning and identity will learn different things from those experiences and develop identity and disposition differently than others because of what they are already familiar with as well as because of the other experiences they have. And given the variability in the activities and communities our learners participate in, we have little control over the opportunities they will have to try out what they are learning and therefore little control over whether they will feel confident or competent in those situations or have the capabilities to be successful in those situations.

My conclusion, then, is that our best chances of fostering positive Jewish identity development will come from a combination of (a) helping our youngsters have experiences with the qualities discussed above over a variety of environments and as part of a variety of communities and community members; (b) helping them reflect on how what they are learning and becoming might be called on in the variety of other situations they encounter in their lives; (c) helping them reflect on their expression (or lack thereof) of values and ways of doing things between the Jewish environments they engage in and other environments; and (d) helping them anticipate and negotiate the tensions and challenges involved in the expression of their Jewish values and ways of doing things in non-Jewish environments and situations. To make that happen, we need to clarify the values and practices we and the organizations we belong to subscribe to and what we want our youngsters to know and to know how to do, we need to clearly articulate the ways of being Jewish that we want our youngsters to consider and make their own, and we need to design experiences for them that will help them both learn what we want them to learn and internalize the values in those beliefs, attitudes, and practices. It is not simple, but it is not impossible either. It will require, I believe, development of educational and social opportunities across organizations (e.g., camps and schools) and across usually siloed departments or divisions within those organizations (e.g., youth group and education functions of synagogues). It will benefit, as well, from involving experts in the conceptual foundations of identity development (i.e., the literature I cite here) and in designing for identity development as members of educational planning groups along with Jewish education professionals.

Whatever the specific Jewish outcomes we are aiming for in Jewish education, we want learners to become competent and capable within those domains, to have confidence in what they can do and what they know, to be aware of the Jewishness of what they are doing, to take pride and enjoy what they are doing, and to find it meaningful. The literature above and what was learned through the KSI experience suggest building blocks for achieving such goals.

Bibliography

Barton, Angela Calabrese, and Edna Tan. "We Be Burnin'! Agency, Identity, and Science Learning." *Journal of the Learning Sciences* 19, no. 2 (2010): 187–229.

Bereiter, Carl. "A Dispositional View of Transfer." In *Teaching for Transfer: Fostering Generalization in Learning*. Edited by Anne McKeough, Judy Lupart, and Anthony Marini, 21–34. Mahwah, NJ: Lawrence Erlbaum Associates, Inc., 1995.

Blumenfeld, Phyllis C., Elliot Soloway, Ronald W. Marx, Joseph S. Krajcik, Mark Guzdial, and Annemarie Palinscar. "Motivating Project-Based Learning: Sustaining the Doing, Supporting the Learning." *Educational Psychologist* 26, no. 3–4 (1991): 369–98.

Brown, Bryan A. "'It Isn't No Slang That Can Be Said about This Stuff': Language, Identity, and Appropriating Science Discourse." *Journal of Research in Science Teaching* 43, no. 1 (2006): 96–126.

Carlone, Heidi B., and Angela Johnson. "Understanding the Science Experiences of Successful Women of Color: Science Identity as an Analytic Lens." *Journal of Research in Science Teaching* 44, no. 8 (2007): 1187–218.

Clegg, Tamara, L. "Kitchen Science Investigators: Promoting Identity Development as Scientific Reasoners and Thinkers." PhD diss., Georgia Institute of Technology, 2010.

Clegg, Tamara L., and Janet L. Kolodner. "Bricoleurs and Planners Engaging in Scientific Reasoning: A Tale of Two Groups in One Learning Community." *Research and Practice in Technology Enhanced Learning* 2, no. 3 (2007): 239–65.

———. "Scientizing and Cooking: Helping Middle-School Learners Develop Scientific Dispositions." *Science Education* 98, no. 1 (2014): 36–63.

Clegg, Tamara L., Christina Gardner, Janet L. Kolodner. "Playing with Food: Moving from Interests and Goals into Scientifically Meaningful Experiences." In *Learning in the Disciplines: Proceedings of the 9th International Conference of the Learning Societies*. Edited by Kimberly Gomez, Leilah Lyons, and Joshua Radinsk, 1135–42. Chicago: International Society of the Learning Sciences, 2010.

Erikson, Erik H. *Dimensions of a New Identity*. New York: W. W. Norton & Company, 1979.

Fordham, Signithia. "Racelessness as a Factor in Black Students' School Success: Pragmatic Strategy or Pyrrhic Victory?" *Harvard Educational Review* 58, no. 1 (1988): 54–85.

Gardner, Christina M. "Supporting Cognitive Engagement in a Learning-by-Doing Learning Environment: Case Studies of Participant Engagement and Social Configurations in Kitchen Science Investigators." PhD diss., Georgia Institute of Technology, 2011.

Gee, James Paul. "Identity as an Analytic Lens for Research in Education." *Review of Research in Education* 25 (2000–2001): 99–125.

Gresalfi, Melissa Sommerfeld. "Taking Up Opportunities to Learn: Constructing Dispositions in Mathematics Classrooms." *Journal of the Learning Sciences* 18, no. 3 (2009): 327–69.

Gresalfi, Melissa Sommerfeld, and Adam Ingram-Goble. "Designing for Dispositions." In *Cre8ing a Learning World: Proceedings of the 8th International Conference for the Learning Sciences*. Edited by Paul A. Kirschner, Geroen J. G. van Merrienboer, and Ton de Jong, 576–83. Utrecht, the Netherlands: International Society of the Learning Sciences, 2008.

Gresalfi, Melissa Sommerfeld, and Paul Cobb. "Cultivating Students' Discipline-Specific Dispositions as a Critical Goal for Pedagogy and Equity." *Pedagogies: An International Journal* 1, no. 1 (2006): 49–57.

Hazari, Zahra, Gerhard Sonnert, Philip M. Sadler, and Marie-Claire Shanahan. "Connecting High School Physics Experiences, Outcome Expectations, Physics Identity, and Physics Career Choice: A Gender Study." *Journal of Research in Science Teaching* 47, no. 8 (2010): 978–1003.

Holland, Dorothy, William Lachicotte Jr., Debra Skinner, and Carole Cain. *Agency and Identity in Cultural Worlds*. Cambridge, MA: Harvard University Press, 1998.

Kolodner, Janet L. "The Roles of Scripts in Promoting Collaborative Discourse in Learning by Design." In *Scripting Computer-Supported Collaborative Learning: Cognitive, Computational and Educational Perspectives*. Edited by Frank Fisher, Ingo Kollar, Heinz Mandl, and Jorg M. Haake, 237–62. New York: Springer Science+Business Media, 2007.

Kolodner, Janet L. et al. *Project-Based Inquiry Science (PBIS)*. 13 vol. Mt. Kisco, NY: It's About Time, 2013.

Kolodner, Janet L., Jacquelyn T. Gray, and Barbara Burks Fasse. "Promoting Transfer through Case-Based Reasoning: Rituals and Practices in Learning by Design Classrooms." *Cognitive Science Quarterly* 3, no. 2 (2003): 183–232.

Kolodner, Janet L., Mary L. Starr, Daniel Edelson, Barbara Hug, David Kanter, Joseph Krajcik, Juliana A. Lancaster et al. "Implementing What We Know About Learning in a Middle-School Curriculum for Widespread Dissemination: The Project-Based Inquiry Science (PBIS) Story." *Proceedings of the 8th International Conference for the Learning Sciences (ICLS)*. Edited by Paul A. Kirschner, Geroen J. G. van Merrienboer, and Ton de Jong, 274–281. Utrecht, the Netherlands: International Society of the Learning Sciences.

Kolodner, Janet L., Paul J. Camp, David Crismond, Barbara Fasse, Jackie Gray, Jennifer Holbrook, Sadhana Puntambekar, and Mike Ryan. "Problem-Based Learning Meets Case-Based Reasoning in the Middle-School Science Classroom: Putting Learning by Design into Practice." *Journal of the Learning Sciences* 12, no. 4 (2003): 495–547.

Lave, Jean, and Etienne Wenger. *Situated Learning: Legitimate Peripheral Participation*. Cambridge, UK: Cambridge University Press, 1991.

Nasir, Na'ilah Suad. "But When is an Identity: Challenges and Tensions in Operationalizing Identity in the Study of Learning." Paper presented at the meeting of the International Society for Cultural and Activity Research, Seville, Spain, August 2006.

———. "Identity, Goals, and Learning: Mathematics in Cultural Practice." *Mathematical Thinking and Learning* 4, no. 2–3 (2002): 213–47.

Nasir, Na'ilah Suad, and Victoria Hand. "From the Court to the Classroom: Opportunities for Engagement, Learning, and Identity in Basketball and Classroom Mathematics." *Journal of the Learning Sciences* 17, no. 2 (2008): 143–79.

Polman, Joseph L. "The Zone of Proximal Identity Development in Apprenticeship Learning" ("La zona de desarrollo próximo de la identidad en entornos de aprendizaje de oficios"). *Revista de Educación* 353 (2010): 129–55.

Polman, Joseph L., and Diane Miller. "Changing Stories: Trajectories of Identification Among African American Youth in a Science Outreach Apprenticeship." *American Education Research Journal* 47, no. 4 (2010): 879–918.

Schön, Donald A. *The Reflective Practitioner: How Professionals Think in Action*. New York: Basic Books, 1983.

Vygotsky, L. S. *Mind in Society: The Development of Higher Psychological Processes*. Cambridge, MA: Harvard University Press, 1978.

Wenger, Etienne. *Communities of Practice: Learning, Meaning, and Identity*. Cambridge, UK: Cambridge University Press, 1998.

Wortham, Stanton. *Learning Identity: The Joint Emergence of Social Identification and Academic Learning*. New York: Cambridge University Press, 2006.

Learning about Learning in Jewish Education

Ari Y. Kelman

In this chapter, Kelman begins with a critique of Jewish educational researchers' relative neglect of learning processes, and points his readers to the work of Lave and Wenger as a framework for understanding Jewish learning and its outcomes. He suggests five directions that emerge from Lave and Wenger's sociocultural learning theory: learning about and from a variety of "experts" in realms of Jewish activity or engagement; deep examination of the way learning happens in different Jewish educational settings; exploration of the broader ecology of Jewish learning; a focus on technology and Jewish learning; and the way in which "non-Jewish Jews" learn about Jewish communal participation. Through charting these directions, Kelman builds his case for the importance of greater attention to Jewish learning as a focus for Jewish educational research.

Nobody is born Jewish. Everyone who sees themself as Jewish or who engages with Jewish culture, Judaism, or Jewishness in some way, has learned to do so. For some, it is the result of their family of origin or the context of their upbringing. Others choose to be Jewish as adults. Still others marry into Jewish families, become friends with Jews, or otherwise find themselves participants in Jewish communities and rituals in spite of identifying otherwise. In any event, engaging in Jewish life results from an array of acquired skills, cultivated in classes or summer camping, constructed from knowledge gathered from any number of sources, nurtured in the practice of family-based rituals or through participation in a synagogue, community, or Jewish social organization. The data and discourse favoring families with two Jewish parents over those with one Jewish and one non-Jewish parent support this perspective, insofar as they argue for a fundamentally sociological definition of Jewishness, rather than a genetic or theological (or even *halakhic*) one, while scholars debate whether Jews are an ethnicity, a religion, a people, a nation, or some uniquely syncretic example of a combination of social categories. Jewish education has developed as one response these sociological realities, and it has emerged as one programmatic answer to the question of how to facilitate the process by which people learn to be Jewish.

Across the range of Jewish educational sites and settings, responses to this question have taken any number of forms: through the teaching of classical Jewish texts, by domestic mimesis of home-based ritual, by creating structures of Jewish education that mimicked the "grammar of schooling" observed in public education, by modernizing Jewish schools, by organizing educational tours, by focusing on training elites, by writing new curricula, by creating multimedia, by teaching Hebrew, by empowering people to practice their own "hands on" Judaism, and so on. Each of these represents a response to the question of how best to facilitate Jewish education, and, consequently, they tend to cluster on the programmatic side of the question posed above.

Absent from literature on Jewish education, insightful and inspiring though it might be, and missing from the incredible diversity of educational programs, efforts, and institutions is any sustained attention to the question of how people learn to engage in Jewish life. What does such learning look like and what does it entail? How does one cultivate a sense of connection with Jewishness, Judaism, or Jewish people? In what ways might it resemble learning math or history, and in what ways might learning to be Jewish resemble learning to be a lawyer or an engineer or a basketball player? Little, if anything, is known about the answers to these questions. Looking across the literature, so much effort has been expended on ensuring curriculum and programs, but nobody seems to ask whether or not all of those offerings helped people learn, perhaps because nobody seems to ask *how* people learn.

This is a significant shortcoming in the literature on Jewish education, and this chapter—along with other chapters in this book—offers the beginnings of an effort to fill this lacuna. It begins by providing an overview of the situation as it has evolved by focusing on significant studies of Jewish education. From there, it will offer five possible directions for future research projects that, together, could begin to contribute to our understanding of learning in Jewish education. In this effort, it draws strongly on literature from the Learning Sciences, the insights of which have encouraged me to write this chapter in the first place. Drawing on the work of Jean Piaget and Lev Vygotsky, it seems that the most successful learning endeavors engage learners in "constructivist" activities, in which the learners are not imagined as empty vessels to be filled, but active participants in the construction of meaning and new knowledge. Understood in this way, learning becomes a fundamentally social endeavor, insofar as individual-level learning cannot be extracted from the social context in which it happens. To explore this phenomenon further, scholars have studied the crews of ships at sea,[1] Girl Scouts selling cookies,[2] skiers skiing,[3] tailors learning their craft and alcoholics in recovery,[4] professional dairy workers,[5] high school students becoming track athletes,[6] and more. Each of these settings provided a site for inquiry into the ways in which people developed new knowledge and capacities, and each revealed the social dimensions of that process.

So, consider this an initial attempt to outline some possible avenues by which the field of Jewish education could begin paying attention to learning.

What We've Learned About Learning in Jewish Education

The short answer to the question of what we've learned about the actual learning that takes place in Jewish educational settings is: not much. Research on Jewish education has largely neglected to engage with the question. The *International Handbook on Jewish Education*[7] does not contain a single contribution that closely examines the dynamics of learning. Both *What We Know About Jewish Education*,[8] and its successor, *What We Know Now About Jewish Education*[9] offer little insight into how people learn or the experiences of learners in Jewish educational settings. Despite their breadth in other areas, none of those three collections contains a single article that focuses on learning.

Literature on educational philosophy in Jewish education has similarly avoided discussions of learning and focused instead on broader questions

---

1 Edwin Hutchins, *Cognition in the Wild* (Cambridge, MA: The MIT Press, 1995).
2 Barbara Rogoff et al., "Mutual Contributions of Individuals, Partners, and Institutions: Planning to Remember in Girl Scout Cookie Sales," *Social Development* 11, no. 2 (2002): 266–89.
3 Richard R. Burton et al., "Skiing as a Model of Instruction," in *Everyday Cognition: Development in Social Context*, ed. Barbara Rogoff and Jean Lave (Cambridge, MA: Harvard University Press, 1984), 139–50.
4 Jean Lave and Etienne Wenger, *Situated Learning: Legitimate Peripheral Participation* (New York: Cambridge University Press, 1991).
5 Sylvia Scriber, "Studying Working Intelligence," in Rogoff and Lave, *Everyday Cognition*, 9–40.
6 Na'ilah Suad Nasir and Jamal Cooks, "Becoming a Hurdler: Low Learning Settings Afford Identities," *Anthropology and Education Quarterly* 40, no. 1 (2009): 41–61.
7 Helena Miller et al., eds., *International Handbook of Jewish Education* (New York: Springer, 2011).
8 Stuart L. Kelman, ed., *What We Know About Jewish Education: A Handbook of Today's Research for Tomorrow's Jewish Education* (Los Angeles: Torah Aura Productions, 1992).
9 Roberta Louis Goodman et al., *What We Now Know About Jewish Education: Perspectives on Research for Practice* (Los Angeles: Torah Aura Productions, 2008).

about the underlying principles of the enterprise and how it ought to be carried out.[10] Research on pedagogy has followed a similar approach, tending to emphasize what teachers ought to know or how they ought to approach their practice rather than seeking to understand how people learn and then developing appropriate pedagogies to suit those modes of learning.[11] Perhaps the largest body of literature in the field of research in Jewish education has focused on the impact of site-specific educational experiences including families,[12] day schools,[13] summer camps,[14] heritage tourism,[15] supplementary schooling,[16]

---

10 Seymour Fox, "Toward a General Theory of Jewish Education," in *The Future of the Jewish Community in America*, ed. David Sidorsky (Philadelphia: Jewish Publication Society, 1973), 239–59; Seymour Fox et al., eds., *Visions of Jewish Education* (New York: Cambridge University Press, 2003); Joseph S. Lukinsky and Philip W. Lown School, "'Structure' in Educational Theory," *Educational Philosophy and Theory* 2, no. 2 (1970): 15–31; Joseph S. Lukinsky, *Integrating Jewish and General Studies in the Day School: Philosophy and Scope* (New York: Jewish Theological Seminary, 1978); Michael Rosenak, "Jewish Religious Education and Indoctrination," *Studies in Jewish Education* 1 (1983): 117–38; Michael Rosenak, *Commandments and Concerns: Jewish Religious Education in Secular Society* (Philadelphia: Jewish Publication Society, 1987).

11 Barry W. Holtz, *Textual Knowledge: Teaching the Bible in Theory and in Practice* (New York: Jewish Theological Seminary, 2003); Sharon Feiman-Nemser, "Preparing Teachers for Jewish Schools: Enduring Issues in Changing Contexts," in Helena Miller et al., *International Handbook*, 937–58.

12 Jack Wertheimer, ed., *Family Matters: Jewish Education in an Age of Choice* (Waltham, MA: Brandeis, 2007); Alice Goldstein and Sylvia Barack Fishman, *When They Are Grown They Will Not Depart: Jewish Education and the Jewish Behavior of American Adults*, CMJS Research Report 8 (Waltham, MA: Cohen Center for Modern Jewish Studies, Brandeis University, 1993).

13 Geoffrey Bock, "The Jewish Schooling of American Jews: A Study of Non-Cognitive Educational Effects" (EdD diss., Harvard University, 1976); Geoffrey Bock, "Does Jewish Schooling Matter?" (New York: The American Jewish Committee, 1977); Harold S. Himmelfarb, "The Impact of Religious Schooling: The Effects of Jewish Education Upon Adult Religious Involvement" (PhD diss., The University of Chicago, 1974); Steven M. Cohen, "The Impact of Jewish Education on Religious Identification and Practice," *Jewish Social Studies* 36, no. 3/4 (1974): 316–26; Fern Chertok et al., *What Difference Does Day School Make?* (Boston: PEJE and the Cohen Center for Modern Jewish Studies, May 2007); Alex Pomson and Howard Deitcher, eds., *Jewish Day Schools, Jewish Communities: A Reconsideration* (Portland, OR: Littman Library of Jewish Civilization, 2009).

14 Steven M. Cohen et al., "Camp Works: The Long-Term Impact of Jewish Overnight Camp" (New York: Foundation for Jewish Camp, 2011); Amy L. Sales and Leonard Saxe, *"How Goodly Are Thy Tents": Summer Camps as Jewish Socializing Experiences* (Hanover: Brandeis University Press and the AVI CHAI Foundation, 2003).

15 Leonard Saxe and Barry Chazan, *Ten Days of Birthright Israel: A Journey in Young Adult Identity* (Waltham, MA: Brandeis, 2008); Shaul Kelner, *Tours That Bind: Diaspora, Pilgrimage, and Israeli Birthright Tourism* (New York: NYU Press, 2012).

16 David Schoem, "Jewish Schooling and Jewish Survival in the Suburban American Community," in *Studies in Jewish Education* vol. 2, ed. Michael Rosenak (Jerusalem: Magnes Press, 1984),

b'nai mitzvah,[17] and "experiential education."[18] Each of these scholarly responses to the question of how to educate American Jews emphasizes a different modality for doing so, but they have done so without attending to the question of learning in any sustained way.

Even Jon Woocher's[19] critique of this situation failed to engage the question of learning. In his essay, "Reinventing Jewish Education for the 21st Century," he argued that the principles of Jewish education in the twentieth century placed Jewish educators at the center and "intentionally or unintentionally prioritized their ideas about what is important to learn and their needs and desires to 'hold on' to learners." The result has been a Jewish educational model that "has been largely a top-down, professionally driven enterprise."[20] He concluded that broad social and cultural changes have rendered this model of Jewish education inadequate to address the needs and interests of American Jews, and that in order to stay "relevant,"[21] Jewish education had to reorient itself around the needs, capabilities, and desires of learners.

This marks one of the first departures from much of the scholarship that has tended to take a more prescriptive approach to Jewish education. In his article, Woocher challenges Jewish educators to consider the needs of those they teach. "How," he asks, "can we help Jews find in their Jewishness resources that will help them live more meaningful, purposeful, and fulfilling human lives?"[22] This is a welcome shift in perspective, as it posits Jewish education as a "learner centered" enterprise, rather than one that focuses on what teachers should teach or broad notions about what Jews should know.

52–64; Madeline Heilman, "Sex Bias in Work Settings: The Lack of Fit Model," *Research in Organizational Behavior* 5 (Greenwich, CT: JAI Press, 1983); Joe Reimer, *Succeeding at Jewish Education: How One Synagogue Made It Work* (Philadelphia: Jewish Publication Society, 1997).

17 Stuart Schoenfeld, "Folk Judaism, Elite Judaism and the Role of the Bar Mitzvah in the Development of the Synagogue and Jewish School in America," *Contemporary Jewry* 9, no. 1 (1987): 67–85.

18 Barry Chazan, "The Philosophy of Informal Jewish Education," *The Encyclopedia of Informal Education*, accessed November 11, 2017, http://www.infed.org/informaljewisheducation/informal_jewish_education.htm; Joe Reimer, "Experiential Jewish Education," in *What We Now Know about Jewish Education: Perspectives on Research for Practice*, ed. Roberta L. Goodman et al. (Los Angeles: Torah Aura Productions, 2009), 343–52; David Bryfman, ed., *Experience and Jewish Education* (Los Angeles: Torah Aura Productions, 2014).

19 Jonathan Woocher, "Reinventing Jewish Education for the 21st Century," *Journal of Jewish Education* 78, no. 3 (2012): 182–226.

20 Ibid., 195.

21 Ibid., 201.

22 Ibid., 189.

Nevertheless, despite the essay's focus on "learners," it does not quite go far enough, because it retains a focus on a kind of person rather than on an effort to understand the activity that defines them. Woocher wants us to adopt a much more learner-focused stance in Jewish education, but the learners here seem more like consumers (of a product called education) than people who are engaged in a practice that we might call learning, a practice or a process that we desperately need to understand better if we are to make any progress. Focusing on people (learners) over practices (learning) ultimately limits Woocher's critique, insofar as it still organizes the enterprise of Jewish education around the question of who is learning rather than on how they are doing so. In this way, it still fails to address the question of how people learn to be Jewish. Providing them with access to ideas, texts, rituals, experiences, vocabulary, or other people who might help them "live more meaningful, purposeful, and fulfilling human lives" is a worthy project, but it does not offer any insight into the ways in which people make meaning, purpose, or fulfillment out of Jewishly sourced material.

Woocher's essay is an important corrective. It represents a significant departure from the visions of Jewish education that preceded it, owing in large measure to its insistence that learners should matter. Yet, by failing to address the question of learning, Woocher proposes that the remedy to a century of "top-down" educational efforts rests in better-informed versions of those same efforts. But without attending to the ways in which people learn, it seems difficult to truly change Jewish educational practice so that it matches or meets anyone who wishes to learn in ways that serve not just their needs for a meaningful, fulfilling life, but so that it meets their needs as learners.

Toward Learning about Learning

Therefore, I want to spend the remainder of this chapter exploring five directions that research in Jewish education could pursue, in order to begin to engage more seriously with the question of learning. I offer each of these as a possibility for new opportunities for research, with much more to be done in terms of research design, sampling, methods, and so on. Those details, of course, will determine the validity of the research and the generalizability of the findings generated by each project, and I trust good researchers to take these questions up in a serious manner, should the field take seriously the dearth of reliable information about learning. The ideas that follow should therefore be read as proposals, suggestions, or indications of possible research directions.

Collectively, however, these five directions point toward a more nuanced and complicated theoretical framework for what we mean by learning in Jewish education.

1. Learning Expertise

To understand learning requires a conceptual framework that allows scholars to observe the development of learners as they move from one set of understandings to another. As a result, much of the scholarship on learning has taken shape around understanding the differences between novices and experts, and the behaviors and capacities that constitute expertise within a particular construct.[23] Research has focused on questions like: What do expert players or surgeons or historians do that is different from people with far less experience? What kinds of habits of mind do they practice when they practice their craft? If it is possible to discern those skills, approaches, or practices, then it might be possible to create a scaffold around which one could become, progressively, more adept at using them. In these studies, the language of learning refers to the process by which one adopts skills and behaviors that derive from expert practice. The issue is not that all chess players or physicists need to be experts, but rather that the identification of expertise allows the creation of a trajectory for learning that is demonstrable in some real fashion.

Experts and expertise, however, come in many forms. Sometimes, it can be practiced by an individual like a Chess Grand Master or a Nobel Prize winning physicist, each of whom has achieved a level of success within a particular domain that stands in for evidence of expertise. Another approach has been the study of what might be called "working knowledge." This latter mode is deeply contextual and can emerge from the ways in which factory workers or health care professionals have developed time or energy-efficient work-arounds or have jiggered remedies to systemic problems. Both Nobel Prize-winning physicists and factory workers possess a kind of expertise that is highly specialized, and that cannot be understood to be properly "transferrable" to other domains. Knowing how to operate efficiently within the space of an industrial dairy production plant is not necessarily going to go very far in a physics lab, and the same would be true of a physicist in a dairy. Yet, both

---

[23] National Research Council, *How People Learn: Brain, Mind, Experience, and School: Expanded Edition* (Washington, DC: National Academies Press, 2000); Susan A. Ambrose et al., *How Learning Works: Seven Research-Based Principles for Smart Teaching* (San Francisco, CA: Jossey-Bass, 2010).

domains allow for a kind of local expertise that is useful when thinking about Jewish education.

With respect to Jewish education, the analogous question should not be: how do we make Jewish experts? Any attempt to establish the parameters of a generalized Jewish expertise will be wrought with all of the predictable problems and weaknesses. What or who could constitute a Jewish "expert?" Politicians? Religiously observant Jews? Artists? People might argue about whether or not the celebration of certain holidays, engaging with the State of Israel, or reciting prayers in Hebrew constitute desirable behaviors for American Jews, but engaging in those behaviors or holding those beliefs does not necessarily represent expertise of any demonstrable kind. The very notion of a Jewish "expert" in a general sense seems perverse, as the domain is too broadly construed to be particularly helpful.

Consequently, I want to suggest the study of expertise within particular domains of knowledge and practice. So, for example, how does an expert *shalihat zibbur* (prayer leader) do her job? Studying a number of *shlihei tzibbur*, employing a variety of methods, we might begin to understand what kinds of decisions she makes while leading communal prayer, and how she makes them. Surely, "expertise" in this domain is not demonstrated by whether or not her prayers are answered, nor by technical knowledge of Hebrew and melodies. Instead, we might explore how she operationalizes a variety of forms of knowledge with consideration for her congregation, their shared musical repertoire, and the sense of allotted time for congregational prayer, all within context of a prayer service. The ability to negotiate these various considerations in this context is comprised by a set of skills that, together, constitute a kind of expertise in this domain.

We might apply this same approach to a variety of "experts" within the Jewish world: curators, journalists, teachers, Talmud scholars, chefs. Each represents a domain of expertise within Jewish life, and each could be studied with a similar approach to understanding how an expert in each of those fields goes about doing the work that defines it. The Learning Sciences would provide the groundwork for understanding the broad contours of expertise, and close study would contribute more finely grained accounts of expertise in action. With those understandings in place, we could begin to scaffold a course of study that we imagine could help a learner move from being a novice to someone further along a trajectory of development. Regardless of whether or not a person wished to become an expert in that domain, such a study would at least allow for the modeling of informed learning pathways based on what expertise looks like.

2. Learning in Place

Learning always happens in places. We typically measure learning through tests or individual survey responses, which assume that whatever we learn ought to be transported with us from place to place, and ought to be accessible to us as individual respondents. But learning is always a product of social relationships, embedded in cultural contexts. Jean Lave[24] referred to this as "situated learning," in order to emphasize its local nature. Learning, for Lave, is not about the acquisition of abstract knowledge, but about engagements with knowledge as part of a web of other social, cultural, and interpersonal dimensions that shape the nature of learning itself. Knowledge, she argued, could hardly exist out of context; to extract it from its context would rend it from the social structures that make it meaningful. For this reason, John Seely Brown, Allan Collins, and Paul Duguid refer to learning as "enculturation."[25] For them, learning to use a "tool"—a term that includes material as well as conceptual ones—without understanding the value or meaning of that tool in its cultural context renders the tool effectively worthless. "The community and its viewpoint, quite as much as the tool itself, determine how a tool is used."[26] Building on their understanding of tools, they write "conceptual tools similarly reflect the cumulative wisdom of the culture in which they are used and the insights and experience of individuals. Their meaning is not invariant but a product of negotiation within the community."[27] Neither tools nor ideas are transparent and readily meaningful. Instead, they argue, their meaning rests on the specific social and cultural contexts in which they exist. Barbara Rogoff extended this line of thinking to her studies of children, whom she called "cognitive apprentices," in order to emphasize the practical and local dimensions of their learning. She explained, "cognitive activities occur in socially structured situations that involve values about the interpretation and management of social relationships."[28] Together, these arguments point to the significance of studying learning in place.

The majority of empirical research in Jewish education has not pursued this line of inquiry, focusing instead on outcome measures that run across a

---

24 Jean Lave, *Cognition in Practice: Mind, Mathematics and Culture in Everyday Life* (New York: Cambridge University Press, 1988).
25 John Seely Brown et al.,"Situated Cognition and the Culture of Learning," *Educational Researcher* 18, no. 1 (1989): 33.
26 Ibid.
27 Ibid.
28 Barbara Rogoff, *Apprenticeship in Thinking: Cognitive Development in Social Context* (Oxford: Oxford University Press, 1990), 61.

range of normative behaviors and attitudes. As a remedy to this situation, I propose a series of deep studies of learning in place. Focusing on sites designed to facilitate learning—schools, summer camps, adult programming, educational tourism—it is possible to engage in qualitative studies that seek to understand the dynamics of learning in each of these sites. Research in this vein can draw on a wealth of school ethnographies,[29] and Lave and Rogoff, among others, have offered pioneering studies of smaller communities of learning ranging from Girl Scouts selling cookies[30] to British wine merchants in Portugal.[31] Each provides some insight into the ways in which people learn, and the ways in which learning is tied to specific people in context. The field of Jewish education has much to learn from pursuing similar efforts, in an attempt to understand the ways in which people learn. No single site will capture the entire picture of Jewish education, but a few studies might begin to reveal patterns by which people learn to be Jewish within those localized settings.

3. Learning Ecologies

Brigid Barron defines "learning ecologies" as "the set of contexts found in physical or virtual spaces that provide opportunities for learning."[32] For research on Jewish education, which has largely focused on outcomes born of particular institution—schools, camps, tourism, classes, families—moving to an ecological framework means expanding our understanding of the ways in which these sites intersect and interact. A learning ecologies approach does not try to isolate variables and assess the impact of one setting over another, but rather seeks to understand the ways in which people engage in learning across a variety of intentional and unintentional domains. This kind of approach will provide a

---

29 Paul Willis, *Learning to Labor: How Working Class Kids Get Working Class Jobs* (New York: Columbia University Press, 1981); Jay MacLeod, *Ain't No Makin' It: Aspirations and Attainment in a Low-Income Neighborhood*, 3rd ed. (Boulder, CO: Westview Press, 2008); Denise Clark Pope, *Doing School: How We Are Creating a Generation of Stressed-Out, Materialistic, and Miseducated Students* (New Haven, CT: Yale University Press, 2001).
30 Rogoff et al., "Mutual Contributions," 266–89.
31 Jean Lave, "Getting to Be British," in *History in Person: Enduring Struggles, Contentious Practice, Intimate Identities*, ed. Dorothy Holland and Jean Lave (Santa Fe, NM: School of American Research Press, 2001), 281–324.
32 Brigid Barron, "Learning Ecologies for Technological Fluency: Gender and Experience Differences," *Journal of Educational Computing Research* 31, no. 1 (2004): 1–36; Brigid Barron, "Interest and Self-Sustained Learning as Catalysts of Development: A Learning Ecology Perspective," *Human Development* 49, no. 4 (2006): 195.

much more textured account of learning, insofar as it will focus on the ways in which the network of institutions, contexts, or settings enable a learner or a set of learners to generate knowledge.

The ecological approach to studying Jewish learning would home in on the ways in which people engage with and produce knowledge across and within a learning ecology. It is less concerned with the question of whether or not the apparent outcomes of day school can be attributed to the school or to the types of families that send their children to day schools, because such finely grained distinctions do not represent the ways in which learners understand their learning experiences holistically, across rather than defined by particular domains.[33] For example, researchers could study a set of students in a Hebrew School or a collection of families in a congregation or *havurah*, exploring the various ways in which people engage in learning across and through various sites and resources. Students' families probably play a role in enhancing or inhibiting their Jewish learning in ways that extend beyond the Hebrew school setting. Similarly, members of a *havurah* likely engage in not-strictly traditional holiday celebrations which they construct out of and across resources both contemporary (online, print, etc.) and inter-generational (memories of childhood, etc.). At issue in this approach is the question of how people learn across rather than between them, and how the various settings in which they participate in Jewish life (home, school, online, synagogue, museums, etc.) collaborate in facilitating Jewish learning.

4. *Learning Technologies*

To state the obvious: American lives at the beginning of the twenty-first century are intensely and intimately connected to digital technologies. The penetration of digital technology into American life, culture, commerce, and politics has been both widely bemoaned and celebrated. In terms of education, the promises of "online learning" or "blended learning" have sent traditional educational institutions into apoplexy as they attempt to engage in the open education alongside privately funded efforts like Khan Academy, Udacity, or the wide and varying offers available via YouTube. Jewish education has waded into these waters with a number of online efforts, including MOOCs, podcasts, apps, free and subscription services for online content, the digitization of Jewish texts,

---

33 Ari Y. Kelman and Zoe Wolford, "Learning Across Church and State: Student Experience of a Released Time Program," *Religious Education* 111, no. 1 (2016): 49–74.

and many others. These tend to focus on specific channels for the delivery of content and while some are more equipped to measure audience engagement than others, none can adequately assess the ways in which people utilize technology to learn to participate in Jewish life.

People use technologies for a variety of things: to remind them of birthdays, to check the time of sundown for the beginning of Shabbat, to look up whether or not something is kosher, to read pertinent news, or to keep in touch with family and friends. But *how* people use technology to gather and generate information about Jewish life remains largely unknown. How do people use social media technologies to engage in public discourse about American Jewish life? How do people use Skype and other messaging platforms to virtually connect with far-away family during holidays? How do people study or engage with sacred texts online and do they do so differently than they do on paper books? What kinds of information are people seeking and what do they do with that information? All of these are questions that a careful study of technology and its uses would provide researchers interested in understanding how technology is facilitating Jewish education.

This builds on the Learning Ecologies approach but focuses intently on technology, which has enabled greater access to information and people than has been historically possible. The question of access, however, is only one element of the broad impact that digital and mobile technologies have had on Jewish life, and insofar as people now rely on their phones for everything ranging from driving directions to recalling telephone numbers, we think with our technology more than we ever have, and this certainly has some impact on the shape and dynamics of Jewish life, more generally. Measuring website "clicks" or video views might reveal the meaning of a specific mediated interaction, but it cannot illuminate the ways in which people are actually engaging with technology to facilitate their Jewish lives across a variety of domains.

5. Learning of Non-Jewish Jews

What marks this moment in Jewish history, perhaps uniquely so, is the significance of people born of non-Jewish parents in the families and institutions of the Jewish community. For some scholars of American Jewish life, this trend—or exogamy, specifically—raises a concern about the demise of American Jewry,[34]

---

34 Steven M. Cohen, "Intermarriage and the Jewish Future," in *A Statement on the Jewish Future: Text and Responses*, 10–19 (American Jewish Committee, 1997); Steven M. Cohen and

while others advocate for a more sympathetic understanding of the role that Jewish families that include non-Jews can play in Jewish communities.[35] But either way, the demographic reality is that a majority of families in the Jewish community have one or more non-Jewish members. Given this reality, we have an opportunity to examine the ways in which adults learn to join a "community of practice"[36]—that is, how they learn to be, if not Jewish themselves, at least members of Jewish families.

Though Lave and Wenger coined their term to describe a very specific social formation, one that has been organized around a particular practice (tailoring, midwifery), researchers might be able to take advantage of the looseness of the term to explore the ways in which non-Jewish adults learn to engage in Jewish cultural and religious practice, regardless of how they might define it. Roy Pea's[37] concept of "distributed intelligence" may be helpful here. He offers the concept as a way of accounting for the ways in which a social system engages with information. "When I say that intelligence is distributed," he wrote, "I mean that the resources that shape and enable activity are distributed in configuration across people, environments, and situations. In other words, intelligence is accomplished rather than possessed."[38] For non-orthodox Jewish families in the twenty-first century, this must include an account of the ways in which their non-Jewish members participate in this effort.

Edwin Hutchins[39] offers an extended version of Pea's theory that called not only for an account of distributed intelligence, but distributed cognition. Through rigorous ethnographic research, Hutchins argued that individual understanding or skill can only ever be one part of a larger system. "The process by which work is accomplished, by which people are transformed from novices into experts and by which work practices evolve are all the same process."[40]

Jack Wertheimer, "The Pew Survey Reanalyzed: More Bad News, but a Glimmer of Hope," *Mosaic Magazine*, November 2, 2014, https://mosaicmagazine.com/essay/2014/11/the-pew-survey-reanalyzed/.

35 Keren R. McGinity, *Still Jewish: A History of Women and Intermarriage in America* (New York: New York University Press, 2012); Jennifer A. Thompson, *Jewish on Their Own Terms: How Intermarried Couples Are Changing American Judaism* (New Brunswick, NJ: Rutgers University Press, 2013).

36 Lave and Wenger, *Situated Learning*.

37 Roy D. Pea, "Practices of Distributed Intelligence and Designs for Education," in *Distributed Cognitions: Psychological and Educational Considerations*, ed. Gavriel Salomon (New York: Cambridge University Press, 1993), 47–87.

38 Ibid., 50.

39 Hutchins, *Cognition in the Wild*.

40 Ibid., 351.

In the fullest rejection of the approach to learning that celebrates individual cognition, Hutchins concludes "cognition is a cultural process,"[41] arguing that what happens in the mind of a single person within a given context cannot adequately account for the acquisition of knowledge because it ignores the social and cultural dynamics that provide a framework for making that knowledge meaningful. What is often attributed to one person is, in fact, an artifact of the larger systems in which they are operating.[42]

Foregrounding the information-producing and -processing efforts of Jewish communities shifts the emphasis from the ways in which they are not living up to normative standards for behaviors and attitudes, and toward a more nuanced understanding of the ways in which they participate in the creation of Jewish knowledge. This would illuminate the complex landscape of American Jewish communities in light of twenty-first century demographics. Non-Jewish members of Jewish communities provide a site for exploring this kind of learning.

Social Learning

These five interlocking research directions are connected by a shared interest in the social dimensions of learning. Whether based in institutions or ecologies, whether focusing on novices or experts, these proposals for research on Jewish education seek to place learning at the center without reducing it to test scores or outcome measures. As with learning, Jewish life is inherently social, so emphasizing the social and contextual dimensions of learning should be good news for Jewish education, insofar as this approach seeks to understand the ways in which learning and Jewish life might inform one another. However, most of the scholarship on Jewish education, to date, has sought to identify which curricula or experiences have the greatest impact, and thus have inadvertently extracted learners from both their social contexts and the processes that might constitute learning in a social environment. Instead of acknowledging and seeking to better understand the social dimensions of learning, the

---

41 Ibid., 354.
42 See also, R. P. McDermott, "The Acquisition of a Child by a Learning Disability," in *Understanding Practice: Perspectives on Activity and Context*, ed. Seth Chaiklin and Jean Lave (New York: Cambridge University Press, 1993), 269–305; Bruno Latour, *Science in Action: How to Follow Scientists and Engineers through Society* (Cambridge, MA: Harvard University Press, 1987); Bruno Latour and Steve Woolgar, *Laboratory Life: The Construction of Scientific Facts* (Beverly Hills, CA: Sage Publications, 1979).

normative approach isolates and extracts. Focusing on individual learners at the expense of the ways in which those learners engage in the "adaptive reorganization of a complex system"[43] misses the ways in which learning is, itself, a social endeavor.

Studies of Jewish education that avoid attending to learning miss the social dimension of the enterprise and fail to acknowledge the systems within which people learn to be Jewish. Learning is never an artifact of a single input, whether that input is camp or family, tourism or day school. Attempts to prescribe what one person's idea of what a knowledgeable Jew should know or research intended to isolate the "impact" of a single experience cannot account for the social dimensions of learning. These approaches reduce people to outcomes and communities to context, drawing artificial distinctions between people and the social systems in which they participate.

Learning in the Future

For much of the twentieth century, research on Jewish education focused primarily on broad, prescriptive visions of what American Jews ought to know. Around the turn of the twenty-first century, with the increased focus on assessment and accountability in American education more generally, scholars of American Jewish education began utilizing approaches that emphasized the study of specific educational outcomes, and trumpeting those as evidence of the "success" of a particular educational enterprise. Day schools, summer camps, and taglit-birthright have capitalized on this approach particularly well, using data to describe reported outcomes but not engaging in any significant way with anything that could properly be called "learning." This approach persists.

This essay is an effort to shift the discussion in research on American Jewish education away from prescriptions and outcomes and toward a more nuanced and detailed account of the ways in which people learn to engage in Jewish life. Drawing on the work of the Learning Sciences to develop research programs that promise to illuminate dimensions of Jewish learning will make a significant contribution to our understanding of Jewish life in general, as it will provide much needed details about the ways in which people engage with and create meaning from elements of Jewish culture and knowledge. Focusing on learning affords a kind of inside story on socialization in Jewish communities,

---

43   Hutchins, *Cognition in the Wild*, 289.

insofar as it may reveal insights into the ways in which people engage with media, institutions and information.

In order to begin shifting the discourse on Jewish education, I want to propose that we focus on the dynamics of learning—not on its outcomes or motivations, but primarily on learning on its own terms. Until we are able to develop a robust set of theories that can help us conceptualize learning within Jewish education, the enterprise is going to remain mired in functionalist and behavioralist analyses that merely update older educational paradigms. The question facing Jewish educational research in the twenty-first century cannot be phrased in terms of the utility or applicability of the experiences of participants. The question must foreground learning as a dynamic process not only of knowledge acquisition, but as a cultural practice of American Jews. This will require an expanded understanding of learning that draws significantly on the work of the Learning Sciences, in order to embed the study of learning in social networks and cultural contexts. We can affirm that Jewish education is the key to ensuring the future of the Jewish people—but we do not yet understand the full range of ways in which people learn to be Jewish.

Bibliography

Ambrose, Susan A., Michael W. Bridges, Michele DiPietro, Marsha C. Lovett, and Marie K. Norman. *How Learning Works: Seven Research-Based Principles for Smart Teaching.* San Francisco, CA: Jossey-Bass, 2010.

Barron, Brigid. "Learning Ecologies for Technological Fluency: Gender and Experience Differences." *Journal of Educational Computing Research* 31, no. 1 (2004): 1–36.

———. "Interest and Self-Sustained Learning as Catalysts of Development: A Learning Ecology Perspective." *Human Development* 49, no. 4 (2006): 193–224.

Bock, Geoffrey. "Does Jewish Schooling Matter?" New York: The American Jewish Committee, 1977. http://www.bjpa.org/Publications/details.cfm?PublicationID=2229.

———. "The Jewish Schooling of American Jews: A Study of Non-Cognitive Educational Effects." EdD diss., Harvard University, 1976.

Brown, John Seely, Allan Collins, and Paul Duguid. "Situated Cognition and the Culture of Learning." *Educational Researcher* 18, no. 1 (1989): 32–42.

Bryfman, David, ed. *Experience and Jewish Education.* Los Angeles: Torah Aura Productions, 2014.

Burton, Richard R., John Seely Brown, and Gerhard Fischer. "Skiing as a Model of Instruction." In *Everyday Cognition: Development in Social Context.* Edited by Barbara Rogoff and Jean Lave, 139–150. Cambridge, MA: Harvard University Press, 1984.

Chazan, Barry. "The Philosophy of Informal Jewish Education." *The Encyclopedia of Informal Education,* 2003. http://www.infed.org/informaljewisheducation/informal_jewish_education.htm.

Chertok, Fern, Leonard Saxe, Charles Kadushin, Graham Wright, Aron Klein, and Annette Koren. *What Difference Does Day School Make?* Boston: PEJE and the Cohen Center for Modern Jewish Studies, May 2007.

Cohen, Steven M. "Intermarriage and the Jewish Future." In *A Statement on the Jewish Future: Text and Responses,* 10–19. American Jewish Committee, 1997.

———. "The Impact of Jewish Education on Religious Identification and Practice." *Jewish Social Studies* 36, no. 3/4 (1974): 316–326.

Cohen, Steven M., and Jack Wertheimer. "The Pew Survey Reanalyzed: More Bad News, but a Glimmer of Hope," *Mosaic Magazine,* November 2, 2014. http://mosaicmagazine.com/essay/2014/11/the-pew-survey-reanalyzed/

Cohen, Steven M., Ron Miller, Ira M. Sheskin, and Berna Torr. "Camp Works: The Long-Term Impact of Jewish Overnight Camp." New York: Foundation for Jewish Camp, 2011.

Feiman-Nemser, Sharon. "Preparing Teachers for Jewish Schools: Enduring Issues in Changing Contexts." In *International Handbook of Jewish Education*. Edited by Helena Miller, Lisa D. Grant, and Alex Pomson, 937–58. New York: Springer, 2011.

Fox, Seymour, Israel Scheffler, and Daniel Marom, eds. *Visions of Jewish Education*. New York: Cambridge University Press, 2003.

Fox, Seymour. "Toward a General Theory of Jewish Education." In *The Future of the Jewish Community in America*. Edited by David Sidorsky, 239–59. Philadelphia: Jewish Publication Society, 1973.

Goldstein, Alice, and Sylvia Barack Fishman. *When They Are Grown They Will Not Depart: Jewish Education and the Jewish Behavior of American Adults, CMJS Research Report 8*. Waltham, MA: Cohen Center for Modern Jewish Studies, Brandeis University, 1993. http://www.bjpa.org/Publications/details.cfm?PublicationID=2896.

Goodman, Roberta Louis, Paul A. Flexner, and Linda Dale Bloomberg. *What We Now Know About Jewish Education: Perspectives on Research for Practice*. Los Angeles, CA: Torah Aura Productions, 2008.

Heilman, Madeline. "Sex Bias in Work Settings: The Lack of Fit Model." *Research in Organizational Behavior* 5. Greenwich, CT: JAI Press, 1983.

Himmelfarb, Harold S. "The Impact of Religious Schooling: The Effects of Jewish Education Upon Adult Religious Involvement." PhD diss., The University of Chicago, 1974.

Holtz, Barry W. *Textual Knowledge: Teaching the Bible in Theory and in Practice*. New York: Jewish Theological Seminary, 2003.

Hutchins, Edwin. *Cognition in the Wild*. Cambridge, MA: The MIT Press, 1995.

Kelman, Ari Y., and Zoe Wolford. "Learning Across Church and State: Student Experience of a Released Time Program." *Religious Education* 111, no. 1 (2016): 49–74.

Kelman, Stuart L., ed. *What We Know About Jewish Education: A Handbook of Today's Research for Tomorrow's Jewish Education*. Los Angeles, CA: Torah Aura Productions, 1992.

Kelner, Shaul. *Tours That Bind: Diaspora, Pilgrimage, and Israeli Birthright Tourism*. New York: New York University Press, 2012.

Latour, Bruno, and Steve Woolgar. *Laboratory Life: The Construction of Scientific Facts*. Beverly Hills, CA: Sage Publications, 1979.

Latour, Bruno. *Science in Action: How to Follow Scientists and Engineers through Society*. Cambridge, MA: Harvard University Press, 1987.

Lave, Jean, and Etienne Wenger. *Situated Learning: Legitimate Peripheral Participation*. New York: Cambridge University Press, 1991.

Lave, Jean. "Getting to Be British." In *History in Person: Enduring Struggles, Contentious Practice, Intimate Identities*. Edited by Dorothy Holland and Jean Lave, 281–324. Santa Fe, NM: School of American Research Press, 2001.

———. *Cognition in Practice: Mind, Mathematics and Culture in Everyday Life*. New York: Cambridge University Press, 1988.

Lukinsky, Joseph S. *Integrating Jewish and General Studies in the Day School: Philosophy and Scope.* New York: Jewish Theological Seminary, 1978.

Lukinsky, Joseph S., and Philip W. Lown School. "'Structure' in Educational Theory." *Educational Philosophy and Theory* 2, no. 2 (1970): 15–31.

MacLeod, Jay. *Ain't No Makin' It: Aspirations and Attainment in a Low-Income Neighborhood*, 3rd Edition. Boulder, CO: Westview Press, 2008.

McDermott, R. P. "The Acquisition of a Child by a Learning Disability." In *Understanding Practice: Perspectives on Activity and Context*. Edited by Seth Chaiklin and Jean Lave, 269–305. New York: Cambridge University Press, 1993.

McGinity, Keren R. *Still Jewish: A History of Women and Intermarriage in America.* New York: New York University Press, 2012.

Miller, Helena, Lisa D. Grant, and Alex Pomson, eds. *International Handbook of Jewish Education.* New York: Springer, 2011.

Nasir, Na'ilah Suad, and Jamal Cooks. "Becoming a Hurdler: Low Learning Settings Afford Identities." *Anthropology and Education Quarterly* 40, no. 1 (2009): 41–61.

National Research Council. *How People Learn: Brain, Mind, Experience, and School: Expanded Edition.* Washington, D.C: National Academies Press, 2000.

Pea, Roy D. "Practices of Distributed Intelligence and Designs for Education." In *Distributed Cognitions: Psychological and Educational Considerations*. Edited by Gavriel Salomon. New York: Cambridge University Press, 1993.

Pomson, Alex, and Howard Deitcher, eds. *Jewish Day Schools, Jewish Communities: A Reconsideration.* Portland, OR: Littman Library of Jewish Civilization, 2009.

Pope, Denise Clark. *Doing School: How We Are Creating a Generation of Stressed-Out, Materialistic, and Miseducated Students.* New Haven, CT: Yale University Press, 2001.

Reimer, Joe. "Experiential Jewish Education." In *What We Now Know about Jewish Education: Perspectives on Research for Practice*. Edited by Roberta L. Goodman, Paul A. Flexner, and Linda D. Bloomberg, 343–52. Los Angeles: Torah Aura Productions, 2009.

———. *Succeeding at Jewish Education: How One Synagogue Made It Work.* Philadelphia: Jewish Publication Society, 1997.

Rogoff, Barbara, Karen Topping, Jaquelyn Baker-Sennett, and Pilar Lacasa. "Mutual Contributions of Individuals, Partners, and Institutions: Planning to Remember in Girl Scout Cookie Sales." *Social Development* 11, no. 2 (2002): 266–89.

Rogoff, Barbara. *Apprenticeship in Thinking: Cognitive Development in Social Context.* Oxford: Oxford University Press, 1990.

Rosenak, Michael. "Jewish Religious Education and Indoctrination." *Studies in Jewish Education* 1 (1983): 117–38.

———. *Commandments and Concerns: Jewish Religious Education in Secular Society.* Philadelphia: Jewish Publication Society, 1987.

Sales, Amy L., and Leonard Saxe. *"How Goodly Are Thy Tents": Summer Camps as Jewish Socializing Experiences.* Hanover: Brandeis University Press and the AVI CHAI Foundation, 2003.

Saxe, Leonard, and Barry Chazan. *Ten Days of Birthright Israel: A Journey in Young Adult Identity*. Waltham, MA: Brandeis, 2008.

Schoem, David. "Jewish Schooling and Jewish Survival in the Suburban American Community." In *Studies in Jewish Education* vol. 2. Edited by Michael Rosenak, 52–64. Jerusalem: Magnes Press, 1984.

Schoenfeld, Stuart. "Folk Judaism, Elite Judaism and the Role of the Bar Mitzvah in the Development of the Synagogue and Jewish School in America." *Contemporary Jewry* 9, no. 1 (1987): 67–85.

Scribner, Sylvia. "Studying Working Intelligence." In *Everyday Cognition: Development in Social Context*. Edited by Barbara Rogoff and Jean Lave, 9–40. Cambridge, MA: Harvard University Press, 1984.

Thompson, Jennifer A. *Jewish on Their Own Terms: How Intermarried Couples are Changing American Judaism*. New Brunswick, NJ: Rutgers University Press, 2013.

Wertheimer, Jack, ed. *Family Matters: Jewish Education in an Age of Choice*. Waltham, MA: Brandeis, 2007.

Willis, Paul. *Learning to Labor: How Working Class Kids Get Working Class Jobs*. Morningside edition. New York: Columbia University Press, 1981.

Woocher, Jonathan. "Reinventing Jewish Education for the 21st Century." *Journal of Jewish Education* 78, no. 3 (2012): 182–226.

Old Traditions, New Practices: A Proposal for a Return to Text Study as a Centerpiece of Jewish Community and Family Life

Daniel P. Resnick and Lauren B. Resnick

While study of classical Jewish texts has always been central to the traditional curriculum, that study has waxed and waned among liberal Jews. In this chapter, Daniel and Lauren Resnick offer their own critical survey of that phenomenon. In particular, they hypothesize that the status of classical text study waned in part due to the erosion of the educational norm of textual discussion in general education. In other words, as information-delivery models came to dominate pedagogy in schools—as textbooks crowded out texts—Jewish education followed suit. However, they suggest that the tide has turned in the last decades, with a wave of research in general education that focuses on "dialogic instruction" and that emphasizes participatory discussion of texts. Texts, then, are making a comeback against textbooks, and the prospects for Jewish education are positive.

Introduction

The period of post-Holocaust life in America is unlike any known before in the history of the Jewish diaspora. Jews are actively engaged in every phase of American life and are widely respected in their professional and social lives. The great majority of non-orthodox American Jews—Reform, Conservative, and Reconstructionist—marry freely with partners of other faiths and often create new kinds of Jewish families in the process. And yet, we are different, and many of us seek to maintain that difference.

A major distinction between Jews and those of other faiths has been our relationship to sacred texts. Iconic representations of the Ten Commandments on tablets adorn our places of worship, the ark containing Torah scrolls occupies center stage in our synagogues, our doorposts are hung with rolled-up pieces of parchment from Deuteronomy, calling on us to harken to our past, remember our commandments, and educate our children. All of these are symbols of the centrality of Torah to Judaism and the Jewish community.

Jewish identity and survival as a people have been intimately connected with the study of texts: Torah, its many layers of commentary, and other classical Jewish texts. We have historically been a "people of the book" with high literacy rates and a curiosity about words, stories, and meaning, although the "book" in question has never only been the Pentateuch or even the entire Hebrew Bible.[1] Through encounters with a variety of Jewish sacred texts, we engage in a process of dialogue with the past that affirms our membership in the stream of Jewish experience. Community study of sacred texts has lent Judaism in the diaspora dignity and depth, distinguishing it in positive and self-sustaining ways from the surrounding Christian and Muslim communities.

Most of today's American Jewish community, however, seems to have lost its connection to traditional text study. The bond between Jewish identity and text study is strongest for the orthodox, and weaker among Conservative, Reform, and other denominations. Notwithstanding the "back to the sources" movement beginning in the 1980s, community surveys indicate that no more than one quarter of all adults who identify as Jewish take part in "structured Jewish learning activities." These can include going to a class, attending a lecture, or discussing a text.[2] When a more specific question is posed about how important text study itself is to "being Jewish," the portion affirming its importance is even smaller. Lisa Grant, a prominent evaluator of adult Jewish learning concludes: "... it appears that formal study just is not a high priority

---

[1] Barry Holtz has made the case strongly and clearly: "Torah and its study is the dominant religious preoccupation throughout the history of Judaism. . . ." See Barry Holtz, ed., *Back to The Sources: Reading the Classic Jewish Texts* (New York: Summit Books, 1984), 12. For Amos Oz and his daughter Fania, "Ours is not a bloodline but a textline." See Amos Oz and Fania Oz-Salzberger, *Jews and Words* (New Haven, CT: Yale University Press, 2012), 1.

[2] According to Laurence Kotler-Berkowitz et al., "National Jewish Population Survey (NJPS) 2000–2001," "Among all adults in the more strongly connected Jewish population, 24 percent (just over 800,000 total people) attended an adult Jewish education class or other kind of adult Jewish learning. . . ." See http://www.jewishdatabank.org/studies/details.cfm?-StudyID=307. Neither the 2000–2001 NJPS nor the Pew Study of 2013 pose questions about regular text study as a Jewish practice.

among most American Jews."[3] In its fullest and deepest form, Jewish text study is a lengthy process with no shortcuts; it calls for more time than families with busy schedules now think they can afford. And what place could it have, some will say, in a society concerned with digests, visuals, key words, and the "bottom line?"

In this essay we remain optimistic, nonetheless, that text study will remain a central part of Jewish learning and community participation, and we are even optimistic that its appeal to adults and families within the liberal Jewish community can grow. We confirm the persistence of Torah study with modern study aids in the liberal community, and argue that traditional types of analysis, argument, and discussion can be applied to a variety of new "texts." Jews in America have become engaged with short stories, novels, histories, and poetry along with theater, serious journalism, and film. Liberal Jews may not be spending enough time with the traditional body of Torah writings and commentary, but they have been engaged with many other kinds of texts that illuminate the story of the Jewish people.

Beyond these points, however, we also want to pursue an argument based on developments in the theory and practice of text study within secular educational contexts. We are encouraged by these developments, which are making a larger place for discussion, listening, and responding to texts of many different kinds. We believe that these developments can help make text-based discussion and argument part of the curriculum of Reform and Conservative educational programs. Efforts in this direction have already begun.

In our first section below we offer a brief perspective on the evolution of discussion and argument in the study of our traditional Jewish texts, particular in liberal Jewish communities. We want to offer a view of the landscape, calling

---

3   See Lisa Grant, "Jewish Men and Adult Jewish Learning," 5. Accessed in the Berman Jewish Policy Archive, https://www.bjpa.org/search-results/publication/4803 [Originally published in *The Gender Gap* (New York: URJ Press 2007)]. Grant reports that In a Long Island survey, only 13 percent to 18 percent assigned high priority to text study as a practice, with significant gender differences among Reform and Conservative respondents. "Simply put, it appears that women act on being Jewish more than men." When a question is asked about "Jewish study," without specification of texts as such, the portion responding positively is higher, but does not rise above 25 percent. The denominational differences are confirmed in the Pittsburgh Jewish Community Study, 2002. When asked in a telephone survey whether they had been "regularly engaged" in Jewish study during the preceding year or two, 25 percent of the Conservatives said "yes," as did 19 percent of the Reform, 56 percent of the orthodox, and 8 percent of the others. This survey did not seek out differences in the practices of men and women. See Ukeles Associates, "The 2002 Pittsburgh Jewish Community Study Final Report" (updated December 2002): 86, http://www.jfedpgh.org/document.doc?id=13.

attention to certain features that we believe are significant. In the second section, we consider the changes that are taking place in the education of children, where social theory and theories of language and learning are changing school practice. In the third section, we call attention to the ways that the new focus on textual engagement in mainstream American education echoes and adapts traditional Jewish approaches to text, as well as propose some new ways that it might do so. Finally, we conclude by expressing optimism about the future of Jewish text exploration and its contribution to the cultural life of our people.

The Evolution of Jewish Text Study in Non-Orthodox Settings

Despite the relatively few people participating in it, few practices have evolved in style and focus in the non-orthodox community as much as text study. A variety of tools have emerged to support the study of texts in multiple venues. Outside of a small scholarly community, most Jews in America are unable to read and understand the sacred texts in the language in which they were written. However, side-by-side Hebrew/English pages of the Pentateuch, with notes and commentary, now allow American Jews to approach the printed word closely and critically. A variety of online study aids have also come into widespread use. The impact of these tools, providing access to those without traditional training, cannot be underestimated.

The habits of study, interpretation, and discussion have persisted and are now in evidence as Jews engage with a variety of texts in many languages and many disciplines. These habits of mind were shaped in Torah study. As Ismar Schorsch wrote in his foreword to *Etz Hayim: Torah and Commentary*, the important Hebrew-English volume of annotated Torah text and commentaries from the Conservative movement:

> Judaism is above all a life of dialogue. Revelation destined Israel to become a nation of readers and interpreters. ...Jews learned to read deeply rather than quickly, disjunctively as well as contextually. Each generation and every Jew was bidden to pore over the text afresh to internalize its normative force and to garner another layer of undetected meaning.[4]

While the Jewish interpretive tradition has always been diverse, non-scholarly readers now have more than one pair of eyes to read the text.

---

4 Ismar Schorsch, forward to *Etz Hayim: Torah and Commentary*, ed. David L. Lieber (Philadelphia: Jewish Publication Society, 2001), xvii.

Translators' notes and observations about historical context appear below the line and in appended essays. Literary theory, moreover, has changed the very definition of a text, obliging the reader to engage with it to give it meaning. Women's authority to interpret text has challenged what had been a male monopoly, increasing empathy for Biblical characters and heightening appreciation for human agency.

The Bar/Bat Mitzvah

To take one prominent context as an example, text study for the Bar/Bat Mitzvah has benefited from these developments by providing young students with a wealth of approaches and interpretive stances that, just a few decades ago, would not have been available. Much has been written about the social side of celebrating this rite of passage, and many jokes made about the gift-giving associated with it. But in liberal Jewish communities, the heart of the Bar/Bat Mitzvah is study of the Torah. Preparation for the ceremony of Bar/Bat Mitzvah begins with the traditional patterns of Torah study. The young person will carefully examine the portion of the week for the Saturday on which the ceremony will be held, usually with a rabbi or educator from the congregation. After studying the text, with notes and commentary, the boy or girl has two tasks. The first is to read from the Torah scroll and the second is to prepare a talk to the congregation—a *d'var Torah*—on the meaning of the text. To make this "coming of age" ceremony possible, many members of the congregation contribute their knowledge and skills, and family members who come before the opened Torah scroll rehearse their Hebrew to offer their blessings. But of equal importance, the effort to articulate some meaningful perspective on the text depends on a set of new intellectual resources that are readily available. To be sure, in many cases the social elements seem to displace the religious and intellectual ones. Nevertheless, the ceremony is a validation of the role played by Torah study in maintaining Jewish identity across generations, even as the *d'var Torah* is frequently a fascinating example of how to read old texts in new ways.

Looking beyond the Bar/Bat Mitzvah, we can see evolving modalities of text study that help Jews—particularly adults—to keep text study vibrant. What follow are some other examples drawn from our experiences and observations of contexts of text study that seem to draw increasing, and increasingly diverse, numbers of participants.

Tikkun Leil Shavuot/Shavuot Eve Study

Every Sabbath is a special day for Torah study, but one holiday marks the central experience of receiving the Torah, the holiday of Shavuot. In many Jewish communities across America, the evening of Shavuot has become an occasion for late night Jewish learning, on a community-wide as well as a congregational basis, adapting the kabbalah-influenced practice of an all-night study session (or "tikkun").[5] The diversity of backgrounds of attendees at such events offers evidence that a traditional observance can extend its reach to non-orthodox members of the community. Many denominations can recognize what they have in common, and that text study, short lectures by the learned, and Jewish argument can have a continuing appeal. Moreover, the texts studied at a Shavuot Eve Study may range broadly, from Torah and Talmud, to medieval philosophy, to modern poetry. In this way, Shavuot Eve Study has become, in some locations, a kind of mini-festival of Jewish culture.

Weekly and Daily Study

At the congregational level, Jewish text learning through rabbi-led study of the weekly portion, often before Saturday morning services, and rabbi-led Talmud courses appear to be growing significantly, although still drawing only a small committed core. In addition, in large cities, there is a growth in lay-led *minyanim*, some of which meet separately for text study. Doctors and lawyers, within their own professional groups, sometimes meet to study text, often focused on medical and legal ethics. Jewish agencies may sponsor some of this activity, but it is often grassroots and bottom-up. Some of those who participate in Torah study prepare in advance by consulting the many online commentaries readily available to them.

    The Conservative and Reform movements have both produced volumes that include not only the Torah and its translation but also aids for study. The Conservative *Etz Haim* includes 160 pages of essays that reflect the movement's

---

5 Community-wide Shavuot observances in many American cities are posted on the Internet and organized at the local level. For some reporting on how this has proceeded in a middle-sized city like Pittsburgh, see Toby Tabachnick, "Community Shabbaton Will Cross Denominational Lines," *The Pittsburgh Jewish Chronicle,* April 25, 2012, and Andrew Goldstein, "Jewish Pittsburgh Studies All Night and into the Morning to Mark Shavuot," *The Pittsburgh Jewish Chronicle,* June 3, 2012, http://www.thejewishchronicle.net/view/full_story/18843574/article-Jewish-Pittsburgh-studies-all-night-and-into-the-morning-to-mark-Shavuot.

effort to absorb critical biblical scholarship without challenging the divinely inspired character of the work. The discussion of Revelation, Torah, and Mt. Sinai in the essays by Daniel Gordis and Elliot Dorff illustrates this well.[6] In the Reform movement, David Stein's *The Torah: A Modern Commentary*, an updating of Gunther Plaut's earlier work,[7] and Tamara Cohn-Eskenazi's *The Torah, A Women's Commentary*[8] likewise provide tools for study along with the text.

Since the 1980s, Federations, denominations and Congregations have mounted educational programs for adults, children, and families. Formal text study has many sponsors and is available in many formats. Me'ah programs developed by Hebrew College in the 1990s are now getting support from the Combined Jewish Philanthropies of Greater Boston and are being reconceived for different demographics. The Florence Melton Adult Jewish Mini-School program developed at the Hebrew University of Jerusalem now offers courses, according to its website, to 5,500 adults in almost fifty sites.

Beyond the weekly rhythm of classes, there is also a pattern of daily study, known as *Daf Yomi*, literally, "the daily page." The page in question refers to a page of Talmud, and the Daf Yomi curriculum is a standardized schedule of daily Talmud study that was formalized almost a century ago. But now it is supported on the web, with English-language translations and websites dedicated to the practice, making it accessible far beyond its core audience of orthodox men.

We note that Chancellor Arnold Eisen of the Jewish Theological Seminary, in a Wall Street Journal op-ed, called for renewing and revising the practice. He did not critique Talmud study, but said that we need "a different page of Jewish learning, one that is open to the larger world and bears the impact of modern thinking." That "different page" would be both traditional and modern. "It would cleave faithfully to texts, rituals, history and faith while being informed by art, music, drama, poetry, politics and law." But crucially, Eisen's vision maintained the daily rhythm of Daf Yomi. "Imagine if every Jew who wished to do so

---

6 David L. Lieber, ed., *Etz Hayim: Torah and Commentary* (Philadelphia: Jewish Publication Society, 2001). See Hillel Halkin's nuanced and sometimes grudging assessment of this achievement in Hillel Halkin, "'Boiling a Kid': Reflections on a New Bible Commentary," *Commentary* 115, no. 4 (April 2003), 37–43.

7 W. Gunther Plaut and David E. S. Stein, *The Torah: A Modern Commentary* (New York: Union for Reform Judaism, 2005).

8 Tamara Cohn Eskenazi, *The Torah: A Women's Commentary* (New York: URJ Press and Women of Reform Judaism, 2008).

could awake to a platform of daily Jewish text not limited to Talmud—and to Jewish media not limited to text."[9]

The Search for Ethical Teachings

Many contemporary Jews study Torah or other classical texts not for mastery of the subject or coverage of a corpus, but rather, in order to seek guidance in living their lives, and wisdom about how to do so well. The Pew Research Center's 2013 Survey of American Jews indicated that, for those in the large sample, "Leading an ethical and moral life," along with remembering the Holocaust, were the most essential elements in "being Jewish."[10] Where some might turn to self-help literature, others turn to the Jewish tradition. Torah study for adults, premised on discussion, argument, and example, can play an important role in building that ethical consciousness, especially when specifically oriented toward that function. As Rabbi David Teutsch recently reminded us:

> The purpose of studying Torah is to gain insight and wisdom about how to lead a good life. While all forms of learning are laudable, the kind that qualifies as Torah study aims not primarily at increased knowledge or analysis, but at deeper understanding and deeper devotion to living out a commitment to goodness and authenticity.[11]

Torah study to guide decision-making can have a powerful appeal and a spiritual dimension. But there is also a literature, captured in the *Mussar* (self-discipline, moral conduct) movement, that argues that Torah is not enough, and that valuable ethical and spiritual guidance can be found in the last thousand years of medieval and rabbinic writings, from Ibn Gabirol and Maimonides to Chaim Luzzatto. Mussar was introduced in eighteenth century Lithuanian traditionalist *yeshivot* by Israel Salanter, a significant figure in the emergence of modern Jewish psychology and philosophy. Reform and Conservative scholars

---

9 Arnold M. Eisen, "A New Page for Jewish Learning," *Wall Street Journal*, August 9, 2012, http://www.wsj.com/articles/SB10000872396390443404004577578960721021888.
10 Pew Research Center, "A Portrait of Jewish Americans" (2013), 56, http://www.pewforum.org/files/2013/10/jewish-american-full-report-for-web.pdf.
11 David A. Teutsch, *A Guide to Jewish Practice Vol. I: Everyday Living* (Wyncote, PA: RRC Press, 2011), 70. Rabbi David A. Teutsch is the Wiener Professor of Contemporary Jewish Civilization and director of the Levin-Lieber Program in Jewish Ethics at the Reconstructionist Rabbinical College (RRC) in Philadelphia. He served for more than a decade as President of the RRC.

and educators after the Second World War assumed leadership in spreading the program of study.[12] Mussar introduced a now familiar set of Jewish values—humility, generosity, kindness, thankfulness, order, empathy, holiness, community, and others—as the object of study, meditation, and practice. The most visible contemporary leaders among the non-orthodox are Alan Morinis and Ira F. Stone.[13]

Books and Film

Thus, while it is still the case that a majority of liberal American Jewish adults do not engage in anything that resembles text study, an impressive minority do so, through one or more of the avenues delineated here. Far from being a relic of a traditionalist society with uncritical assumptions about the meaning of the texts in question, something that we can identify as "text study" is alive and well in modern (liberal) Jewish America. This is fascinating, and it is deserving of both further study and further development.

At the same time, it is also worth calling attention to a complementary cultural phenomenon, the ways in which Jews engaged in consuming, discussing, and exploring other kinds of texts and text-analogues. Jews read all sorts of contemporary literature, and they like to talk about what they are reading. Novels, histories, memoirs, short stories, and poetry are all the focus of group study in a myriad of book clubs. "Jewish book clubs" as a Google query produced almost ten million hits, compared to three million hits for "African American book clubs," two million for Presbyterian, and under two million for Catholic.[14] The places where the clubs convene are more likely to be homes

---

12 See Geoffrey Claussen, "The American Jewish Revival of Musar," *The Hedgehog Review: Critical Reflections on Contemporary Culture* 12, no. 2 (2010), http://iasc-culture.org/THR/THR_article_2010_Summer_Claussen.php; Corinne E. Blackmer, "Transforming Ethical Behavior: The Musar Movement and the Care of the Self," *Judaica Ukrainica* 3 (2014), 24–36.
13 Alan Morinis is Dean of the Mussar Institute, which he founded more than a decade ago. He is the author of *Climbing Jacob's Ladder: One Man's Journey to Discovery of a Jewish Spiritual Tradition* (New York, Broadway Boosk, 2002), *Everyday Holiness: The Jewish Spiritual Path of Mussar* (Boston: Trumpeter, 2007), and *Every Day, Holy Day* (Boston: Trumpeter, 2010). See www.mussarinstitute.org for his online guidance of individual, *havruta* and group study. Rabbi Ira F. Stone has been working to strengthen Mussar practice within the Conservative movement. He is the author of *A Responsible Life: The Spiritual Path of Mussar* (Eugene, OR: Wipf and Stock Publishers, 2005).
14 On June 11, 2015, a Google query produced 9,830,000 hits for Jewish book clubs, 2,850,000 for African American, 2,180,000 results for Presbyterian, and 1,700,000 for Catholic book clubs.

than congregations or community centers. The web is an important source for book titles, discussion guides, interviews with authors, and blogs about books. The interrogatory style, the questioning habits of mind, and the delight in argument, cultivated in Torah text study, are all in play when Jewish book clubs meet, although for many it can be mainly a social occasion.

The wide reach of Jewish book clubs, and the discussions they generate, are a prime example of how some of the methods used in the study of sacred text can be applied to novels, biographies, and memoirs. Book clubs help to build up knowledge of history, leadership, immigration, Zionism, gender roles, and cultural conflicts that is relevant for American Jews in the open society in which they live.

Film is recognized as a special kind of "text" by literary and media critics,[15] and it has evolved over the past century under the guiding hand of Jewish producers whose names are now legends. Neal Gabler's *An Empire of their Own* (1988),[16] tells that story. There is now a contagion to film festivals that celebrate Jewish themes and producers from around the world. According to a film reviewer in *The Forward,* eighty Jewish film festivals were scheduled in fifty states in 2014. The list of the twenty best included Baton Rouge, Charlotte, and Mobile, as well as New York, Miami, and San Francisco. The eleven-day JFilm festival in Pittsburgh has run for over twenty years, and a recent version included twenty films, twenty-eight screenings, and about four thousand attendees.[17] Films have provided American Jews perspectives on the Holocaust, Israeli life, and diaspora conditions that they would otherwise be denied, and have extended considerably the sense of Jewish family and community.

The Changing Face of Education: From Recitation to Structured Text Discussion

Throughout this chapter, we are oscillating between highlighting the centrality of text study to Jewish community and acknowledging that text study is a

---

15 Stanley Fish made a significant contribution to reader-response theory and the practice of interpretive reading. See Fish, *Is There a Text in This Class? The Authority of Interpretive Communities* (Cambridge, MA: Harvard University Press, 1980).
16 Neal Gabler, *An Empire of Their Own: How the Jews Invented Hollywood* (New York: Crown, 1988).
17 See Sheerly Avni, "The Best Jewish Film Festivals of 2014," *The Forward,* January 3, 2014 http://forward.com/culture/190088/the-best-jewish-film-festivals-of-2014/. For information about JFilm in Pittsburgh, see http://jfilmpgh.org/programs-events/festivals/jfilm-festival/.

practice that is pursued by only a minority of the liberal Jewish community. We might wonder why the latter is the case. There are surely many reasons, but we want to call attention to one reason in particular that we believe has been underappreciated. The reason is this: Text study for children diminished in Reform and Conservative religious education over decades of trying to bring Jewish education into closer alignment with the formalized patterns of American education. Classroom discussion, until recently, was not an active part of American classroom practice. There was no recognized place for structured text-based discussions, discussions in which students were guided through—and had the opportunity to practice—rigorous consideration of problems, data, or written texts. On the contrary, the model that dominated formal American education was an information-delivery model. The textbook reigned supreme, with an authority that could not be questioned. It is no surprise that Jewish religious education mimicked the norms of general American education. A good Jewish religious educational environment was a classroom with a textbook (about Jewish history or thought or practice) from which the teacher could instruct and from which the students could absorb information.

Now, however, the tide has turned. In secular education, there is growing understanding of the limitations of textbooks, and growing interest in learning through active discussions of texts broadly considered. Interest in dialogic discussion-based methods of teaching and learning began in US lay education in the 1960s and 1970s and has grown since to become a major theme of scholarly research and applied education efforts. At the base of the new methods are theories of language as *communication* rooted in specific cultural traditions and of reading as an *interpretive* undertaking. Science and mathematics in this vein became *reasoned argumentation* rather than a collection of facts and procedures.

This nascent scholarly movement was already in process when a major compilation of the work of Lev Vygotsky (1896–1934), a Russian-Jewish educator and scholar of language and thinking, appeared in an English translation in 1978.[18] Vygotsky put forth a theory of language and intelligence as inherently *social* constructions. His work reached America just as the explosion of research on language, often collaborations between linguists and anthropologists, provided a stream of publications documenting the different ways that

---

18 See L. S. Vygotsky, *Mind in Society: The Development of Higher Psychological Processes*, ed. Michael Cole et al. (Cambridge, MA: Harvard University Press, 1978). An earlier translated compilation of his work, published in 1962, did not have the same impact.

mostly oral language functioned in home, community, and school settings. In virtually all of these studies a marked difference in language between lower class and minority families and those of the ascendant groups was noted. Almost everyone observed that children from working or minority populations confronted language in school that was very different from that used at home. Yet, evidence mounted that certain kinds of classroom discussion could draw out significant reasoning abilities among even the poorest and most culturally isolated students.

Educators, and some political activists, gradually seized on these ideas as a way of simultaneously increasing the overall level of learning in American schools and, at the same time, the power of the schools to provide more equitable results across different populations of students. These were both important education agendas in the 1980's and '90s, furthered by publication of *A Nation at Risk* (1983)[19] and the growing centrality of educational opportunity to the civil rights movement. The suggestions emerging from research on student discussion of problems or texts became more relevant to educators. In secular education, there was growing understanding of the limitations of textbooks and a rising interest in learning through active, teacher-guided but "student-owned" discussions.

Teacher-guided student discussions of literary texts (in English class and sometimes history), concepts and problems (in mathematics), and data sets (in science) are now among the most heavily promoted and researched practices in the learning sciences. This is true in North America and Western Europe especially, but to some extent in any part of the world that is investing in education. Academic conferences and teacher development workshops are likely to include multiple sessions on revising classroom practice to include much more discussion and argumentation.

Dialogic forms of teaching have theoretical roots in cognitive psychology, linguistics, child development, and social theories of mind. As teaching methods, they may be called Accountable Talk, Academically Productive Talk, argumentation, or several other titles.[20] Because of the way it features

---

19 National Commission on Excellence in Education, *A Nation at Risk: The Imperative for Educational Reform* (US Department of Education: 1983).

20 Lauren B. Resnick et al., "How (Well-Structured) Talk Builds the Mind," in *Innovations in Educational Psychology: Perspectives on Learning, Teaching, and Human Development*, ed. David D. Preiss and Robert J. Sternberg (New York: Springer, 2010), 163–94. Accountable Talk® is a registered trademark of the University of Pittsburgh. Lee Shulman has made his own case for accountability in pedagogy: "A persistent problem of most forms of education

argumentation and philosophical reasoning, Matthew Lipman's Philosophy for Children, introduced to American schools in the 1970s, belongs with this group of discussion-rich pedagogies. It is worth looking in depth at this form of talk—what it is and what it is not—because of its similarities to the Jewish critical approach to text.

In this still small but rapidly growing field of research, almost everyone agrees on three points about effective classroom talk. Each has a reasonably strong body of supporting research evidence, much of it now assembled in a volume published by the American Education Research Association (2015) based on a conference held in Pittsburgh.[21]

1. The talk is argumentative, sometimes noisily so, as children struggle to express ideas that are new to them, outside of their "comfort zone."
2. It is teacher-*structured*, but student-*owned*. Teachers set problems and "standards" for debating them, but students develop the ideas, "turning them and turning them again" in an echo of Jewish religious text study.
3. There are clear standards for what counts as a good discussion, often described as the "three accountabilities:" *accountability to knowledge*, getting the "facts" right even if it is a struggle to find exactly the right wording; *accountability to reasoning*, being able to provide a rational justification for a claim or explanation; *accountability to community*, speaking in ways that respect the ideas and feelings of other students.

In this form of talk, students think out loud: noticing something about a problem, puzzling through a surprising finding, or articulating, explaining, and reflecting upon their own reasoning. The teacher works to elicit a range of ideas, which may be emergent or incomplete. With teacher guidance, other students take up their classmates' statements: building on, challenging, or clarifying a claim (including a teacher's claim); posing questions; reasoning about a proposed solution; or offering a counter claim or an alternate explanation.

---

is that they permit student invisibility, which breeds disinterest and leads to zoning out and non-learning. Learning requires that students feel visible and accountable." See Lee Shulman, "Pedagogies of Uncertainty," *Liberal Education* 91, no. 2 (2005), 18–25.

21 See Lauren B. Resnick et al., eds., *Socializing Intelligence Through Academic Talk and Dialogue* (Washington, DC: American Educational Research Association, 2015). Contributors to thirty-four chapters present our current understanding of the theory, practice, and effectiveness of discussion teaching in different forms, disciplines, and countries.

All students are positioned as intellectual agents in the discussion; all students are expected to use their minds. Overall, the teacher's goal is to sustain a process of shared reasoning that ultimately leads to a more fully developed, evidence-backed conclusion, solution, or explanation.

These forms of dialogic teaching and learning are quite different from the traditional American and European traditions of recitation that migrated out of Christian religious training into lay schools in many countries beginning in the eighteenth century. The school-based version of recitation is widely used to teach a defined body of knowledge to students who may be only weakly literate and in any case are expected to learn only simple ideas. Although such exchanges may sometimes probe for meaning, there is little of the intellectual challenge that characterizes lively Torah study. Correct answers are sought, without aiming for deep understanding. Unfortunately, this recitation model is still widely used in American classrooms, although it is under challenge for reasons we have indicated.

The key difference between recitation and dialogic learning lies in who owns the storyline—who is allowed to change it. In Accountable Talk, teachers do not merely repeat what students say, they ask students whether their own "re-voicing" faithfully captured the student's intended meaning. A teacher might say, "I'm not sure I understand. Did you mean. . .?" or "I'm not sure I have your thinking right. Are you saying. . .?" These moves not only engage students in co-constructing an argument, they reinforce for students that they "own" their own ideas, that they have minds that can change and grow. Decades of research have shown that students who believe that the mind can grow are more successful academically than those who see intelligence as fixed.

Bridging Jewish Text Study and Contemporary Dialogic Education

Accountable Talk and other forms of dialogic education share some features with *havruta*, a form of paired text study considered a signature Jewish pedagogy. *Havruta* has been documented and analyzed in orthodox yeshivas by Baruch Schwarz and in a non-orthodox after-school program by Orit Kent.[22]

---

22 See Baruch B. Schwarz, "Discussing Argumentative Texts as a Traditional Jewish Learning Practice," in Resnick, *Socializing Intelligence*, 157–66, as well as his chapter in this volume. Eli Holzer and Orit Kent describe methods and concepts in A Philosophy of Havruta: Understanding and Teaching the Art of Text Study in Pairs, Jewish Identities in Post-Modern Society (Boston: Academic Studies Press, 2013). See also Orit Kent, "A Theory of Havruta Learning," in *Turn It and Turn It Again: Studies in the Teaching and Learning of*

In both *havruta* settings, pairs of students are co-constructing the meaning of texts. They agree and disagree, negotiate rewordings, and look for resources within the assembled texts to support their interpretations or challenge those of their partners. When they can't resolve their disagreements they ask for help. This process allows students to make decisions or enlarge their interpretive options.

Kent has worked with both teachers and students. Her pilot with middle school students has some unique features. Students follow guidelines. They use note cards to prompt attention to listening, paraphrasing (re-voicing), attending to the evidence, and dealing with different interpretations. In her model, the text is assumed to have a voice in the discussions, several pairs are at work in the same classroom, and the teacher is present to guide the work of the pairs when needed.[23]

The interpenetration of traditional Jewish approaches to text and modern literary approaches to reading and discussion can also be seen in Shira Horowitz's description of how she has taught the weekly Torah portion to young children. Her sessions of "Torah talk" begin to structure, for those who are only six and seven years old, the features of Torah study for more mature children and adults. Incorporating the work of Lucy Calkins[24] on reading instruction for children, she has had her students ask questions, attend to what is in the text, listen to one another, paraphrase, summarize, and find their own voice. Even very young children can develop an appreciation for the interplay of reader and text.

These examples demonstrate an impressive degree of coherence between the central aspects of contemporary dialogic education and the features of traditional Jewish text study, even when that text study is carried out in not-exactly-traditional settings. But we believe that there are further, untapped opportunities to bridge Jewish text study and dialogic education.

Classical Texts, eds. Jon A. Levisohn and Susan P. Fendrick (Boston: Academic Studies Press, 2013), 286–322.

23 For an excellent video presentation of how this works in the classroom, see Allison Cook and Orit Kent, "Learning Torah Through Partnership (9.5-minute version)," Mandel Center for Studies in Jewish Education, 2014, as well as their accompanying viewer's guide, found at http://www.brandeis.edu/mandel/pdfs/2014-10-24_Video-companion_Learning_Torah_through_Partnership.pdf. See also Orit Kent and Allison Cook, "Leveraging Resources for Learning Through the Power of Partnership," Working Paper (Beit Midrash Research Center, Jack, Joseph and Morton Mandel Center for Studies in Jewish Education, Brandeis University, 2014).

24 For more on Lucy Calkins and the Writing Workshop, see her background, publications, and interests in http://www.tc.columbia.edu/academics/index.htm?facid=lmc71.

One example may be the kinds of Jewish book clubs or discussion groups to which we referred earlier. Within these groups, leaders and participants benefit from discussion questions, often included in published works. The online National Jewish Book Club offers its own set of questions for selected titles, along with other aids to facilitate discussion.[25] But discussion questions alone are not sufficient to structure the kind of genuinely dialogic environment that we would like to see. To be sure, many skilled facilitators intuit on their own how to make a comfortable space for textual exploration. But others need help. They need guidance about how to structure dialogue in ways that will empower the discussants and yet respect the text. The "three accountabilities" of Accountable Talk would certainly reduce the conversational wanderings that threaten poorly guided discussions. There is an art, we know from our Jewish tradition, to productive discussion of text. Articulating the desired norms and making them easily comprehensible would go a long way to enriching this setting for the study of texts.

Here it is also important to note that just as digital technology has helped to widen and deepen for more readers the discussion of sacred text, so has it also changed discussions of other Jewish writings. Before a book club meeting, many attendees have had access to reviews, accessed online. And once the discussion begins, if they have their book in tablet form, they can challenge one another by referring easily to specific passages, searching for phrases, or even doing word counts. In other words, it is now easier for more readers to argue from the text. When we envision Jewish book groups as sites for dialogic textual investigation, we should actively integrate the technology at our fingertips to help make readers more active in establishing meaning and owning an interpretation.

This is one example of a way of deepening and enriching text study within Jewish communities. Are there others? Surely there are—but we may need to adopt a more experimental approach than we are used to. One aspect of an experimental approach is to seek out "natural experiments," undertaken without design or oversight, responding to local needs. Where is text study flourishing? Who has undertaken a novel approach? These natural experiments can and must be documented and analyzed, generating a knowledge base for others. Beyond the naturally occurring experiments, however, a

---

25 Among the many Jewish book clubs, The National Jewish Book Club stands out for the quality of its offering and the many study aids. See http://www.jewishbookcouncil.org/bookclub/national-jewish-book-club. For the Yale UP Jewish biography series, see http://www.jewishlives.org/

second aspect of an experimental approach is more intentional innovation, undertaken with the express purpose of trying out new methods and documenting the process. We suggest, therefore, a project that attempts to explore text study in a series of learning experiments, conducted in pilot form in a small number of communities.

Skilled educators have an opportunity to devise short courses, outdoor experiences, and one-off experiences that enlarge the opportunity for discussion of texts. Adults and young people might study together or separately. The groups may be guided by rabbis and other trained educators or by lay members willing to put in time to learn the texts and available resources in depth. The texts studied might follow the traditional Jewish calendar of study, or a study group may choose texts that explore certain ethical themes. The study groups may meet in synagogues or other specifically Jewish spaces, or in countryside campgrounds, retreat settings, or homes. We can experiment with calendars that will make the experience maximally available to those who would like to participate. We imagine a spreading leadership—with new groups being formed as new interests are recognized.

Eventually, presumably, there will need to be some reliable funding streams to grow these experimental study programs and provide study materials that help people access the ideas—traditional and new—that study will itself produce. But the program in any given city could begin with almost no funding at all—meeting in homes and synagogues and using study materials that are easily available on the web.

Maintaining, extending, and deepening the study of texts of all kinds at all ages is a challenge for congregations, community centers, Jewish media, and inter-denominational collaboration. The potential for exciting text study experiences, however, is substantial, even for school-age children who find school-based study "boring." We can see how animated children become when engaged in close analysis and discussion of texts. This is true for text study in secular classrooms as well as for the study of Jewish texts in Jewish learning environments. Those who seek "a renewal of spirit" may find that it begins in the pedagogy of small-group learning in school programs, summer camps, and retreats.

In many ways what we are proposing is something so old—for the Jews—that we wonder whether we need to propose it. Maybe it is happening already. If so, our main task will be to discover it, document it, promote it, enlarge it, make it so exciting that everyone is talking about the study of texts as a central feature of Jewish communal life.

Conclusion

We expect widening expressions of Jewish cultural life, extending within and beyond currently recognized venues. Each of us has in our home the power to call up the great library of Alexandria, the galleries of the Louvre, and the latest expressions of stand-up Jewish comedy. With our digital devices, we can also create rallies for worthy causes, protest injustice, support the needy, and explore the relationship of religious communities and the state. The world appears to be unfolding before us.

Learning and study have a central place in this expansion of Jewish life. We have continued to explore our Torah, in all its dimensions. In the words of Rabbi David Teutsch:

> Torah study is not limited to Bible, midrash and Talmud. It can include medieval Jewish philosophy and poetry, kabbala (medieval Jewish mysticism) and hasidut (the works of Hasidism)… contemporary thought and so on. Many of us would include works by Jewish and non-Jewish artists, writers and spiritual masters as well.[26]

Our sages established study, prayer, and good deeds as the foundation of a Jewish life, but they did not place limits on where to pray, fix the boundaries of what to study, or circumscribe where we would perform our acts of kindness. We have respected life as a continuing creation, and acknowledged our responsibility to invent and adapt, even as we celebrate our tradition. There is an amazing fullness to the variety of Jewish life in North America.

We believe that the growing interest in Jewish study of all kinds will find a locus in homes, community centers, movie theatres, camps, and places we cannot now imagine. As it grows, more adults and families will enjoy discussion and argument around texts of all kinds. The focus on study has brought many benefits to American Jews in family life, daily habits, and educational goals. It has extended the Jewish presence and influence in the professions and the broader society. Maintaining a heritage, however, requires practice.

We have seen that traditional Jewish learning methods (for both children and adults) share many features with the styles of Accountable Talk and other forms of dialogic education that are emerging in general education: discussion of texts; commitment to a "knowledge based" form of reasoning and argumentation; and willingness to approach difficult topics. It is time to harvest these learning techniques across boundaries of age and denomination.

---

26 Teutsch, *A Guide to Jewish Practice Vol. I*, 70.

Bibliography

"A Portrait of Jewish Americans." Pew Research Center, 2013. http://www.jewishdatabank.org/studies/downloadFile.cfm?FileID=3088.

Avni, Sheerly. "The Best Jewish Film Festivals of 2014." *The Forward*, January 3, 2014. http://forward.com/culture/190088/the-best-jewish-film-festivals-of-2014/.

Blackmer, Corinne E. "Transforming Ethical Behavior: The Musar Movement and the Care of the Self." *Judaica Ukrainica* 3 (2014). http://judaicaukrainica.ukma.edu.ua/ckfinder/userfiles/files/JU_3_2013_Blackmer.pdf.

"Calkins, Lucy." *Teachers College: Columbia University*. http://www.tc.columbia.edu/faculty/lmc71/.

Claussen, Geoffrey. "The American Jewish Revival of Musar." *The Hedgehog Review: Critical Reflections on Contemporary Culture* 12, no. 2 (2010). http://iasc-culture.org/THR/THR_article_2010_Summer_Claussen.php.

Cohn Eskenazi, Tamara. *The Torah: A Women's Commentary*. URJ Press and Women of Reform Judaism, 2008.

Cook, Allison, and Orit Kent. "'Learning Torah through Partnership' A Viewer's Guide." Mandel Center for Studies in Jewish Education, 2014. http://www.brandeis.edu/mandel/pdfs/2014-10-24_Video-companion_Learning_Torah_through_Partnership.pdf.

———. "Learning Torah Through Partnership (9.5 minute version)." Mandel Center for Studies in Jewish Education, 2014. https://vimeo.com/97982899.

Eisen, Arnold M. "A New Page for Jewish Learning." *The Wall Street Journal*, August 9, 2012. https://www.wsj.com/articles/SB10000872396390443404004577578960721021888.

Fish, Stanley. *Is There a Text in This Class? The Authority of Interpretive Communities*. Cambridge, MA: Harvard University Press, 1980.

Gabler, Neal. *An Empire of Their Own: How the Jews Invented Hollywood*. New York: Crown, 1988.

Goldstein, Andrew. "Annual Shavuot Study Draws Hundreds." *The Jewish Chronicle*, 2013. http://thejewishchronicle.net/pages/full_story/push?article-Annual+Shavuot+-study+draws+hundreds%20&id=22681762.

———. "Jewish Pittsburgh Studies All Night and Into the Morning to Mark Shavuot." *The Jewish Chronicle*, 2012. http://www.thejewishchronicle.net/view/full_story/18843574/article-Jewish-Pittsburgh-studies-all-night-and-into-the-morning-to-mark-Shavuot.

Halkin, Hillel. "'Boiling a Kid': Reflections on a New Bible Commentary." *Commentary* 115, no. 4 (April 2003), 37–43.

Holtz, Barry W., ed. *Back to The Sources: Reading the Classic Jewish Texts*. New York: Summit Books, 1984.

Holzer, Eli, and Orit Kent. *A Philosophy of Havruta: Understanding and Teaching the Art of Text Study in Pairs*. Jewish Identities in Post-Modern Society. Boston: Academic Studies Press, 2013.

"Jewish Lives: Biographies that Illuminate Jewish Experience." *JewishLives.org*. https://www.jewishlives.org/.

JFilm Festivals Pittsburgh. http://filmpittsburgh.org/.

Kent, Orit. "A Theory of Havruta Learning." In *Turn It and Turn It Again: Studies in the Teaching and Learning of Classical Texts*. Edited by Jon A. Levisohn and Susan P. Fendrick. Boston: Academic Studies Press, 2013.

Kent, Orit, and Allison Cook. "Leveraging Resources for Learning Through the Power of Partnership." Working Paper. Beit Midrash Research Center, Jack, Joseph and Morton Mandel Center for Studies in Jewish Education, Brandeis University, 2014.

Kotler-Berkowitz, Laurence, Steven M. Cohen, Vivian Klaff, Frank Mott, Lorraine Blass, Jim Schwartz, Jonathan Ament. "National Jewish Population Survey (NJPS) 2000-01." United Jewish Communities, 2001. http://www.jewishdatabank.org/studies/details.cfm?StudyID=307.

Lieber, David L. *Etz Hayim: Torah and Commentary*. Philadelphia: Jewish Publication Society, 2001.

Lisa Grant. "Jewish Men and Adult Jewish Learning." In *The Gender Gap: A Congregational Guide for Beginning the Conversation about Men's Involvement in Synagogue Life*. Edited by Hara E. Person with Carolyn Bricklen, Owen Gotlieb, and Melissa Zalkin Stollman. New York: URJ Press 2007. http://www.bjpa.org/Publications/downloadFile.cfm?FileID=4701.

Morinis, Alan. *Climbing Jacob's Ladder: One Man's Rediscovery of a Jewish Spiritual Tradition*. Broadway Books: 2002.

———. *Every Day, Holy Day: 365 Days of Teachings and Practices from the Jewish Tradition of Mussar*. Shambhala: 2010.

———. *Everyday Holiness: The Jewish Spiritual Path of Mussar*. Shambhala: 2007.

National Commission on Excellence in Education. *A Nation at Risk: The Imperative for Educational Reform*. US Department of Education: 1983.

"National Jewish Book Club." *Jewish Book Council*. http://www.jewishbookcouncil.org/book-club/national-jewish-book-club.

Oz, Amos, and Fania Oz-Salzberger. *Jews and Words*. New Haven, CT: Yale University Press, 2012.

Plaut, W. Gunther, and David E. S. Stein. *The Torah: A Modern Commentary*. Union for Reform Judaism, 2005.

Resnick, Lauren B., Christa S. C. Asterhan, and Sherice N. Clarke, eds. *Socializing Intelligence Through Academic Talk and Dialogue*. Washington, DC: American Educational Research Association, 2015.

Resnick, Lauren B., Sarah Michaels, and M. C. O'Connor. "How (Well-Structured) Talk Builds the Mind." In *Innovations in Educational Psychology: Perspectives on Learning, Teaching, and Human Development*. Edited by David D. Preiss and Robert J. Sternberg. New York: Springer, 2010.

Schorsch, Ismar. Forward to *Etz Hayim: Torah and Commentary*. Edited by David L. Lieber. Philadelphia: Jewish Publication Society, 2001.

Schwarz, Baruch B. "Discussing Argumentative Texts as a Traditional Jewish Learning Practice." In *Socializing Intelligence Through Academic Talk and Dialogue*. Edited by Lauren B. Resnick, Christa S. C. Asterhan, and Sherice N. Clarke. Washington, DC: American Educational Research Association, 2015.

Shulman, Lee S. "Pedagogies of Uncertainty." *Liberal Education* 91, no. 2 (2005).

Stone, Ira F. *A Responsible Life: The Spiritual Path of Mussar*. Eugene, OR: Wipf and Stock Publishers, 2005.

Tabachnick, Toby. "Community Shabbaton Will Cross Denominational Lines." *The Jewish Chronicle*, 2012. http://thejewishchronicle.net/view/full_story/18356336/article-Community-Shabbaton-will-cross-denominational-lines.

Teutsch, David A. *A Guide to Jewish Practice Vol. I: Everyday Living*. Wyncote, PA: RRC Press, 2011.

Ukeles Associates. "The 2002 Pittsburgh Jewish Community Study Final Report." United Jewish Federation of Greater Pittsburgh and Jewish Healthcare Foundation, December 2002, revised. http://www.jfedpgh.org/document.doc?id=13.

Vygotsky, L. S. *Mind in Society: The Development of Higher Psychological Processes*. Edited by Michael Cole, Vera John-Steiner, Sylvia Scribner, and Ellen Souberman. Cambridge, MA: Harvard University Press, 1978.

Part Two

LEARNING FROM JEWISH EDUCATION

Observing *Havruta* Learning from the Perspective of the Learning Sciences

Baruch Schwarz

In this chapter, Baruch Schwarz applies the lens of the learning sciences to analyze the havruta *(paired) learning that is characteristic of ultra-orthodox yeshivot. He begins with a description of the learning that takes place in these settings, providing a glimpse into a context unseen by many Jewish educational researchers. In these yeshivot, havruta learning is marked by intense interpersonal engagement and argumentation, often motivated by what Schwarz calls the learners'* sense of the worthiness *of the activity. Though aware of the important differences between ultra-orthodox and liberal educational settings, he nonetheless argues that they can inform one another. For example, Schwarz addresses the relevance of the* sense of the worthy *as a motivational factor even in settings, such as pluralistic schools, where one may imagine that there is less consensus about what is worthy.*

The present chapter presents Havruta learning—the traditional dyadic learning of Talmudic texts—in *Haredi* (i.e., ultra-orthodox) *yeshivas* from a Learning Sciences perspective. This educational setting is very unusual in comparison with practices of study in other societies: learners practice the collective reading of argumentative texts, initiate critical discussions on their interpretations as the most central educational practice, and, since Talmudic texts are normative within the culture, try to infer from their interpretations how to behave. In addition, Havruta learners enact these practices intensively as they pursue their studies for years from early adolescence to adulthood. Rabbis first control Havruta learning, but along the years, learners become autonomous. The thorough engagement of learners and their tenacity contrast with the ways students typically learn in schools.

Through the analysis of several interactions between Havruta learners, as well as interviews of yeshiva students, we identify the motivation that moves Havruta learners in their complex studies for years, as well as some learning mechanisms that characterize the argumentative dialogue as it deploys itself in the conversation. The interviews point at an intensive motivation we call *sense of the worthy*, a kind of motivation not observed in schools and not accounted for in motivation theories. The mechanisms directly observed are unique, especially in the ways Havruta learners capitalize on the texts as resources in their argumentative dialogue. Ironically, the mechanisms observed, as well as the motivation reported, have important implications for liberal education, and for Jewish education, but not in directions that leaders of the yeshiva would likely endorse.

We will also draw conclusions concerning the relevance of yeshiva learning to the Learning Sciences. The recent developments in the organization of the social setting of classrooms favor teacher-guided and autonomous small-group work.[1] However, studies that explore the effects of long term small group work practices are badly missing. The yeshiva context is an interesting environment for studying the development of knowledge, argumentative skills, autonomy and identity over the long term, from early adolescence to early adulthood. Such studies may provide insights for educators interested in the intensive fostering of small group learning. Finally, we will briefly reflect on a more integrative perspective of yeshiva learning and the Learning Sciences to consider novel and constructive directions in Jewish education.

Havruta: A Central Practice in Yeshivas

Havruta, also pronounced *Havrussa* (from the Aramaic for "friendship"), is a traditional approach to Talmudic study in which a pair of students autonomously learn, discuss, and debate a shared text. While this is not the place for a history of the practice, it is worth noting that Havruta was not very popular in the heyday of the Lithuanian Yeshivas in the nineteenth century,

---

[1] Noreen M. Webb, "The Teacher's Role in Promoting Collaborative Dialogue in the Classroom," *British Journal of Educational Psychology* 79, no. 1 (2009), 1–28.

as many elite students preferred learning individually.[2] However, the transformation of *Haredi* society into a community of learners in the middle of the twentieth century positioned Havruta as the focal point of yeshiva-based study of the Talmud.

In Haredi yeshivas, dyads learn in the study hall—the *Beit Hamidrash* or *Beis Medrash*. The *Beit Hamidrash* is a special space, with a certain sanctity but also, during study, a dull roar of voices. Depending on the size of the yeshiva, dozens or even hundreds of Havruta dyads can be heard discussing and debating each other's opinions. The head of the yeshiva or other senior rabbis typically sit in the back of the *Beit Hamidrash* and study alone. Students sometimes consult them, when dyads get stuck on a difficult point or need further clarification, but *Havruta* learning is primarily an autonomous activity for dyads.

Havruta learning in this setting tends to be loud and animated, as the study partners read the Talmudic text and the commentaries aloud to each other and then analyze, question, debate, and defend their points of view to arrive at a mutual understanding of the text. Given that students typically spend the whole day, or most of the day, learning beside hundreds of other dyads, the term "total institution" coined by Erving Goffman[3] seems to perfectly fit this setting. At times, groups of advanced dyads gather in a *Habura* to hear about new interpretations by others, and to present to other learners the conclusions of their dyadic efforts. This auto-organization has social implications: it is in *Haburas* that bright students are identified through peer evaluation. The *Habura* provides social validation for the efforts of the dyad, for better or for worse. Daily Havruta learning cannot be understood without taking into account that the interpretations of dyads are regularly evaluated, and these evaluations impinge on the image of the learners in their yeshiva, and more generally, in their society.

In the general structure of a day of study in yeshivas, the only activity that resembles school learning is the *Shiur*—a kind of lecture led by an instructor. But even the *Shiur* is different from teacher-led discussions in classrooms: the instructor asks difficult questions of the students, advances arguments, and is asked harsh questions in turn as students vie to refute his

---

[2] Immanuel Etkes and Shlomo Tikochinski, eds. *Memoirs of the Lithuanian Yeshiva* (Jerusalem: Zalman Shazar Center for Jewish History, 2004).

[3] Erving Goffman, *Asylums: Essays on the Condition of the Social Situation of Mental Patients and Other Inmates* (New York: Anchor Books, 1961).

arguments. And challenges and refutations are always based on commentators of the Talmud.

In the yeshivas designed for unmarried young men, learners typically study Talmudic texts without accounting for the application of their new understanding to any objective. They embrace a norm within rabbinic literature on the central religious importance of Torah study, rather than learning Torah for extrinsic purposes. Learning Torah is a commandment, and fulfilling the commandments is a central goal demanded from all (religious) Jews. Thus, the motivation of Torah learning should be total obedience as a way to express one's belief in God. At the same time, members of this community tend to see the fulfillment of the commandments as an honor rather than a burden, as reflected in the following Talmudic saying: "One who acts because he is commanded to do so is greater than one who acts without being commanded" (b. Kiddushin 31b).

Another leitmotiv of the rabbinic literature on Torah learning is that, in spite of the apparently coercive nature of this and other practices, they lead to freedom. A Midrashic interpretation of the biblical verse that the word of God "was inscribed on tablets of stone" (Exodus 32:16) plays with the word "inscribed" (*harut*) to make the point: "Do not read it as 'inscribed" (*harut*) but rather 'freedom' (*herut*)" (Exodus Rabbah 41). Obedience as a way to express one's belief, learning for its own sake, and attaining freedom are three major themes of rabbinic literature on Torah learning.

And yet, even given this cultural context, we may wonder how adolescents or young adults can sit together for ten or even twelve hours per day, six days a week, for years, poring over the tomes of the Talmud. Moreover, the content of the Talmudic text—the fact that the material is often obsolete and often obscure—augments the strangeness of this phenomenon. As we proceed, we will identify what Havruta learners say about their motivation for their daily learning. We were convinced, initially, that since yeshiva students know well the rabbinic literature about the importance of Torah study, they would be inclined to recite by heart what they read and heard about the topic. And indeed, many learners have internalized those messages. However, our interviews uncover a richer picture, which goes beyond the mere recitation of memorized formulae.

But before turning to this data, we would like to note an important characteristic of Talmudic texts that is highly relevant to the question of motivation, namely, their strongly normative character: The discussions among sages in the Talmud are very often about how one should behave in religious or civil matters. We might think, therefore, that yeshiva students engage in the study of Talmud in order to improve their behavior, to bring it into conformity with the dictates of the tradition. However, the situation is not so simple.

The *Halakha*—the collective body of Jewish religious law derived from a number of sources, but especially from the Talmud—is compiled in post-Talmudic codes and responsa literature. *Poskim,* decisors, of whom there are only a few who are acknowledged in any generation, have done the job of inferring the law from the Talmud on virtually any human activity, and the new and challenging questions that arise—due to new technologies, for example—are considered to be the exclusive domain of those leading *poskim*. What is left for the yeshiva student to do? To understand how the already-known Jewish law can be inferred from the Talmud.

Such an activity can be a bit dangerous because the learner is exposed to a literature in which legislators often disagree and present the reasons for their decisions. Learners might be inclined to take sides, something that endangers the strict hierarchy in the very conservative world of *Haredi* Jewry. This kind of activity (which is called "*Aliba de-hilkheta*") was very rare in *Haredi* yeshivas for the reasons just mentioned. However, it is now flourishing in many *kollels* (yeshivas for married men). In these *kollels,* in-depth learning of Talmudic texts is replaced by the analysis of *halakhic* texts, rapid review of texts is replaced by reconsideration of Talmudic texts already learned in the past, and the preparation toward tomorrow's in-depth learning is replaced by in-depth learning of relevant Talmudic texts toward the forthcoming analysis of *halakhic* texts.

Research on *Havruta* Learning

In 1986, Courtney Cazden claimed that no research had been done at that time on this important practice, and stressed that research should focus ". . . on the coincidence of intellectual, emotional, and religious experience and not only on the ensuing (and presumably more intellectual) discussion."[4] Since then, a research program undertaken by Elie Holzer, Orit Kent, and their colleagues has focused on pedagogies and teacher education programs to introduce

---

4   Courtney B. Cazden, "Classroom Discourse," in *Handbook of Research on Teaching,* 3rd ed., ed. Merlin C. Wittrock (New York: Macmillan Publishing Company, 1986), 133.

students outside the yeshiva to dyadic study of ancient texts.[5] These interesting programs share in common a focus on interactional components, or what is called a "relational epistemology"[6] combined with a "relational paradigm of teaching and learning."[7] The texts are short, tailored to the context, and are provided with extensive scaffolding, including translation from the original Aramaic and Hebrew.[8]

In some other publications, general ideas about the suitability of Havruta learning to modern pedagogies are articulated.[9] Sometimes, important details from observations of Havruta learners are stressed. For example, Susan Tedmon[10] notices the vividness of Havruta learning among middle school youngsters who refer to the exegete Rashi (1040–1106) by saying "Rashi says. . ." instead of "Rashi said. . ." and who collaborate in the construction of new interpretations of their own. However, such descriptions are episodic rather than systematic, or aspire to develop models of what Havruta learning ought to be as opposed to what it is. Recently, Holzer and Kent[11] have clearly articulated this idealized model in the light of advances in modern pedagogies and theories of learning.

Some researchers have initiated systematic analyses of actual Havruta learning in *Haredi* and orthodox yeshivas. For example, Menahem Blondheim

---

5   For example, Sharon Feiman-Nemser, "Beit Midrash for Teachers: An Experiment in Teacher Preparation," *Journal of Jewish Education* 72, no. 3 (2006), 161–81; Elie Holzer, "What Connects 'Good' Teaching, Text Study and Hevruta Learning? A Conceptual Argument," *Journal of Jewish Education* 72, no. 3 (2006), 183–204; Orit Kent, "Interactive Text Study: A Case of Hevruta Learning," *Journal of Jewish Education* 72, no. 3 (2006), 205–32; Orit Kent, "A Theory of Havruta Learning," *Journal of Jewish Education* 76, no. 3 (2010), 215–45; Miriam Raider-Roth and Elie Holzer, "Learning to be Present: How Hevruta Learning Can Activate Teachers' Relationships to Self, Other and Text," *Journal of Jewish Education* 75, no. 3 (2009), 216–39.
6   Raider-Roth and Holzer, "Learning to be Present," 219–20.
7   Ibid., 220.
8   See also, Moshe Abelesz, "Encouraging Successful Gemara Learning for Boys of Religious Zionist and Modern Orthodox Backgrounds in Israeli State Religious High Schools," *ATID Journal* (2000), http://www.atid.org/journal/journal00/default1.asp; Moshe Genuth et al., "Hora'at haTalmud vehahakhanah labagrut: Sihot im Misrad haHinnukh, morim, venituah homerei ezer," *ATID Journal* (2001), http://www.atid.org/journal/journal01/default1.asp.
9   Steven M. Brown and Mitchel Malkus, "Hevruta as a Form of Cooperative Learning," *Journal of Jewish Education*, 73, no. 3 (2007), 209–26.
10 Susan Tedmon, "Collaborative Acts of Literacy in a Traditional Jewish Community" (PhD diss., University of Pennsylvania, 1991).
11 Elie Holzer and Orit Kent, *A Philosophy of Havruta: Understanding and Teaching the Art of Text Study in Pairs* (Boston: Academic Studies Press, 2014).

and Shoshana Blum-Kulka[12] have provided fine-grained descriptions of Havruta discussions among young learners from a National-Religious yeshiva, that demonstrate how learners successfully handle disagreements in interaction. These descriptions are instructive, but they focus on novice students within the mainstream education system who have not yet mastered the techniques of Havruta learning. Likewise, Segal[13] describes Havruta interactions in institutional settings in which learners are novices, focusing on relations between the lessons of the Rabbi and Havruta sessions rather than on the learning processes involved in Havruta settings. My own research has focused specifically on experienced Havruta learners in *Haredi* institutions: the Mir Yeshiva[14] and in a Slobodka *kollel*.[15]

These studies have uncovered the following interesting phenomena:

- The *high argumentativeness* of the learners, including the deployment of impressive argumentative practices: the reconstitution of complex arguments agreed upon in a previous session (to initiate a new discussion); critical evaluation of sources; critical discussions governed by high-level dialectic rules;[16]
- The relatively aggressive style of learners when handling disagreements;[17]

---

12   Menahem Blondheim and Shoshana Blum-Kulka, "Literacy, Orality, Television: Mediation and Authenticity in Jewish Conversational Arguing, 1–2000 C.E.," *The Communication Review* 4, no. 4 (2001), 511–40; Shoshana Blum-Kulka et al., "Traditions of Dispute: From Negotiations of Talmudic Texts to the Arena of Political Discourse in the Media," *Journal of Pragmatics* 34, no. 10–11 (2002), 1569–94.

13   Aliza Segal, "Schooling a Minority: The Case of Havruta Paired Learning," *Diaspora, Indigenous, and Minority Education: Studies of Migration, Integration, Equity, and Cultural Survival* 7, no. 3 (2013), 149–63.

14   Baruch B. Schwarz, "'Hevruta' Learning in Lithuanian Yeshivas: Recurrent Learning of Talmudic Issues," in *Education and Religion: Authority and Autonomy*, ed. Immanuel Etkes et al. (Jerusalem: Magnes Publishing House, 2011), 279–308; Baruch B. Schwarz, "Discussing Argumentative Texts as a Traditional Jewish Learning Practice," in *Socializing Intelligence Through Academic Talk and Dialogue*, ed. Lauren B. Resnick et al. (Washington, DC: American Educational Research Association, 2015), 153–62.

15   Baruch B. Schwarz, "Authoritative or Authoritarian Voices in Traditional Learning in Jewish Institutions," in *Activities of Thinking in Social Spaces*, ed. Tania Zittoun and Antonio Iannaccone (Hauppauge, NY: Nova Science Publishers, 2014), 129–46.

16   Schwarz, "'Hevruta' Learning in Lithuanian Yeshivas," 279–308; Schwarz, "Discussing Argumentative Texts," 153–62.

17   Blondheim and Blum-Kulka, "Literacy, Orality, Television," 511–40. Like Blondheim and Blum-Kulka, we observed that very often disagreements occurred in Havruta interactions by asserting that the claim contested is not relevant to the issue at hand. A linguistic study has shown that disagreements on arguments in conversations are of four types: irrelevancy claims, challenges,

- The *high level of collaboration* between peers: although the Talmudic text is often adversarial, and despite the aggressiveness mentioned above, students tend to adopt a collaborative atmosphere rather than a disputational style in their interactions.[18]
- *A high level of autonomy and independence*: learners indicate that they feel a great deal of freedom in the interpretative realm, and try not to approach helpers (instructors, more able students, or even written material that eases the comprehension of texts) in their Havruta learning when they encounter difficulties;[19]
- *Audacious reference to authority*: learners express the freedom to uncover interpretations that differ from the interpretations of even senior rabbis in their yeshivas, and point out that the rabbis are human like them and may make mistakes (although dissidence does not impinge on rules of behavior that are decided by the rabbis only). Also, among experienced learners, there is a clear autonomous stand toward the authority of rabbis, or even from recent texts written by contemporary religious leaders.[20] Some of the moves of the interactions even show an unsubordinated approach as for interpretation of texts.[21]

The above insights are glimpses of a world of study whose nature is still not very well understood. With my research group, I have begun a systematic analysis of the learning in Havruta as it deploys itself in argumentative dialogue. Most of the insights we reach relate to recurrent patterns of interactions between learners. For example, the collaborative character of Havruta learning is visible in a dialectical pattern in which one learner brings forward an argument (a reasoned claim), his peer asks for clarifications, and the first

---

contradictions and counterclaims. See Peter Muntigl and William Turnbull, "Conversational Structure and Facework in Arguing," *Journal of Pragmatics* 29, no. 3 (1998), 225–56. In countries such as the United States, irrelevancy claims are considered very aggressive in comparison with counterclaims, contradictions or even challenges. Blondheim and Blum-Kulka analyzed conversations among Jews to conclude that conversational arguing in Jewish culture is more antagonistic than in other cultures, and suggest that this difference might be imputed to perennial dialectical practices of Torah study culturally rooted even among secular Jews.

18 Reuven Ben-Haim et al., "Making the Written Text Oral by Collaborating in Argumentation: Towards Detecting Chavruta Processes Among Ultra-Orthodox Learners," in *Studies in Jewish Education*, ed. Jonathan Cohen. (Jerusalem: The Melton Center for Jewish Education, (in press)).
19 Schwarz, "'Hevruta' Learning in Lithuanian Yeshivas," 279–308.
20 Schwarz, "Authoritative or Authoritarian Voices," 129–46.
21 Schwarz, "'Hevruta' Learning in Lithuanian Yeshivas," 279–308.

learner expands on his argument. Another pattern consists in the bringing of an argument and an expansion by the peer. The high argumentativeness was visible in a ubiquitous dialectical pattern consisting on an argument, a counter-argument or a challenge (rather than a request for clarification), and a refutation. My research group is currently collecting data to document other patterns that point at processes that characterize Havruta learning in a distinctive way.

The overwhelming presence of argumentation in Havruta interactions is particularly impressive in the light of research that shows that argumentation is rare in learning contexts because learners have difficulties maintaining their motivation to argue.[22] Moreover, the autonomy and independence of students in Havruta settings deepens the question about what motivates learners in yeshivas, to which we now turn.

Motivation for Learning in Yeshivas

Not all yeshiva students are equally motivated, of course. But among those students who are identified (by their teachers and fellow students) as being highly motivated, who demonstrate that motivation even in the havruta setting characterized by autonomy and argumentation, what is the nature of that motivation? In interviews of *Haredi* men and boys living in Israel conducted by Mordecai Nisan and Yishai Shalif [23] and by my research group[24], these students were asked questions such as these: Why are you studying Torah? What does this study give you? What is missing for young men who do not study Torah? Is Torah study challenging and, if so, in what way? Are there times when you are not studying Torah? How do you feel then, and why? Is the problem of "what other people think" an important factor in your wish to study Torah? Are there times when studying is difficult? How do you convince yourself to keep on studying?

The interviewees tended to explain their motivation to study Torah first and foremost in terms of the religious commandment, their sense of obligation, and their notion of what is worthy and what is good. They considered

---

22 Baruch B. Schwarz and Amnon Glassner, "The Blind and the Paralytic: Fostering Argumentation in Social and Scientific Domains, in *Arguing to Learn: Confronting Cognitions in Computer-Supported Collaborative Learning Environments*, ed. Jerry Andriessan et al. (Dordrecht, Netherlands: Kluwer Academic Publishers, 2003), 227–60.
23 Mordecai Nisan and Yishai Shalif, "The Sense of the Worthy as a Motivation for Studying: The Case of the Yeshiva," *Interchange* 37, no. 4 (2006), 363–94.
24 Ben-Haim et al., "Making the Written Text Oral," in Cohen, *Studies in Jewish Education*.

this explanation to be totally obvious, and offered various formulations of the basic assertion, "We have to study the Torah because God said so, and there is a commandment to study the Torah."

Perceiving Torah study as a worthy pursuit motivates the students directly and immediately in the study situation, and at the same time has the status of a meta-conception that determines the value and legitimacy of activities at the yeshiva and the feelings associated with them. This sense of the worthy is manifested in its influence on other motivational factors. The interviewees are aware of these other factors and mention them: considerations of utility and long-term interests (such as obtaining a good teaching position at the yeshiva or being given the opportunity to marry a worthy woman), social pressure and assessment, intellectual challenge and interest, and what sounds to the psychologist like a need for self-actualization. In other words, these other factors are based on the assessment of yeshiva studies as worthy and good. Without such an assessment, all the other considerations lose their power.

What is the basis of the sense that Torah study is a worthy pursuit? Most of the men and boys never even asked themselves this question. The life style of Torah study has been a basic fact of their lives for as long as they can remember. As one of the Yeshiva students declared in his interview: "Why do I study the Torah? Because 'this is our life' [a quotation from the daily prayer service].... You should ask the fish why they want to be in the water—because that is how they live." Nevertheless, when they are asked to explain the value of Torah study, yeshiva students offered well-developed justifications. The answers can be categorized into three views: (a) it is a commandment, (b) it is necessary for self-improvement and growth, and (c) it is a fulfillment of the purpose of life.

In the first view, obedience to a commandment without any other reason for acting is the greatest manifestation of the worship of God, or the worthy life. Torah study is done purely for its own sake, as opposed to doing it for the sake of some extrinsic reward. In the second view, the value of Torah study stems from its contribution to human improvement. It is seen as the natural way to promote human development and perfection—not as an instrument that can be replaced by some other, but as an activity that embodies human development and flourishing. Development is not limited to intellectual achievement, such as understanding the Torah or sharpening the mind, but expands to include the acquisition of virtues and proper ways of behaving toward others. In the third view, Torah study is seen as the purpose of human life. The goal is to know the true and the good, and this knowledge is achieved through study of the Torah. Torah study in and of itself constitutes the individual's humanity, the realization of his ultimate purpose and the meaning of life. This view of the motivation for Torah study goes beyond the fulfillment of the commandment and attempts to reach its meaning.

The view of Torah study as worthy is considered obvious in the interviews. In general in human activities, obviousness obstructs awareness. In our interviews, it was the contrary, as learners were fully aware of the worthiness of Torah study. The answer to this oddity may be found in the prevalent view at the yeshiva that Torah study must always be accompanied by awareness that it is a divine commandment and consciousness of its worth. Many of the interviewees mentioned the distinction between "studying Torah for its own sake," and "studying Torah not for its own sake," for some extrinsic purpose, such as attaining social esteem. Many of the interviewees quoted the aforementioned Talmudic saying, "Doing it not for its own sake leads to doing it for its own sake." This saying defends studying Torah not for its own sake yet at the same time expresses reservations about this practice. The "sense of the worthy" is thus nourished by the normative expectation of such awareness—an explicit demand that Torah study be based on the sense of the worthy rather than extrinsic reasons.

Moreover, in the interviews, what we are calling the "sense of the worthy" comfortably co-exists with a sense of autonomy: students see the commandment of studying Torah not as lessening their freedom but as enhancing it. The contradiction between the idea that the Torah was forced on the Jewish people (e.g., in b. Shabbat 88a) and the status of free will in the fulfillment of the commandments is a familiar dilemma among yeshiva students. The commandments do not limit human freedom but make it possible and even enhance it, as they free the individual from coercions that he may not even be aware of and open up new opportunities. *Haredi* Jews feel that, within the "coerced" setting of the commandment to study the Torah, the yeshiva not only allows for, but even encourages, a space for personal expression. Structurally, students have autonomy to choose their own Havruta partners, and as noted above, the *Habura*—the gathering of different dyads every two weeks to report on progress in learning—is student-organized and led. When a student presents an interpretation in a *Habura* that is recognized as novel and particularly worthy, it is disseminated among other *Haburas*.

There are also other positive motivations for learning in yeshiva. For example, the Yiddish word *geschmack*—meaning a sort of superior flavor—is used to describe the pure pleasure or satisfaction gained from the act of Torah study itself. Some of the types of satisfaction may appeal to Western psychological theories of motivation:

- "The material itself exerts a pull on you" (curiosity and interest);
- "You discover strengths within yourself, you are renewed and also reveal a new person" (self-discovery and identity creation);
- "I can express myself.... I can realize myself" (self-actualization).
- Other types of satisfaction are anchored in religious views:
- "You feel closeness to the thing you are studying.... You feel close to the one who gave us the Torah";
- "Someone who studies Torah feels that he is holding the world together.... I am involved in bringing rain to the world, I am involved in bringing peace to the land."

My own working hypothesis is that the feeling of *geschmack* partly relates to the dialectical character of Havruta argumentation, involving tension (disagreement, challenge) and relaxation (resolution, explanation). Researchers in argumentation have recognized this alternation as being accompanied by pleasant emotional states.[25]

What can Liberal Education Learn from Yeshiva Learning?

The unusual enthusiasm and the tenacity of Havruta learners in yeshiva may easily generate envy among promotors of liberal education, including liberal Jewish education. Is yeshiva learning relevant to liberal education? What can liberal education learn from yeshivas? To be sure, from the perspective of liberal educators, the yeshiva embodies major defects such as the indoctrination of students to a narrow, closed worldview. Also, liberal educators may be repelled by the very notion of normative motivation in schools. We will return to these major issues later on. However, we can also identify other aspects of Havruta learning that are highly relevant to modern pedagogies.

Most fundamentally, of course, Havruta learning is based on a collaborative setting in dyads. Progressive pedagogies are committed to reducing both teacher-led discussions and individual work, in favor of small-group work.[26]

---

25 Jerry Andriessen et al., "Socio-Cognitive Tension in Collaborative Working Relations," in *Learning Across Sites: New Tools, Infrastructures and Practices*, ed. Sten R. Ludvigsen et al. (London: Routledge, 2011), 222–42.
26 For example, Webb, "The Teacher's Role," 1–28.

Schools often implement collaboration among students—but far less comprehensively than in yeshivas.

Beyond this dyadic structure, the learning task in the yeshiva is organized around texts that present different and often conflicting viewpoints, whereas school learning has traditionally been organized around canonical, monological texts. This may be changing. For example, in history classes, activities may be designed around the comparison of texts representing different narratives.[27] In science education, socio-scientific dilemmas are presented through texts that convey divergences of opinion concerning science-based solutions to socially relevant issues.[28] The pedagogy to be adopted, to lead students into consideration of conflicting views, has been recognized as argumentative. However, this pedagogy is still embryonic, and the preliminary free questioning which is so common in yeshiva learning is an important practice to be considered.

Relatedly, the texts studied in yeshiva often show how different religious authorities have reached their conclusions, including their doubts, dead ends and rebutted arguments, and the challenges they faced when confronting the views of antagonists. Some researchers have recently adopted a similar approach in science education: Students are presented *Adapted Primary Literature* (APL) texts that report not only on results but also the process through which these results were discovered, including doubts or hypotheses rejected after being tested.[29] But the use of APL texts in science classrooms has been tested with high-level students only, and for a short period of time. Can such a practice be democratized?

Let us consider, next, the question of motivation. Of course, I have not focused on disengaged students, or on students who have difficulties in following the daily pace imposed by the yeshiva. Nevertheless, the interviews performed by Nisan and Shalif[30] confirmed my own overall impression, which was the

---

27 For example, Janet van Drie and Carla van Boxtel, "Historical Reasoning: Towards a Framework for Analyzing Students' Reasoning about the Past," *Educational Psychology Review* 20, no. 2 (2008), 87–110; Sam Wineburg, "On the Reading of Historical Texts: Notes on the Breach Between School and Academy," *American Educational Research Journal* 28, no. 3 (1991), 495–519.

28 For example, Troy D. Sadler and Dana L. Zeidler, "The Significance of Content Knowledge for Informal Reasoning Regarding Socioscientific Issues: Applying Genetics Knowledge to Genetic Engineering Issues," *Science Education* 89, no. 1 (2005), 71–93.

29 For example, Ayelet Baram-Tsabari and Anat Yarden, "Text Genre as a Factor in the Formation of Scientific Literacy," *Journal of Research in Science Teaching* 42, no. 4 (2005), 403–28.

30 Nisan and Shalif, "The Sense of the Worthy," 363–94.

overwhelming motivation generated by a *sense of the worthy*. Yeshiva students are products of an authoritative society. Toddlers in that society learn unequivocally what is good and bad; they recite by heart prayers and psalms, and are taught to fulfill commandments as ways to obey their Creator. Yeshivas are total institutions that isolate students from outside influences. They function to strengthen cohesion in communities: learning well in the Yeshiva ensures social recognition, and alliance with good families. However, within this context, during the arduous Havruta learning that lasts ten or twelve hours a day, the motivation expressed as a sense of worthy remains steady, and authoritative voices are not perceivable. This is a remarkable achievement from which liberal education can learn.

But what to learn? Pluralism encourages openness to many views and cultures, and recognizes their legitimacy, apparently obviating any possibility of adopting an ethical orientation or all-embracing educational approach based on uncontested goals and consistent views among all participants. I want to claim that this is incorrect: a sense of the worthy can and should serve as a motivational factor in liberal, pluralistic schools. For example, Galston[31] argues that, beyond all the controversies about what is good, there is still a considerable set of behaviors that are widely agreed to be worthy and appropriate. Also, even though liberal thinkers hesitate to impose their ideas on schoolchildren, there is still broad agreement that non-instrumental subjects should be included in the school curriculum. Moreover, even if one denies that some texts are sacred, there are nevertheless texts that are valued as prime creative works in a particular culture. Finally, despite reservations about character education in schools, I would argue that education should aim at developing good traits without being self-righteous or indoctrinating. Pluralism and its apparent ramifications, such as recognizing the legitimacy of other people's values and undermining the authority of the educator, do not eliminate the entire realm of the good and the worthy; rather, they too become values. Liberal schools may never look like yeshivas, but they can still aspire to cultivate a sense of the worthy in their own ways.

The fact that the yeshiva embodies a number of aspects that progressive educators find problematic (indoctrination, imposition of a normative motivation, social conservatism) should not prevent them from drawing lessons from it, including from the basic idea of normative motivation—the sense of the worthy. The yeshiva students observed in their studies and interviewed tend

---

31 William Galston, "Civic Education in the Liberal State," in *Philosophers on Education*, ed. A. Oxenberg Rorty (London: Routledge, 1998), 470–80.

not to feel any sense of coercion or impairment of their autonomy. They feel good about their studies, which are not focused on measurable aspects of the material to be learned, and their intrinsic motivation is enhanced by their sense of the worthy. The normative motivation in the yeshiva does indeed act in the direction of cultural conservatism, but there is no reason to believe that this direction—which stems from the yeshiva's educational purpose—is a necessary aspect of all forms of normative motivation. The sense of the worthy in one's studies can be realized in different ways, and there can be negotiations and compromises about the degree to which it should be taken into account. It is thus worth investigating whether there can be normative motivation that leaves room for negotiation between the teachers and the students about the sense of the worthy itself, the justifications for it, and the ways of realizing it.

What should be the messages of liberal schools? The first step is to be aware of the fact that liberal educators have a message. A second step would be that they should strive for a greater degree of clarity and consistency in the conceptions of the worthy that constitute, or that are embodied by, school curricula and extracurricular activities. Providing a clear message—to students, to parents, and to teachers—about the purposes of school studies and the reasons for these purposes is a must, especially those that are not instrumental. It is also important to institute activities connected with the goals, to coordinate lessons and activities with regard to their ethical significance, and to explain the reasons for these purposes and the studies associated with them.

But what are the master ideas of liberal education in the twenty-first century? What are the normative commitments around which education can be organized, in the way that yeshiva education is organized around the centrality of Torah study? Beyond the idea of pluralism, which is totally absent from *Haredi* yeshivas, our observation of Havruta learning makes salient three other, central characteristics of progressive pedagogies. First, liberal educators are committed to *dialogism*. Operationally, this means the obligation to express one's own view to the other, to respect the other and account for the other's view, and to construct one's account on the basis of previous contributions. The second characteristic of Havruta learning that is relevant here is its *collaborative* character. Liberal educators have emphasized the importance of collaboration, not only as a conduit for better learning but as a goal for its own sake. However, collaboration brings a consensual view of dialogism which constrains liberal education[32], so a *dialectic-critical approach* to resolve conflicts is also necessary.

---

32 Robin J. Alexander, *Towards Dialogic Teaching: Rethinking Classroom Talk* (York: Dialogos, 2005).

In my own work, I have developed pedagogies involving different forms of argumentative talk to enact these four commitments—pluralism, dialogism, collaboration, and dialecticity.[33] Notably, these four ideas have been articulated differently by Sarah Michaels, Catherine O'Connor, and Lauren Resnick as *Accountable Talk*.[34] For them, Accountable Talk means (1) accountability to the learning community, in which participants listen to and build their contributions in response to those of others, (2) accountability to accepted standards of reasoning, that is, talk that emphasizes logical connections and the drawing of reasonable conclusions; and (3) accountability to knowledge, that is, talk that is based explicitly on facts, written texts, or other public information. Accountable Talk has been enacted in hundreds of schools in the United States. One of the reasons of this success, we propose, is the clarity and the assertiveness of its proponents. Like our colleagues in yeshivas, they communicate their own sense of the worthy.

Of course, there is no place in a liberal school for a strict ethical orientation in which all lessons and activities are subordinated to a worldview directed at the worthy. Nevertheless, liberal education will benefit from a clear articulation of learning goals that incorporate pluralism, dialogism, collaboration, and dialecticity as worthy goals per se, beyond the acquisition of knowledge.

---

33 Baruch B. Schwarz, "Argumentation and Learning," in *Argumentation and Education: Theoretical Foundations and Practices*, ed. Nathalie Muller Mirza and Anne-Nelly Perret-Clermont (New York: Springer, 2009), 91–126; Baruch B. Schwarz and Christa S. C. Asterhan, "Argumentation and Reasoning," in *International Handbook of Psychology in Education*, ed. Karen Littleton et al.(Bingley, UK: Emerald Group Publishing, 2010), 137–76.

34 Sarah Michaels et al., "Deliberative Discourse Idealized and Realized: Accountable Talk in the Classroom and in Civic Life," *Studies in Philosophy and Education* 27, no. 4 (2008), 283–97.

Bibliography

Abelesz, Moshe. "Encouraging Successful Gemara Learning for Boys of Religious Zionist and Modern Orthodox Backgrounds in Israeli State Religious High Schools." *ATID Journal*, 2000. http://www.atid.org/journal/journal00/default1.asp.

Alexander, Robin. J. *Towards Dialogic Teaching: Rethinking Classroom Talk*. York: Dialogos, 2005.

Andriessen, Jerry, Michael Baker, and Chiel van der Puil. "Socio-Cognitive Tension in Collaborative Working Relations." In *Learning Across Sites: New Tools, Infrastructures and Practices*. Edited by Sten R. Ludvigsen, Andreas Lund, Ingvill Rasmussen, and Roger Säljö, 222–42. London: Routledge, 2011.

Baram-Tsabari, Ayelet, and Anat Yarden. "Text Genre as a Factor in the Formation of Scientific Literacy." *Journal of Research in Science Teaching* 42, no. 4 (2005), 403–28.

Ben-Haim, Reuven, Zvi Bekerman and Baruch B. Schwarz. "Making the Written Text Oral by Collaborating in Argumentation: Towards Detecting Chavruta Processes Among Ultra-Orthodox Learners. In Studies in Jewish Education. Edited by Jonathan Cohen. The Melton Center for Jewish Education. Jerusalem, in press.

Blondheim, Menahem, and Shoshana Blum-Kulka. "Literacy, Orality, Television: Mediation and Authenticity in Jewish Conversational Arguing, 1–2000 C.E." *The Communication Review* 4, no. 4 (2001), 511–40.

Blum-Kulka, Shoshana, Menahem Blondheim, and Gonen Hacohen. "Traditions of Dispute: From Negotiations of Talmudic Texts to the Arena of Political Discourse in the Media." *Journal of Pragmatics* 34, no. 10–11 (2002), 1569–94.

Brown, Steven M., and Mitchel Malkus. "Hevruta as a Form of Cooperative Learning." *Journal of Jewish Education*, 73, no. 3 (2007), 209–26.

Cazden, Courtney B. "Classroom Discourse." In *Handbook of Research on Teaching*, 3rd ed. Edited by Merlin C. Wittrock, 432–63. New York: Macmillan Publishing Company, 1986.

Etkes, Immanuel, and Shlomo Tikochinski, eds. *Memoirs of the Lithuanian Yeshiva*. Jerusalem: Zalman Shazar Center for Jewish History, 2004.

Etkes, Immanuel, Michael Heyd, Tamar Elor, and Baruch Schwarz. *Education and Religion: Authority and Autonomy*. Jerusalem: Magness Publishing House, 2011.

Feiman-Nemser, Sharon. "Beit Midrash for Teachers: An Experiment in Teacher Preparation." *Journal of Jewish Education* 72, no. 3 (2006), 161–81.

Galston, William. "Civic education in the liberal state." In *Philosophers on Education*. Edited by A. Oxenberg Rorty, 470–80. London: Routledge, 1998.

Genuth, Moshe, Avital Hockstein, Adina Luber, and Yael Wieselberg. "Hora'at haTalmud vehahakhanah labagrut: Sihot im Misrad haHinnukh, morim, venituah homerei ezer." *ATID Journal*, 2001. http://www.atid.org/journal/journal01/default1.asp.

Goffman, Erving. *Asylums: Essays on the Condition of the Social Situation of Mental Patients and Other Inmates*. New York: Anchor Books, 1961.

Holzer, Elie, and Orit Kent. *A Philosophy of Havruta: Understanding and Teaching the Art of Text Study in Pairs*. Boston: Academic Studies Press, 2014.

Holzer, Elie. "What Connects 'Good' Teaching, Text Study and Hevruta Learning? A Conceptual Argument." *Journal of Jewish Education* 72, no. 3 (2006), 183–204.

Kent, Orit. "A Theory of Havruta Learning." *Journal of Jewish Education* 76, no. 3 (2010), 215–45.

———. "Interactive Text Study: A Case of Hevruta Learning." *Journal of Jewish Education* 72, no. 3 (2006), 205–32.

Mercer, Neil. "Words and Minds: How We Use Language to Think Together." London: Routledge, 2000.

Michaels, Sarah, Catherine O'Connor, and Lauren B. Resnick. "Deliberative Discourse Idealized and Realized: Accountable Talk in the Classroom and in Civic Life." *Studies in Philosophy and Education* 27, no. 4 (2008), 283–97.

Muntigl, Peter, and William Turnbull. "Conversational Structure and Facework in Arguing." *Journal of Pragmatics* 29, no. 3 (1998), 225–56.

Nisan, Mordecai, and Yishai Shalif. "The Sense of the Worthy as a Motivation for Studying: The Case of the Yeshiva." *Interchange* 37, no. 4 (2006), 363–94.

Raider-Roth, Miriam, and Elie Holzer. "Learning to be Present: How Hevruta Learning Can Activate Teachers' Relationships to Self, Other and Text." *Journal of Jewish Education* 75, no. 3 (2009), 216–39.

Sadler, Troy D., and Dana L. Zeidler. "The Significance of Content Knowledge for Informal Reasoning Regarding Socioscientific Issues: Applying Genetics Knowledge to Genetic Engineering Issues." *Science Education* 89, no. 1 (2005), 71–93.

Schwarz, Baruch B. "Argumentation and Learning." In *Argumentation and Education: Theoretical Foundations and Practices*. Edited by Nathalie Muller Mirza and Anne-Nelly Perret-Clermont, 91–126. New York: Springer, 2009.

———. "Authoritative or Authoritarian Voices in Traditional Learning in Jewish Institutions." In *Activities of Thinking in Social Spaces*. Edited by Tania Zittoun and Antonio Iannaccone, 129–46. Nova Science Publishers, 2014.

———. "Collective Reading of Multiple Texts in Argumentative Activities." *International Journal of Educational Research* 39, no. 1–2 (2003), 133–51.

———. "Discussing Argumentative Texts as a Traditional Jewish Learning Practice." In *Socializing Intelligence Through Academic Talk and Dialogue*. Edited by Lauren B. Resnick, Christa S. C. Asterhan, and Sherice N. Clarke, 153–62. Washington, DC: American Educational Research Association, 2015.

———. "'Hevruta' Learning in Lithuanian Yeshivas: Recurrent Learning of Talmudic Issues." In *Education and Religion: Authority and Autonomy*. Edited by Immanuel Etkes, Michael Heyd, Tamar Elor, and Baruch Schwarz, 279–308. Jerusalem: Magness Publishing House, 2011.

Schwarz, Baruch B. and Christa S. C. Asterhan. "Argumentation and Reasoning." In *International Handbook of Psychology in Education*. Edited by Karen Littleton, Clare Wood, and Judith Kleine Staarman, 137–76. Bingley, UK: Emerald Group Publishing, 2010.

Schwarz, Baruch B., and Amnon Glassner. "The Blind and the Paralytic: Fostering Argumentation in Social and Scientific Domains. In *Arguing to Learn: Confronting Cognitions in Computer-Supported Collaborative Learning Environments*. Edited by Jerry Andriessen, Michael Baker, and Daniel Suthers, 227–60. Dordrecht, Netherlands: Kluwer Academic Publishers, 2003.

Segal, Aliza. "Schooling a Minority: The Case of Havruta Paired Learning." *Diaspora, Indigenous, and Minority Education: Studies of Migration, Integration, Equity, and Cultural Survival*, 7, no. 3 (2013), 149–63.

Tedmon, Susan. "Collaborative Acts of Literacy in a Traditional Jewish Community." PhD diss., University of Pennsylvania, 1991.

van Drie, Janet, and Carla van Boxtel. "Historical Reasoning: Towards a Framework for Analyzing Students' Reasoning about the Past." *Educational Psychology Review* 20, no. 2 (2008), 87–110.

Walton, Douglas. *Appeal to Expert Opinion: Argumentation from Authority*. University Park, PA: Penn State Press, 1992.

Webb, Noreen M. "The Teacher's Role in Promoting Collaborative Dialogue in the Classroom." *British Journal of Educational Psychology* 79, no. 1 (2009), 1–28.

Wineburg, Sam S. "On the Reading of Historical Texts: Notes on the Breach Between School and Academy." *American Educational Research Journal* 28, no. 3 (1991), 495–519.

Learning the Whole Game of Shabbat

Joseph Reimer

What does Shabbat at camp look like, when viewed through the eyes of a learning theorist? In this chapter, Reimer calls our attention to the way in which Shabbat at camp is a practice with its own norms and behaviors, some related to Shabbat elsewhere but many of which are distinct, into which younger students are inducted over time. On the other hand, a comparison to the theatre program at camp reveals the limitations of the present induction model for Shabbat. Reimer concludes with some recommendations for how Shabbat at camp might be designed more aspirationally. Beyond the specifics of the case, however, Reimer helped us to see how a particular Jewish educational setting may benefit from an analysis that is grounded in a theory of learning.

> At 6:15 p.m. every Friday . . . a miracle happens.
> Everyone in camp is in the same place, at the same time. . .
> We are all dressed in our finest summer threads; and with that well-known approving smile of our director . . . the community opens their *siddurim* and begins to chant "Yedid Nefesh."[1]

Celebrating Shabbat at Jewish summer camps is a great triumph for Jewish education in North America. How often have Jewish educators designed a Jewish ritual celebration that has taken hold in virtually all non-profit residential Jewish camps? For all its varieties, Shabbat at camp is broadly recognizable. A vast majority of these camps[2] have incorporated these features: preparing for Shabbat, Friday evening services, a festive meal followed by

---

1 Stacey Cohen, "Reflections," in *Ramah at 60: Impact and Innovation*, ed. Mitchell Cohen and Jeffrey S. Kress (New York: National Ramah Commission, 2010), 333.

2 These camps are the non-profit overnight camps in North America that self-identify as Jewish camps. Jdata follows the growth of these camps. One can see that data for 121 such camps at www.jdata.com on March 6, 2012.

singing and dancing, a relaxed Shabbat schedule, and a *Havdalah* ceremony to close the day.[3]

The Shabbat memory cited above is from an alumna of a Ramah camp. If we were to collect comparable memories from alumni of other Jewish camps, surely the details of celebration would differ, but the general contours might not be so varied. One way to view Shabbat at summer camps is to suggest that more non-orthodox Jewish youth in North America are likely to experience a full day of Shabbat in camp than in any other context in their lives.

There is much we do not know about Shabbat at camp—about the variation of Shabbat practices at the diverse camps, or how staff members guide their campers to experience Shabbat,[4] or what campers actually learn from participating in this special day and how it affects them afterwards. But in this chapter, I will investigate how camp educators *could* design Shabbat at camp to enhance how campers and staff learn the practices of Shabbat.

Why? As a scholar of Jewish camps who has regularly visited camps to observe their practices[5] I am deeply impressed by the power of the Shabbat celebrations I have witnessed. At the same time, I am also convinced that most Jewish camp educators have yet to systematically consider the rich learning potential that Shabbat at camp represents. But the purpose of the chapter actually goes beyond camp itself. I want to propose that Shabbat at camp is an instance of a particular kind of learning environment. Were we to better understand the relationship between participating in a communal ritual like Shabbat at camp and the learning from that participation, we could enhance Jewish learning across many other Jewish educational settings.

Perkins' Theory of Learning by Wholes

One reason Jewish educators have yet to realize the full educational potential of Shabbat at camp is that the questions involved have yet to be properly conceptualized. Amy Sales and Leonard Saxe[6] have put forward the dominant

---

[3] Amy L. Sales and Leonard Saxe, *"How Goodly Are Thy Tents": Summer Camps as Jewish Socializing Experiences* (Hanover, NH: Brandeis University Press, 2004).

[4] Zachary Adam Lasker, "The Camp Counselor as Educator and Role Model for Core Jewish Values and Practices of the Conservative Movement" (EdD diss., University of California Los Angeles, 2009).

[5] Joseph Reimer, "Vision, Leadership, and Change: The Case of Ramah Summer Camps," *Journal of Jewish Education* 76, no. 3 (2010), 246–71; Joseph Reimer, "Providing Optimal Jewish Experiences: The Case of Camp Ramah in Wisconsin," *Journal of Jewish Education* 78, no. 2 (2012), 114–34.

[6] Sales and Saxe, *"How Goodly Are Thy Tents."*

paradigm for how the structural features of camp life set up the possibilities for new learning, a "socialization" model according to which counselors and staff socialize campers into camp practices. They help us appreciate how a young and non-professional staff of counselors can help further the camp's educational agenda. But what the socialization paradigm lacks is a theory of learning within a camp setting: how children between the ages of nine and sixteen make sense of their camp experience and learn from their participation in the essential features of camp life. There is yet much theoretical and empirical work to be done in exploring campers' learning.

To begin that work, we might turn to David Perkins. As a cognitive scientist and educational theorist, Perkins is primarily interested in how to educate for a deeper understanding of whatever subject or area one is presenting. Perkins[7] observes that educators often settle for a shallow version of what constitutes understanding. They are willing to allow learners to repeat a few phrases or answer a few set questions as if that demonstrated their understanding. The cost of settling is that too often learners walk away believing they have learned a subject when in fact, were you to ask them to use their knowledge in another context, they would prove unable to do so. Their knowledge is inert. By contrast when educators design opportunities for learners "to perform their understanding" by drawing on what they have learned to respond to a variety of questions that arise from a variety of frameworks, there is a much greater chance that those learners will attain both a deeper understanding and a better capacity to apply what they have learned to situations outside that specific learning setting.

In his more recent work, Perkins[8] asks what it means to understand something deeply. When he asked his students when they felt they understood something deeply, most pointed to life situations outside their schooling. That was a huge clue: to understand what best promotes deeper understanding, Perkins had to start with life situations outside of formal education.

Perkins' personal answer was that he felt that deeper understanding when he was learning to play baseball as a child, and he uses the example of baseball to great effect.

> I enjoyed playing and learning. In a more analytic sense, it was pretty good because from the beginning I built up a feel for the whole game. I knew

---

7 David Perkins, *Smart Schools: Better Thinking and Learning for Every Child* (New York: The Free Press, 1992).
8 David Perkins, *Making Learning Whole: How Seven Principles of Teaching Can Transform Education* (San Francisco: Jossey-Bass, 2009).

what hitting or missing the ball got you. I knew about scoring runs and keeping score. I saw how it fit together.[9]

"How it fit together" is the key phrase. Often, especially in school, young learners do not see how it all fits together. They learn this and that, but lack an integrative frame that helps to put it all together. And without that whole framework there can be no deep understanding. "Learning by wholes" stresses that building that whole framework is essential for deep learning to proceed.

And so, Perkins invites educators to design "whole games," games that promote learning by wholes, that help to *initiate* learners into the disciplines that these educators represent. What draws Perkins to games as his central metaphor is not that they are fun to play. Rather, they provide a structured way to introduce beginners into a whole activity that makes sense to the players, engages their interest, and motivates them to keep improving their level of performance. What matters in learning baseball is not simply that the players enjoy playing and want their team to win, but that they may be motivated to do more—to attend batting practice to work on their swing, for example, so that when the time comes, they might knock in the winning run.

Perkins argues that the best way to initiate new learners into any complex domain is by immediately involving them in playing a simplified version of the whole game. When coaches get kids out on a baseball field, they do not wait until the novices have mastered the basics of hitting and fielding before allowing them to play. Quite the opposite: the novice players start playing at their beginner level and get excited about being part of the game. They gain a feel for how the game is played and can see that what they are doing can lead to playing like their older peers. Only when that basic framework has been established do the coaches work on improving their skill level.

The whole game approach overlaps with what many have called "experiential learning."[10] But Perkins goes beyond common approaches to "experiential education" by asking that educators build into these whole games features that derive from cognitive science. For if adults simply let children play these

---

9   Ibid., 2.
10 David Bryfman, "Experiential Jewish Education: Reaching the Tipping Point," in *International Handbook of Jewish Education Part Two*, ed. Helena Miller et al. (London: Springer, 2011), 767–84; Joseph Reimer and David Bryfman, "Experiential Jewish Education," in *What We Now Know About Jewish Education: Perspectives on Research for Practice*, ed. Roberta Louis Goodman et al. (Los Angeles: Torah Aura Productions, 2008), 343–52.

games, the learners will learn the basics and get a feel for the game, but may not get much better at the skills of the game. Perkins is aiming for the design of whole games where, by using "the principles of learning"[11] that he has identified, educators will promote deeper learning opportunities to give learners the confidence to play with increasing skill, understanding, and flexibility.

Shabbat at Camp as a Whole Game

Most Jewish educators would agree that it is hard to teach *about* Shabbat to learners who have never experienced a Shabbat.[12] The great advantage of Shabbat education at a residential Jewish camp is that even the new campers get to live Shabbat each week. I would call living Shabbat a "whole game" for at camp there are clear practices and rules that everyone knows and that defines "celebrating Shabbat." What is crucial is that by playing a whole game, the novice gets a *tacit sense* of the whole experience, learns its rules, becomes proficient at its practices, and senses the enjoyment of being part of a group that celebrates Shabbat together.

By calling Shabbat a whole game, I have no intention of reducing what is holy to the level of the mundane. But since my interest is in how campers learn to participate in the celebration of Shabbat, I am positing that for many campers learning how to celebrate may not be much different than learning how to participate in other all-camp activities. In this respect, learning to do Shabbat is no different than learning how to do Color War when it "breaks out." You get with the flow, stay alert to the directions, and follow the crowd until you get the hang of the activities.

Perkins' image of learning to play a whole game recalls Jean Lave and Etienne Wenger's[13] well-known description of learning in a community of practice as "legitimate peripheral participation." Jewish camps function as communities of practice; by starting to participate in the practices of this community, novice campers learn what they will need to know to become fuller participants in this camp culture. Part of that is how to participate in the weekly rituals of celebrating Shabbat. But "learning by wholes" goes beyond

---

11 Perkins, *Making Learning Whole*, 9.
12 Isa Aron, "Visionary Learning: Schooling for Everyone," in *Sacred Strategies: Transforming Synagogues from Functional to Visionary*, ed. Isa Aron et al. (New York: Rowman and Littlefield, 2010), 77–114.
13 Jean Lave and Etienne Wenger, *Situated Learning: Legitimate Peripheral Participation* (New York: Cambridge University Press, 1991).

"legitimate peripheral participation" and points to the way to a more ambitious approach to learning.

Consider the following. Let's imagine that after two seasons at a Jewish camp,[14] most campers have become fairly adept at participating in the rituals of Shabbat at camp. They know the routine. They know when to stand and sit at services and how to sing along with the tunes. They have learned to enjoy the Friday night celebrations and the more relaxed pace of Saturdays at camp. They even look forward to the *Havdalah* ceremony that caps the Sabbath day. They have learned all this through their legitimate peripheral participation during their first two summers.

If so, what comes next? For the many campers who attend for multiple summers, what do they learn from participating in Shabbat once they have mastered the basic routines? My hypothesis is that their learning curve has flattened out. They are happy to repeat the same patterns each week. From the perspective of the socialization model proposed by Sales and Saxe,[15] this repetition is good when it reinforces that participating in Jewish life can be a pleasurable aspect of their lives. But there is precious little new learning happening, within the domain of Shabbat, as campers return for four to six summers and even, for some, go on to become staff.

Need Jewish camp educators settle for this minimal level of Jewish learning or might they aim for more? While one cannot set a single set of aims for diverse Jewish camps, some camps may aim to create Jews who in diverse ways will want to build a Shabbat practice for their adult lives. They may want to teach campers not just to be participants but to be more, to become competent practitioners of Shabbat rather than just amateur players. For my purposes, it is not important what competence in the domain of Shabbat looks like, and it may look different from camp to camp. But I am suggesting that Perkins offers an alternative model that could lead to redesigning Shabbat at camp so that campers have the opportunity to deepen their learning of Shabbat and are better prepared to take that learning into their future lives.

Junior Versions of Whole Games

The primary way to enrich an educational program in Perkins' view is by the educators' designing successive "junior versions" of the whole game.

---

14 A season at camp lasts from as short as ten days for younger campers to eight weeks for older campers. Four weeks is probably the modal season.
15 Sales and Saxe, *"How Goodly Are Thy Tents."*

> The junior version is less technically demanding. The timelines are much shorter. The activity often substitutes simulations for the real thing. . . . However, these junior versions capture a range of basic structural features of the whole game . . . [and] involve learners meaningfully in whole games from the beginning.[16]

In introducing learners to any complex domain, there is a long road to travel from being a novice to becoming a competent practitioner, much less an expert. Perkins[17] proposes that to help learners to progress beyond the elemental versions, educators should design a set of instructional steps or "junior versions," each of which captures crucial elements of the whole and allows the learners to play the game at a level of complexity appropriate for their level. While Perkins offers examples of educators who in school settings have managed to do this, the structure of schooling actually makes it quite difficult. By contrast we can point to multiple examples in camp. For example, at a well-designed waterfront, the campers try out new practices and learn new skills in a set of steps that helps them to become more competent and confident in swimming and boating. Each step is a "junior version" in the sense that the children are actually swimming or boating, but each one is a designed instructional step that allows the children to gain greater competencies.

What often goes unarticulated is that both the waterfront educators and the campers share an implicit vision of what this whole game looks like, and hence, what an adult who has gained the requisite skills in swimming and boating can do in the water. Moreover, not only do they share a vision of what an adult version of the whole game looks like, but in addition, it is taken for granted than many adults will keep using their swimming and boating skills in life contexts outside of camp. So no one asks the question: Why are we investing so much in getting these children to develop these competencies?

The same applies to learning in sports and the arts. In well-developed camp programs there are sports and arts faculty who are adept at teaching these skills in what can be called "junior versions" and who have an implicit idea of what this whole game entails and what it would look like for a camper to become increasingly competent in that domain. As the campers gain greater competence, they move to a next level of participating where more is asked and the game looks increasingly like what competent adults play.

---

16 Perkins, *Making Learning Whole*, 37.
17 Ibid.

But what is the comparable example in camp for mastering new Jewish skills? I have seen Ramah camps where some of the oldest campers have become competent in Torah reading. I have seen Union for Reform Judaism (URJ) campers where some of the oldest campers have become competent in song leading. But as compared to developing skills in sports or at the waterfront, there are only a handful of campers who develop these Judaic skills while the majority of campers do not. Indeed many camps do not have any junior versions where fourteen-year-old campers are challenged to learn new Judaic competencies. They are only asked to repeat what they already learned at camp in their first couple of summers.[18]

Historically there were Jewish camps that were founded with clear visions of how the campers would grow in the camp's chosen Jewish competencies.[19] But today, in most Jewish camps, there is no progressive acquiring of defined skills that have application to living rich Jewish lives outside of camp. In these camps the analogue between learning to play sports and learning to celebrate Shabbat has broken down. Most campers know that the skills they build on the camp's athletic fields can be used in their home communities, and are actually used by some adults. But they may not know adults who regularly celebrate Shabbat and cannot imagine their families would use the Shabbat competencies that they learn at camp. So why would they exert effort to become more skilled at celebrating Shabbat?

Some Jewish camp educators have struggled with the social distance between the Jewish life they create at camp and the Jewish lives that most live the rest of their lives.[20] But they have been lacking what Perkins offers: an educational approach to prepare learners to become more skilled in the practices of Shabbat so they could, if they wished, adapt those to other contexts in their lives.

Before investigating how Perkins' approach to whole learning could lead Jewish camp educators to restructure aspects of Shabbat celebration, let me turn to a model camp program that I have studied that exemplifies designing

---

18 Clear exceptions to this observation can be found at URJ Camps: the Chalutzim program at OSRUI and Jewish leadership program at Kutz Camp.
19 Jenna Weissman Joselit, *A Worthy Use of the Summer: Jewish Summer Camps in America* (Philadelphia: National Museum of American Jewish History, 1993); Hillel Gamoran, "The Road to Chalutzim: Reform Judaism's Hebrew-Speaking Program," in *A Place of Our Own: The Rise of Reform Jewish Camping*, ed. Michael M. Lorge and Gary Phillip Zola (Tuscaloosa: University of Alabama Press, 2006), 27–51.
20 Michael Zeldin, "Making the Magic in Reform Jewish Summer Camps," in Lorge and Zola, *A Place of Our Own*, 27–51.

successive junior versions of a whole Jewish game: theatre education at Camp Ramah in Wisconsin.

Theater Education at Camp Ramah in Wisconsin

Since 2008, I have been studying one camp, Ramah in Wisconsin, in greater depth to better understand how they integrate Jewish education into their larger camp program. My focus has not been on Shabbat, but on theatre education. I was drawn to their Jewish theatre program for it exemplifies how a camp arts program can be transformed into an exciting vehicle for Jewish creative expression.[21]

When thinking about Perkins' approach, I realized that the theatre program could be revisited as a model for designing successive junior versions of the whole game of Jewish theatre. As background, let me quote selections from my earlier paper.

> For decades the Ramah camps have had the tradition of staging American Broadway musicals in Hebrew. This tradition accords with the original Ramah vision of placing great emphasis on both the arts and the Hebrew language (Fox, 1997). What better way for campers to appreciate the possibilities of Modern Hebrew than to learn in Hebrew the lines of plays they already know well in English?
>
> At Ramah Wisconsin veteran director Rabbi David Soloff recognized that the traditional Ramah drama program had grown tired, and yet was not prepared to jettison the staging of the Broadway musicals in Hebrew. Soloff decided to invest more heavily in growing the camp's drama staff, diversifying the drama program at camp as well as revivifying the traditional Hebrew production.[22]

What drew my attention in my earlier research was how, in the production of a single Hebrew musical, the coordinated staff effort created for the campers a powerful *optimal Jewish experience*.[23] I had never before seen such a large group of young teens so taken up and excited about performing a musical in Hebrew. I wondered how the camp managed to create that kind of excitement when most of the campers do not even understand the

---

21 Reimer, "Providing Optimal Jewish Experiences," 114–34.
22 Reimer, "Providing Optimal Jewish Experiences," 115–16.
23 Mihaly Csikszentmihalyi, *Flow: The Psychology of Optimal Experience* (New York: HarperCollins, 1990); Reimer, "Providing Optimal Jewish Experiences."

Hebrew they are singing. For the present, though, I am focusing not on any single play but on the succession of theatre experiences in which many campers participate over an extended period of time. What matters from Perkins' perspectives is not how powerful any one learning experience might be, but how the sequence is structured so that campers have multiple opportunities to be immersed at one level and then move on to a more complex level. This theatre program provides campers over the course of seven years with the following successive steps of involvement, or what we can now call "junior versions."

1. For their first two years younger campers serve as audience for the performances of their older peers while also being introduced to theatre at their own level.
2. During their first summers on the camp stage twelve- and thirteen-year-olds are initiated into performing their first Hebrew musical that tends to be simpler with easier music to sing.
3. During the next two summers that division of campers will perform each year a more complex Hebrew musical.
4. At age fourteen, some campers will also work with staff to perform a weekly Shabbat mini-performance called Storahtelling, which is a dramatic commentary in English on the weekly Torah portion.
5. At age fifteen, some campers will also work with the drama staff to help put on the "Tikvah play," the Hebrew play that the special needs campers perform.
6. At age sixteen, during their final summer as campers, the oldest division will perform what the camp staff considers to be the most complex of the Hebrew musicals.
7. In addition some of the oldest campers will volunteer to work intensively on both writing and acting in an original play in English that they will perform before several camp audiences.[24]

This menu of opportunities involves virtually all the campers whatever their skill levels in some aspect of Jewish theatre. Only a small number of campers can star in a feature role in a Hebrew musical. But those musicals are designed to create many different avenues for involvement so that even campers who will never be able to sing a solo will have an active role. And the English drama piece for the oldest campers opens the door to campers who

---
24 J. A. Ross, Personal Interview, 2014.

have interest in drama, but no fluency in Hebrew or singing ability. It gives those oldest campers an unprecedented opportunity to create their own play that helps them reflect on what this camp experience has meant to them as they end their time as campers.

Note how this sequence of theatre experiences is structured. Starting out as part of the audience is an essential first step. It allows the younger campers to be legitimate peripheral participants while they develop an appetite for the camp stage. By the time of their first turn on a camp stage, they are ready to perform in Hebrew. The camp staff monitors each group, selects a play that they can manage and modifies the script to meet their needs. It is a big challenge to perform in Hebrew, but the campers know this is the camp tradition and their staff will not let them fail. This menu of theatre opportunities illustrates how a camp implicitly creates successive junior versions of a whole Jewish game.

From Theatre to Shabbat at Camp

The theatre program at Ramah Wisconsin evolved gradually and deliberately to answer three questions:

- How to involve virtually all the campers in producing a Hebrew play when the campers' Hebrew abilities are so varied;
- How to keep this process interesting and challenging over the five summers that most campers participate in these Hebrew plays;
- How to offer those campers with more serious interests in theatre varied opportunities to perform not limited to the Hebrew musicals.[25]

Let me raise three parallel questions that could guide the redesign of Shabbat celebration at many Jewish camps.

- How can Shabbat at camp be designed to actively engage virtually all the campers given that often campers come from varied Jewish backgrounds?
- How can Shabbat at camp remain challenging and interesting to campers who have already been at camp for a few summers and know well the routines of the communal celebration?
- How can the camp offer those campers who have a more serious interest in Jewish practice the opportunities to develop their Jewish skills through an enhanced participation in Shabbat at camp?

---

25 Reimer, "Providing Optimal Jewish Experiences," 114–34.

Imagine a camp staff taking apart their Shabbat celebration and asking: How can we redesign the component parts so that we can facilitate greater camper participation and learning? When a camp has many campers who do not have much prior experience with celebrating Shabbat, there is a temptation at Shabbat services to ramp up the music, simplify the Hebrew and shorten the event to minimize camper resistance. Perkins, however, offers an alternative conception: you can always make a junior version even "more junior."[26] Perkins distinguishes "more junior" from simplified. The former entails a clear conception of what the whole looks like and the imaginative capacity to offer virtually any learners entry to that whole, but at a level where they can have access.

How might that be done for campers with little prior background? It entails creating services that are elemental in their simplicity but not fragmented, so that they remain representative of the whole game of Shabbat. It entails studying what is overwhelming and incomprehensible to novices about the all-camp celebrations and offering them a taste of the all-camp services that they can enjoy before feeling overwhelmed. It entails learning occasions before Shabbat at which counselors allow the novices to practice the few prayers, songs, and dances they will perform on Shabbat—not to learn *about* Shabbat, but to practice some of the elements, in the way that a father might take his daughter out to the park to field a few grounders or to take some swings before starting T-ball. It entails preparing counselors to be aware of the discomfort that campers might experience and ready to model the expected practices and answer the questions that arise.

Keeping Shabbat Interesting and Challenging

What would this look like? When campers reach age thirteen it is an ideal time for camp educators to approach them with a new message. "Now that you have already celebrated your bar or bat mitzvah and spent a few summers at camp, it is time to go deeper in your Jewish learning. We will challenge you as a group to explore new learning. We will challenge you as a group to explore new ways to celebrate Shabbat. Much of what you love about Shabbat at camp will remain unchanged, but you will be challenged to do Shabbat in new ways."

Imagine, then, that celebrating Shabbat at camp could have distinctive shifts such that when these campers move on to a next division, the way they participate in Shabbat would grow more complex. Beginning with the available

---

26 Perkins, *Making Learning Whole*, 40.

resources that most Jewish camps have to redesign Shabbat, here are two examples for redesigning Shabbat.

Music and dance: Within camp some songs are reserved only for Shabbat. That creates wonderful educational opportunities. Imagine that the music and dance staffs decided to assign each division its own new songs and dances that were special to them and that expressed their growing competencies. The campers in that division would intensively learn these new songs and dances during the first week of camp and they could become their signature pieces. On Shabbat, they would be the ones to lead in that singing or dancing piece. They would know these pieces well and be proud to display their mastery. These presentations could enliven services and be presented at other points during the day.

Theatre and movement: Shabbat is a wonderful occasion for campers to express their creative dramatics and movement. Younger children might dramatize different Jewish folk tales. Older campers could dramatize short stories from Jewish authors. Yet other campers could explore a set of movements that expresses what it means to rest on Shabbat or to greet the Sabbath queen. Campers in a division would choose a medium of expression and work with that medium for their time at camp, each week exploring another aspect of the Shabbat experience.

The goal is to turn Shabbat celebration from an automatic set of rituals that everyone knows to a set of challenges that communicates clearly, "You still have much to learn about Shabbat, and camp provides a wonderful set of opportunities to deepen that learning." The principle is to prepare the staff to help the older campers make Shabbat their own in ways that allow them to reflect on and enact an understanding of Shabbat that is meaningful for them. The analogue is to the English play that oldest campers stage at Ramah Wisconsin. The play is their own creation and provides an opportunity for these adolescents to reflect seriously on what means most to them as they look ahead to the years beyond being campers.

Or consider another example, that emerges from the history of the URJ camps, where there is a tradition of older campers taking an active role in planning "creative services" for Shabbat.[27] That is a wonderful basis for thinking about how to turn "creative" into "creative and skilled." This has already taken place with song leading. Now older adolescents from these camps can attend

---

27 Donald M. Splansky, "Creating a Prayer Experience in Reform Movement Camps and Beyond," in Lorge and Zola, *A Place of Our Own*, 151–72.

workshops where they can learn the skills of effective song leading. Imagine if camps offered similar workshops in leading Israeli dance, Jewish storytelling and giving dvar Torah. Imagine if specialists worked with the older campers to give them opportunities to try out their new skills in camp and then bring those skills to other venues during the year where Shabbat is celebrated. Imagine if the consistent message of the last years at camp was, "You can contribute to creating a richer Shabbat experience at camp that you can also carry home with you."

A basic premise of Perkins' work is that creating successive junior versions allows learners not only to more deeply understand the domain they are exploring but to also have the flexibility to transfer that understanding to contexts other than the ones in which the learning takes place. Perkins is not thinking about summer camps and the difficulties of bringing home what you learn at camp. But his work suggests ways to think about how camp educators could redesign the Jewish learning at camp to heighten the possibility of adaptation to other contexts. We know campers cannot take the bunk or lake or camp spirit home with them. But skills are more transportable. When camp educators focus more on developing transportable Jewish skills, they increase the chances that some of those skills could find expression outside the confines of summer camp.

Conclusion: *Learning from Skill Building*

Throughout this paper I have been walking a fine line of recognizing the power of Shabbat at camp and yet calling for a basic redesign of those experiences. I have been drawing on Perkins'[28] theory of learning by wholes to show that the Shabbat celebrations that might work well as socializing experiences may work less well to promote the deeper understanding that campers will need to adapt what they learned about Shabbat to their lives outside of camp.

The questions considered in this paper have applicability beyond the context of Jewish camps. "Jewish camp" can represent any immersive Jewish learning experience that takes place in a dedicated space for a defined time. Whenever Jewish educators create such learning environments, they face the same learning problems we have explored in this paper. In particular they face the question of how can participants take home some of what they learned in this special context.

---

28   Perkins, *Making Learning Whole*.

As Perkins argues, taking learning home does not happen of its own accord. Many educators continue to believe that when they create powerful learning experiences, learners will so appreciate the "transformative" quality of the experience that they will be motivated to take their learning home. But evidence points in the opposite direction. What Perkins holds out is a slim reed of hope that educators could redesign learning environments so there is a greater focus on the successive learning and practicing of Jewish skills. We want our youth to enjoy participating in these wonderfully rich experiences. But we also want some of them to think, "I could learn how to lead this song or dance or service and bring that back to my home community." For in the Jewish community much rests upon the possibility that what happens at camp does *not* stay at camp.

Bibliography

Aron, Isa. "Visionary Learning: Schooling for Everyone." In *Sacred Strategies: Transforming Synagogues from Functional to Visionary*, edited by Isa Aron, Steven M. Cohen, Lawrence A. Hoffman, and Ari Y. Kelman, 77–114. New York: Rowman and Littlefield, 2010.

Bryfman, David. "Experiential Jewish Education: Reaching the Tipping Point." In *International Handbook of Jewish Education Part Two*, edited by Helena Miller, Lisa Grant, Alex Pomson, 767–84. London: Springer, 2011.

Cohen, Stacey. "Reflections." In *Ramah at 60: Impact and Innovation*, edited by Mitchell Cohen and Jeffrey S. Kress, 332–33. New York: National Ramah Commission, 2010.

Csikszentmihalyi, Mihaly. *Flow: The Psychology of Optimal Experience*. New York: Harper Collins, 1990.

Dolgin Katz, Betsy. "Reflections." In *Ramah at 60: Impact and Innovation*, edited by Mitchell Cohen and Jeffrey S. Kress, 354–55. New York: National Ramah Commission, 2010.

Gamoran, Hillel. "The Road to Chalutzim: Reform Judaism's Hebrew-Speaking Program." In *A Place of Our Own: The Rise of Reform Jewish Camping*, edited by Michael M. Lorge and Gary Phillip Zola, 27–51. Tuscaloosa: University of Alabama Press, 2006.

Joselit, Jenna Weissman. *A Worthy Use of the Summer: Jewish Summer Camps in America*. Philadelphia: National Museum of American Jewish History, 1993.

Lasker, Zachary Adam. "The Camp Counselor as Educator and Role Model for Core Jewish Values and Practices of the Conservative Movement." EdD diss., University of California Los Angeles, 2009.

Lave, Jean, and Etienne Wenger. *Situated Learning: Legitimate Peripheral Participation*. New York: Cambridge University Press, 1991.

Lerner, Stephen C. "Ramah and its Critics." *Conservative Judaism* 25, no. 4 (1971), 1–28.

Perkins, David. *Making Learning Whole: How Seven Principles of Teaching Can Transform Education*. San Francisco: Jossey-Bass, 2009.

———. "What is Understanding?" *Teaching for Understanding: Linking Research with Practice*, edited by Martha Stone Wiske. San Francisco: Jossey-Bass, 1998.

———. *Smart Schools: Better Thinking and Learning for Every Child*. New York: The Free Press, 1992.

Reimer, Joseph, and David Bryfman. "Experiential Jewish Education." In *What We Now Know About Jewish Education: Perspectives on Research for Practice,* edited by Roberta Louis Goodman, Paul A. Flexner, and Linda Dale Bloomberg, 343–52. Los Angeles: Torah Aura Productions, 2008.

Reimer, Joseph. "Providing Optimal Jewish Experiences: The Case of Camp Ramah in Wisconsin." *Journal of Jewish Education* 78, no. 2 (2012), 114–34.

———. "Vision, Leadership, and Change: The Case of Ramah Summer Camps." *Journal of Jewish Education* 76, no. 3 (2010), 246–71.

Ross, J. A. Personal Interview. 2014.

Sales, Amy L., and Leonard Saxe. *"How Goodly Are Thy Tents": Summer Camps as Jewish Socializing Experiences.* Hanover, NH: Brandeis University Press, 2004.

Sales, Amy L., Nicole Samuel, and Matthew Boxer. *Limud by the Lake Revisited: Growth and Change at Jewish Summer Camp.* New York: AVI CHAI Foundation and CMJS, 2011.

Splansky, Donald M. "Creating a Prayer Experience in Reform Movement Camps and Beyond." In *A Place of Our Own: The Rise of Reform Jewish Camping,* edited by Michael M. Lorge and Gary Phillip Zola, 151–72. Tuscaloosa: University of Alabama Press, 2006.

Zeldin, Michael. "Making the Magic in Reform Jewish Summer Camps." In *A Place of Our Own: The Rise of Reform Jewish Camping,* edited by Michael M. Lorge and Gary P. Zola, 27–51. Tuscaloosa: University of Alabama Press, 2006.

What We Can Learn about Learning from Holocaust Education

Simone Schweber

*F*or decades, Jewish education has included the study of the Holocaust in the curriculum of supplementary schools and day schools, as well as in the informal educational programming of synagogues and camps. In this chapter, Schweber asks about the significance of learning from and for extremes. She proposes that one of the goals may be the cultivation of "reasonable Jews," i.e., Jews with the capacity and disposition to reason even about extreme ideas. Furthermore, Holocaust education ought to immerse students in the "messiness" of lives, to help them resist quick and easy moral judgments. Third, the teaching of the Holocaust highlights the importance of context, especially the context of learning about Jews. Finally, she observes that the teaching of the Holocaust brings to the fore the danger of essentialism and absolutism—not only in politics but in education.

The general argument of this book is that Jewish educators and the Jewish community need to think more deeply and more critically about learners and learning outcomes in Jewish educational settings and within Jewish subject areas. They need to ask, what have they been missing or overlooking, regarding learners or learning outcomes? One way to probe this question is to look at what we can learn from cases on the margins of Jewish education—such as instantiations of Holocaust education.

To be sure, the Holocaust is an especially vexed venue through which to come at the question of learning for a variety of reasons. For starters, the Holocaust is not just a marginal case of Jewish education but an extreme event. Regardless of your positioning along now-clichéd historiographical debates over its uniqueness, the Holocaust is nonetheless historically extreme. That is, whether or not you agree to its uniqueness in Jewish history or world history or even only within the boundaries of the history of genocide, it is clearly an extreme case. It is an extreme case of "othering," of genocidal intent, of persecution, mass murder, industrialized killing, the denial of humanity, and totalitarianism.

In some domains, it is important to prepare for extremes. First responders and crisis planners think about extreme scenarios. Legal scholars do too, when thinking through the implications of a particular law. But as educators and educational researchers, we do not tend to think about learning for extremes, but rather learning as oriented toward the typical. An imperfect analogy might be the following: It is strange to imagine teaching beginning drivers to navigate crashes. While it is certainly in the best interest of new drivers to consider how to avoid crashes, learning to drive is more frequently conceptualized as learning the rules of the road, how to maneuver the vehicle, how to attend to trucks and the weather. I do not mean to suggest that learning about the Holocaust is akin to driving, nor that the Holocaust is akin to a car crash, only that learning via extremes is inherently problematic. Extreme events evoke extreme reactions; they propel us to reactionary responses rather than nuanced reasoning or cultivated compassion. Other educational frameworks, likewise, prepare for the typical. Whether due to optimism or naïveté, or whether due to some structural constraint of formal schooling, we tend to think about education as preparing for life within a fairly narrow range of possible futures. In short, we tend to teach for the typical and in avoidance of the extremes.

And yet, what I want to cultivate through Jewish education are what I have come to think of as "reasonable Jews," that is, Jews who are able to reason about their lives, about the lives of others, about their identities and interactions, about Jewish life and practice, and about how religious identities and national and historical landscapes interact. Reasonable Jews, I think, are Jews who are able to reason about Jews, Judaism, Jewish issues, and Jewish history, which necessarily includes non-Jews, non-Jewish issues, and non-Jewish history.

Is this the only way to think about the desired learning outcomes of Jewish education? Surely not. But to whatever extent the cultivation of reasonable Jews is a shared goal, then it seems to me that the content that we teach must be taught in ways that provide our students with opportunities to practice the kinds of reasoning that we want them to be able to do. We ought to be teaching our students to reason, not only about Jewish texts, but about Jewish life, and not only about Jewish life but about what life as Jews in the modern and ancient world means. We ought to be deliberating about Israeli policies, American policies, and controversial issues, all of which are confronting world Jewry. We ought to be cultivating Jews who reason, through opportunities to do so.

The idea of "reasonable Jews" does not presuppose a single, universal standard of reason with a capital R, the kind of Enlightenment conception of rationality that has been subject to much criticism over the last few decades. It does not mean that Jews ought to act in accord with Reason by suppressing emotion, or by following rules of logic. It does not assume that all rational or reasonable people hold the same (intellectually legitimate) beliefs or act in the same (morally legitimate) way. We can instead embrace what Nicholas Burbules calls a "more inclusive and flexible understanding of reason."[1] The reasonable person is not the person who thinks and acts in accord with Reason. Rather, "a person who is reasonable wants to make sense, wants to be fair to alternative points of view, wants to be careful and prudent in the adoption of important positions in life, is willing to admit when he or she has made a mistake, and so on."[2]

Put in less abstract terms and applied to teaching, the very episodes that most rile us with the blatancy of their immorality, I suspect, are the very acts that we ought to teach about with level-headedness, with openness to radically opposing ideas, with the possibility of learning from them compassion rather than superiority. Even in the extremity of its content, the Holocaust needs to be taught in ways that foster reasonableness, rather than moral supremacy or ethnic insularity. If we teach about the Holocaust so as to insulate ourselves from its protagonists—to claim that we are not like Nazis, for example, or could never be collaborators or bystanders or that we could never be morally compromised—we are, inadvertently or purposefully, teaching for hubris rather than humility. In those acts, we deny our own humanity out of fear. We cannot teach about the Holocaust fruitfully from a place of fear without perpetuating disdain, and we cannot learn moral courage by reifying moral outrage.

This is not to say that moral outrage is never appropriate in discussions of genocide. We can affirm that some acts are morally outrageous. We can respect people who demonstrate righteous indignation. But as educators, we must also admit that moral outrage is sometimes lazy and oftentimes shallow. The condition of moral outrage can be a mask for sanctimony and melodrama. "There are some emotions," writes Eamonn Callan, "[that] we earn the right to feel with the consequence that they are truly our own—emotions we have paid for, so to speak, in thought and experience—and others that have in some way been illicitly appropriated or aroused so that they do not belong to us in all but the

---

[1] Nicholas C. Burbules, "Reasonable Doubt: Toward a Postmodern Defense of Reason as an Educational Aim," in *Critical Conversations in Philosophy of Education*, ed. Wendy Kohli (New York: Routledge, 1995), 85.
[2] Ibid., 86.

shallowest sense."[3] Moral outrage can sometimes have that unearned quality, and hence is not a powerful place from which to learn reasonableness.

My first argument, then, is that Holocaust education demonstrates for us the importance of encountering the extreme in the cultivation of reasonableness.

Second, we ought to consider Sam Wineburg's[4] argument for the value of learning about history as do historians rather than shaping history as do politicians. To think like a historian is ultimately to make moral judgments about events, but not to make those pronouncements lightly. Instead, it is the job of the moral historian to make distinctions based on an evidentiary basis that sifts and weighs and winnows documents and data, that makes careful and reasoned claims warranted by that process, allowing for the humanity of people across time and place to emerge, even if—or perhaps *especially* if—their humanity is unlike our own. Citing Primo Levi's inability to explain to a fifth-grade student why he couldn't escape from Auschwitz concentration camp, Wineburg elaborates on the idea that "our 'inability to perceive the experience of others,' as [Levi] put it, applies to the present no less than the past'"[5] continuing:

> This is why the study of history is so crucial to our present day and age, when issues of diversity dominate the national agenda. Coming to know others, whether they live on the other side of the tracks or the other side of the millennium, requires the education of our sensibilities. This is what history, when taught well, gives us practice in doing.[6]

Presentism is ahistorical precisely in its collapse of the sensibilities that change across time; and it is unavoidable precisely because it is in the present that we act as historians. By contrast, historical inquiry done well, as Wineburg explains, is ultimately redemptive by allowing for the revelation of profound difference and surprising sameness at one at the same time. In this way, it gets us closer to the deepest questions of what it means to be not only human, but also what it means to be a human collective. To deny the possibility that we, living in the aftermath of the Holocaust, share traits and likenesses and difficulties and sociality with perpetrators, is to deny the possibility of careful

---

3 Eamonn Callan, *Creating Citizens: Political Education and Liberal Democracy* (Oxford: Oxford University Press, 1997), 103.
4 Sam Wineburg, *Historical Thinking and Other Unnatural Acts* (Philadelphia: Temple University Press, 2002).
5 Ibid., 23.
6 Ibid., 23–24.

learning from history—as it ultimately allows only self-serving moral lessons to emerge rather than profound moral questions to be addressed.

To state the obvious, perhaps, the most important moral quandaries come from precisely the humanity of all the protagonists who act in history. All of us—perpetrators and bystanders, collaborators and neighbors, victims and survivors, Jews and Roma, Sinti and POW's, in the present and the past—lead what Travis Wright[7] has rightly called "messy lives." Holocaust education, done well, pushes us to reckon with that messiness, and it is that reckoning, in turn, that can lead us to be better thinkers and more compassionate people, if not immediately or directly, then eventually and serendipitously.

What Wright discusses as "messy lives" are the ways in which our coping mechanisms, which are visible in social settings, always reflect the realities of the unseen, the backgrounds of abuse, trauma, fear, or neglect that children sometimes bring to school with them. To think that students should behave well in class is to forget that they live "messy lives" out of school. I agree with Wright on the deepest level that to make sense of the mess we live in is illusory but important. To reckon with the mess as a whole has the power to remind us of the ways that our stories and lives, our families and communities, our nations and states are always intertwined. Ironically, perhaps, it is the acknowledgment of our own messy lives in our ineluctable present that should allow us as researchers and educators to minimize the traps of presentism and to downplay the historical hubris that infuses academic work. This, then, is the second argument: Holocaust education immerses us in the challenges of real lives, messy lives, and their inevitable moral morasses.

Third, Holocaust education reminds us of the importance of learning about Jews. The domain of Jewish education is typically understood as the education of Jews, i.e., of Jewish learners, and more specifically, the education of Jews in the subject matter of Judaism to help them enact their Jewishness in various ways. Learning *about* Jews seems much more like the kind of thing that happens in Jewish museums, or in textbooks about the history of religions, sometimes authored by Jews, but often by non-Jews. And yet, I want to argue that learning about Jews, whether those learners are Jewish or not, is important in our current historical moment—a moment when anti-Semitism is on the rise worldwide, where violence is not necessarily more frequent but more

---

7 Travis Wright, "On Jorge Becoming a Boy: A Counselor's Perspective," *Harvard Educational Review* 77, no. 2 (2007), 164–86; Travis Wright, "Learning to Laugh: A Portrait of Risk and Resilience in Early Childhood," *Harvard Educational Review* 80, no. 4 (2010), 444–63.

visible, and where anti-Jewish activity is only sometimes connected to Israeli state policies.

A few months ago, in Madison, Wisconsin, my hometown, there was a spree of racist, pornographic graffiti and minor property damage. It seems unlikely that the swastikas and message of "fuck Jews" spray-painted on garages and driveways was in any way a reflection of anti-Israel sentiments directly. Instead, it seems more likely that these symbols and expressions were symptomatic of a rise in the acceptability of white supremacist ideas generally. When asked if these messages constituted a hate crime, a spokesperson for the Madison Metropolitan Police initially said no, which further infuriated some local residents. They understood the answer of the police spokesperson to be an anti-Semitic extension of the initial acts, a willful ignoring of the real hurt inflicted by the spray-painted images. But to imagine his answer as a "microaggression" is to use the context of reception to trump the context of production; it is to confuse the impulse to defend against attacks by seeing them everywhere as intents to harm.

For the representative of the police was answering correctly, if not carefully; he was answering the question from a legal standpoint rather than a compassionate frame. The graffiti was of course hateful, but not technically a hate crime. The legal process for the acts to be designated a hate crime according to state statute require that a perpetrator be found and interrogated to prove intent before it could be labeled as such. I would like to think that, had this police representative taken into consideration his multiple audiences more fully before answering the query about the classification of the crime, he would have been better able to answer the question more compassionately and not strictly legally. I would like to think, too, that had the graffiti-writers known more about Jews and understood them better as fellow humans, they would have been less likely to perpetrate the harm in the first place.

But my point here is simpler: that in meaning-making, context is everything, and that to respond with compassion takes practice.

That, then, is the fourth lesson that I have learned from studying learners of the Shoah, that contexts always matter and never superficially: what people know about Jews reflects, powerfully, their social contexts. In other words, students' ideas that come into play when they are learning about the Holocaust always reflects their prior knowledge about Jews. And what they know about Jews reflects the social, historical, and cultural contexts in which that knowledge was embedded.

In my various studies of Holocaust education, I have made it always a point to ask students why they think Jews were persecuted during the Holocaust. I ask the question before they have learned about the Holocaust in their formal or informal settings, and I ask the question afterwards. I ask not only as a way to assess what they learn or investigate their knowledge of history, but to see what they think about larger questions of historical meaning: how violence is justified or inexplicable, under what conditions, when it is deserved or fated or incomprehensible. One student answers the question of why Jews were and are persecuted with, "It's because we're the chosen people, and everyone is always jealous of us." Another student answers, "When I think about it, they killed Jesus, . . . it was all fated to happen." These two responses are dramatically different, and moreover, they provide windows into the ways these students see the world, not only the ways they see Jews. For the fundamentalist Catholic girl who said "they killed Jesus," the murder of Jews was justified, at some theological level, given the myth that "the Jews killed Jesus." For her, there was a kind of divine retribution involved in the mass murder of Jews during the Holocaust. For the Lubavitcher girl who told me that "everyone's always jealous of us," the murder of Jews has to do with envy, not necessarily fate, but envy that is driven by a religious claim about the existential condition of the Jews as chosen. As these examples show, context is not only meaningful as a background or setting for their thinking; it shapes their meaning-making.

More like the scriptwriters than the scenery, contexts structure identity work. Thus the fact that eighth graders at a Charismatic, fundamentalist evangelical Christian school are learning about the Holocaust and that eighth graders at an ultra-orthodox girls' yeshiva are learning about the Holocaust does not mean that they are learning the same content. Indeed they did not even learn the same skills. The girls at the yeshiva learned to argue, in keeping with the pedagogical traditions inherited from rabbinic praxis; the students at the Christian school continued to provide short informational answers to the teacher when called upon, in keeping with the tradition of an authoritarian church dedicated to inculcating obedience. Interestingly, it turned out that both groups of students I studied in those contexts were learning toward similar dispositional ends. Students in both places were taught that they are potential victims in history, that perpetrators of violence can't be understood, and that their own eschatological chosenness or religious supremacy was unquestionable. Through the teaching of the Holocaust at both schools, the students were instructed in ways to solidify their in-group boundaries, and by default, to keep their out-groups out.

We sometimes imagine that "content" exists in a kind of Platonic ideal world, knowledge about the world or about history that we then have to figure out how to convey in the real world to real students in real contexts. Holocaust education reminds us that what it is and what it means depends fundamentally on the contexts in which the students find themselves and the meanings that they make.

Reflecting further on what I saw in the evangelical school and the ultra-orthodox school, we might say that it was a form of teaching toward absolutism—the creation of impermeable boundaries between groups—of the sort that many fundamentalisms perpetuate. That is, after all, one of the defining features of fundamentalisms, that fundamentals are absolute: whether of belief or practice or social groupings. To use the Holocaust to teach *toward absolutism* of any kind, it seems to me, is an abuse of education, as at least according to my frame of reference, absolutism is fundamentally unreasonable. Put differently, teaching toward absolutism can never produce reasonable Jews—as teaching for absolutism is antagonistic to reasoning.

I want to argue, then, that teaching toward reasonableness is not only opposed to teaching for absolutism, but may well act as an antidote to teaching for absolutism. Moreover, as ironic a position as it is logically, I also want to argue that teaching toward reasonableness is an absolute good, regardless of the particularities of our politics. For reasonableness is what allows democracies to function based on an informed citizenry, a citizenry that should be opposed to idiocy, as Walter Parker[8] elucidates etymologically. If I want education to be geared toward reasonableness, that commitment is predicated on the notion that reasonableness fosters tolerance and that tolerance is a requirement, not only for democratic citizenship, but for most forms of living amidst difference, Jewish and otherwise.

Pedagogically, deliberation leads to greater reasonableness. That is, learning that puts people in the position of having to inhabit opposing viewpoints, that forces them to argue against their own beliefs and intolerances, that requires them to listen and be listened to, leads them to reasonableness and greater toleration for difference of opinion. And yet reasonableness, and its reflection in the ability to deliberate, it seems clear, is not enough to generate care or compassion for otherness. It is not enough to grow kindness or love. Deliberation can lead to honed abilities to reason only, not necessarily reasoning about others or caring for them regardless of the reasonableness of

---

8   Walter C. Parker, "Teaching Against Idiocy," *Phi Delta Kappan* 86, no. 5 (2005), 344–51.

doing so. Think of the *yeshiva bochers,* the young men in traditionalist houses of study, arguing over Talmudic texts and following a rabbi who argues for the murder of a Jewish leader; or think of the lawyers arguing reasonably for amoral ends given that law and justice are not synonymous. Nor is tolerance alone a worthy goal for education, having been described as the failure of multiculturalism. So even though I have been arguing that education about Jews ought to involve deliberation as a pedagogical approach for instilling reasonableness, reasonableness is not sufficient. Nor is tolerance. Instead, my contrary (and closing) conclusion from Holocaust education is that our educational efforts must transcend reasoning and foster caring and compassion.

It seems likely that we humans are neurally wired (not neutrally wired) to attend to difference and to be attuned to it, instinctually. Organisms that are different from us in form may also have different aims than we do; they are potential threats. This is the case when we meet a tiger, but it also may be the case when we meet another member of our species—and so a phenomenon that may be evolutionarily explicable may also contribute to anti-sociality. In other words, if by virtue of our evolution we have as a species learned to protect ourselves from possible threats, then the corollary is that education for compassion and care probably bumps up against those biological predispositions. It helps to explain why teaching to care for others is so difficult and so necessary; it probably cannot be accomplished easily. Compassion may well be hard to learn.

Orienting education toward care, as Nel Noddings theorized convincingly, is likely to be successful only through repeated attempts and continuous insistence. What Noddings claimed over thirty years ago[9] is only bolstered by more recent understandings of the brain. We may be hard-wired for human connection and attachment, but it's likely that we are also predisposed to violence in the form of self-protection. It is why violence is easily conjured from only imagined threats, because our heightened sensibility to protect against threats is real. Here again, context is everything. Deliberation allows us to understand others' contexts, the contextual frames that make opposing beliefs tolerable; it teaches us to reframe our deeply held ideas toward reasonable, if utterly opposing, explanations. But how, pedagogically, do we instill care?

Richard Davidson, in his expansive research in neuroscience, has shown that within months, even novice meditators can rewire their neural pathways for a greater capacity for compassion, a heightened sense of joy, and a deeper

---

9   Nel Noddings, *Caring, A Feminine Approach to Ethics and Moral Education* (Berkeley: University of California Press, 1984).

sense of calm, following the example of Buddhist monks. And it turns out that young kids when taught to meditate mindfully, report becoming kinder to each other in school, and that researchers observe the same behaviors in children. It is hard to know exactly what to conclude from this empirical evidence, but here's one possibility: if discussion formats like deliberation teach us to navigate differences reasonably and therefore to orient toward each other more productively, perhaps what meditation does is to teach us to orient toward ourselves in similarly healthy ways, lowering our sensitivity to the felt threats that otherness elicits. Though clichéd and in vogue, it may well be the case that mindful practices help us to learn from a place of compassion and, in so doing, enable us as teachers to help our students learn to be more caring with themselves and each other. It may, in other words, be a fruitful method for encouraging compassion when learning about the kinds of otherness that threaten us most deeply. For some of us, the idea that in other circumstances, I, too, could commit murder or "racial cleansing" is the most threatening learning; for others, it is simply the idea that I could end up in poverty or powerless.

Holocaust education, it seems to me, can easily be harnessed to buttress absolutist certainty rather than to inspire enlightenment ideals—as can all educational endeavors. I do not know if extreme events incite absolutist positions more consistently or more frequently than learning about other kinds of events, but I can imagine that that is the case. Extreme events propel us to reject them vociferously for their rejection of our humanity. This is why not all education about extremes encourages shared understandings of humanity—not even all forms of genocide education. Sometimes, inadvertently or not, Holocaust education distills and transmits essentialized notions of Jews, Nazis, perpetrators, victims, God, or violence. With the aim of drawing distinctions, of making sure our students are good, we demonize and dismiss. We reify categories, including even categories of human beings. And yet, education about Jews, like education about Muslims, about Christians, about African Americans, Latinos, Asians, transgender, intersex and gay people, all of us humans, ought to *de*-essentialize us. It ought to teach us to resist categories, to see nuance and complexity, to be suspicious of formulas, to avoid conclusions even about "what makes us all human." It is precisely the essentializing of people that makes genocide possible, that makes particular patterns of violence continue, that confines us to our narrowest frames of thinking. In de-essentializing us, Holocaust education pursued carefully and deliberatively enables us to see complexity, and contributes to compassion without the elision of difference.

Absolutism is necessarily a stripping away of the context that makes difference understandable and that makes essentializing inevitable. Absolutism is the thorough rejection of difference, the rejection of reasonableness, even probably the rejection of compassion, for it makes a claim to omniscience that necessarily divides human groups rather than limiting those divides. Absolutism is unscientific, ahistorical, impolitic, immoral, and inhumane. It reflects the curse of thinking we are godlike rather than human, and as such, bypasses the humility that allows us to imagine a common humanity across important difference, sharing life on an uncommon planet.

I am not arguing in this chapter for greater attention to Holocaust education per se, neither within Jewish education nor within general education. I am not proposing that Holocaust education is the cure for what ails us, that Holocaust education will make students good or moral or democratic or reasonable in some miraculous fashion. But reflecting on two decades of investigating the ways that Holocaust education is pursued, I have come to believe that there is much that Holocaust education can teach us. I have seen the Holocaust taught well, with attention to nuance and complexity, in a manner that seems to foster reasonableness and compassion. And I have seen the Holocaust taught poorly, in a manner than seems to foster essentialism and absolutism. Precisely because of its extreme nature, the Holocaust is subject to extreme pedagogic diversity. But these lessons are not what I've learned about Holocaust education only; they are lessons that I've learned about learning.

Bibliography

Avery, Patricia G. "Tolerance, Political." *International Encyclopedia of the Social Sciences*, 2nd ed. Edited by William A. Darity, 385–86. Detroit, MI: Macmillan Reference USA, 2008.

Burbules, Nicholas C. "Reasonable Doubt: Toward a Postmodern Defense of Reason as an Educational Aim." In *Critical Conversations in Philosophy of Education*. Edited by Wendy Kohli, 82–102. New York: Routledge, 1995.

Callan, Eamonn. *Creating Citizens: Political Education and Liberal Democracy*. Oxford: Oxford University Press, 1997.

Goffman, Erving. *Asylums: Essays on the Social Situation of Mental Patients and Other Inmates*. New York: Anchor Books, 1961.

Hess, Diana, and Patricia G. Avery. "Discussion of Controversial Issues as a Form and Goal of Democratic Education." In *International Handbook on Education for Citizenship*. Edited by James Arthur, Ian Davies, and Carole Hahn, 506–18. London: Sage Publications, 2008.

Hess, Diana, and Paula McAvoy. *The Political Classroom: Evidence and Ethics in Democratic Education*. New York: Routledge, 2016.

Noddings, Nel. *Caring, A Feminine Approach to Ethics and Moral Education*. Berkeley: University of California Press, 1984.

Parker, Walter C. "Teaching Against Idiocy," *Phi Delta Kappan* 86, no. 5 (2005), 344–51.

Schweber, Simone, and Rebekah Irwin. "'Especially Special': Learning About Jews in a Fundamentalist Christian School." *Teachers College Record* 105, no. 9 (2003), 1693–719.

Schweber, Simone. "'Here There Is No Why': Holocaust Education at a Lubavitch Girls' Yeshiva." *Jewish Social Studies* 14, no. 2 (2008), 156–85.

Wineburg, Sam. *Historical Thinking and Other Unnatural Acts*. Philadelphia: Temple University Press, 2002.

Wright, Travis. "Learning to Laugh: A Portrait of Risk and Resilience in Early Childhood." *Harvard Educational Review* 80, no. 4 (2010), 444–63.

———. "On Jorge Becoming a Boy: A Counselor's Perspective." *Harvard Educational Review* 77, no. 2 (2007), 164–86.

Part Three

CONCEPTUALIZING LEARNING OUTCOMES

Is this a *Real* Story? Learning Critical History and Learning Its Limits

Sam Wineburg

The study of history plays a central role in the Jewish educational curriculum. But when we invite students to consider the Jewish past, what are we really after? In this chapter, Wineburg brings a self-critical perspective to the commitments that we might expect from him, as a leading researcher of the teaching and learning of history. Calling on some familiar examples of the tension between what the great Jewish historian Yosef Yerushalmi called "Jewish history" and "Jewish memory," he argues against the standard moves—some because they do not satisfactorily account for Jewish commitments, and others because they do not satisfactorily account for the absence of criteria of personal or national significance within academic history. Eschewing an easy or facile resolution of the problem, Wineburg sharpens it for us: how do we accommodate our interests and values, the very interests and values that bring us to a study of Jewish history, without compromising our intellectual integrity?

Passover marks the freedom of the Jewish people from Egyptian bondage. For four hundred years Pharaoh turned a deaf ear to the Hebrews' cries. Only when God intervened, raining down ten plagues like turning the Nile into blood and unleashing a torrent of frogs so that from every cooking pot and hearth, leaping frogs made daily life hell—only then did Pharaoh relent and let the Hebrews go.

My family tells this story every spring. When our three children were young—too young to sit through a highly ritualized retelling—we would act out the story, one of us playing the brave Moses, another his arch rival Pharaoh, and others the Egyptian taskmasters who demanded that the Jews meet their brick quota or face the lash.

One year, when my youngest son Raphael was seven, he sat on my lap with rapt attention, without any of the visual aids or sit-com sketches that keep a child awake. He followed along in the *Haggadah*, the ancient record of this story. At the end of the evening, the Afikomen found, the fourth cup of wine emptied, Raphael started to nod off. As I picked him up to put him to bed, he awoke, startled. He was perceivably disturbed. By what I was not sure.

As I laid him to bed, he gazed at me, now wide-awake. Something was on his mind. Then, with the unalloyed innocence of a young child, he asked me this question: "Dad, what we read tonight, was that a *real story*?" It was past midnight and I was beat. I promised to get back to him in the morning. That morning has lasted sixteen years. I am still pondering Raphael's question.

Was he asking me, if you will, a question of narratology, a query that accents the word *story*? Did the *Haggadah* conform to what Aristotle in the *Poetics* described as the basic structure of story: a beginning, middle, and end, with a unity of plot and chains of cause and effect sequences? Did its tension state arc before reaching its climax?

If that was what my seven-year-old was asking, then my response should have been, yes, Raphael, this is a real story. This story, the Exodus tale, conforms to the dictates of narratology to a T. In fact, one might even call it a template for all kinds of stories. The Exodus has captured the imagination of generations precisely because of its power as story.

As you might imagine, however, I do not believe that this was what my son was asking.

Sometime between the ages of seven to ten, the child, according to Jean Piaget, transitions from concrete operations and begins to enter the corridor of mature adult thinking, the earliest stages of what he called "formal operations."[1] It is a time when the child moves from a world of make-believe (in which make-believe seems real) to a time when magical thinking falls away and the child begins to see the world veridically. Raphael no longer believed me when I pointed upward and said, "Watch, I'll wipe my hand across the sky and make the sun go down." He already knew better.

---

1 See, for example, Jean Piaget, *Science of Education and the Psychology of the Child* (New York: Orion Press, 1970).

What my son wanted to know was whether everything he had just heard—about a land called Egypt, about garrison cities of Pithom and Ramses (Exodus 1:11), about a ruler named Pharaoh and a rebellious leader of a slave revolt named Moses, about a mountain called Sinai, and a forty-year sojourn in the desert—whether this was a *true* story.

I believe my son's question came untouched by any postmodern taint—the notion that all stories are constructs, that they are fabricated from words, that there is, to invoke Jacques Derrida, nothing outside of the text.[2] Raphael was blithely unaware, I believe, of Hayden White's *Metahistory*, which smudges the line between history and literature by contending that the historian must (in order to use the story form) *emplot* it, calling on conventions like irony, romance, or satire to give form to an otherwise meaningless sequence of events.[3] Such determinations contrast with Leopold von Ranke's imperative to capture history as it really was ("wie es eigentlich gewesen"),[4] and edge the historian closer to the novelist than to the scientist. Raphael was similarly unaware of Michel Foucault, who saw stories and those who stamped them on modern consciousness as tools of oppression, ways to seize and not let go of power by those in authority.[5] No, my son's question was innocent of the anti-foundational undertones that have punctuated academic discourse during the last few decades.

Raphael, I believe, was asking a much more basic question. My son was only a child but he was not asking a childish question. In fact, it's a question that we ask too once we leave our ivied halls and resume our lives as neighbors, citizens, and ordinary people. When we watch *Schindler's List* or *Seabiscuit* or *Selma*, and describe the movie to our next-door neighbors and they ask, "Sounds fabulous, but is it a *true* story?," we know precisely what they mean. Maybe the filmmaker exaggerated; maybe people didn't die exactly in this way; maybe the clothing they wore was more modest than what some Hollywood costume designer dreamt up; maybe the relationship between Martin Luther King and Lyndon Johnson was more amiable than that portrayed on the

---

2 Jacques Derrida, *Limited Inc.* (Evanston, IL: Northwestern University Press, 1988), 144.
3 Hayden White, *Metahistory: The Historical Imagination in 19th-century Europe* (Baltimore, MD: Johns Hopkins University, 1973).
4 Leopold von Ranke, *Geschichten der romanischen und germanischen Völker von 1494 bis 1535* (*History of the Latin and Teutonic nations, 1494–1535*) (Leipzig: Reimer, 1824), v–vi.
5 For example: "Interpretation is the violent or surreptitious appropriation of a system of rules ... in order to impose a direction, to bend it to a new will, to force its participation in a different game, and to subject it to secondary rules...." Michel Foucault, "Nietzsche, Genealogy, History [1971]," in *The Foucault Reader*, ed. Paul Rabinow (New York: Pantheon, 1984).

screen. But a more fundamental question remains: Did Oskar Schindler really manage to save a thousand Jews from the gas chambers? Was there really a horse that at the height of the Depression won race after prestigious race and offered hope to a nation mired in economic despair? Or . . . did the filmmaker "make it up?"

Such questions return us to the evening when Raphael, alternatingly nodding off and still very much awake, asked me if what he had just heard was a *real* story. In 2001, on Passover eve, Rabbi David Wolpe, the spiritual leader of Los Angeles's Temple Sinai, shocked his congregants by asking the same question from the pulpit. His sermon sent shock waves throughout the sanctuary and made such a ruckus that accounts appeared in newspapers from New York City to Jerusalem. "The truth is," said Wolpe, "that virtually every modern archeologist who has investigated the story of the Exodus, with very few exceptions, agrees that the way the Bible describes the Exodus is not the way it happened, if it happened at all."[6]

"If it happened at all."

There you have it. Raphael's question answered. Not only did the Torah, and afterwards the *Haggadah,* screw up the details, but worse. It's not even clear that the whole thing happened at all.

All is not lost however. Wolpe's flock and my son Raphael could take solace in the fact that even if the Exodus had not occurred, even if the story was not "historically" true in the same way that there was a horse named Seabiscuit or a businessman named Oskar Schindler, it was true in other, more sublime, ways. The Exodus contains a "deeper and more central meaning." The story should be revered not because of its facticity but because it has "been regarded by past generations as true."[7] The real Egypt, in other words, is not a geographical territory running westward along the twenty-second parallel from the Red Sea. Rather, Egypt is a metaphor. As one of Wolpe's congregants put it: "We all have our own Egypts—we are prisoners of something, either alcohol, drugs, cigarettes, overeating. We have to use [the story] as a way to free ourselves from difficulty and make ourselves a better person."[8]

After delivering his bombshell, Wolpe offered a follow-up sermon in which he distinguished historical truths from "spiritual truths" and why it's

---

6 David Wolpe, quoted in Teresa Watanabe, "Doubting the Story of Exodus," *Los Angeles Times,* April 13, 2001.
7 David Wolpe, quoted in Gustav Niebuhr, "Religion Journal; A Rabbi's Look at Archaeology Touches a Nerve," *New York Times,* June 2, 2001.
8 Watanabe, "Doubting the Story of Exodus."

important not to get the two mixed up.[9] Wolpe's sermon had the feeling of a parent breaking the news to a child about make-believe. Fairy tales may serve a developmental need, but carried into adulthood they stunt maturation. Grow up, he seemed to say to his flock. "You do not serve God if you do not seek truth."[10] In this case, it was clear which truth Wolpe meant.

By drawing on the modern science of archeology, history, and the social sciences, Wolpe ushered his congregants into the modern era, following a tradition that goes back to Baruch Spinoza. Sitting in his Amsterdam study in 1655, Spinoza used the tools of philology to question the Mosaic authorship of the Torah, setting into motion a movement that emerged in the early nineteenth century as *Wissenschaft des Judentums*, the scientific study of Judaism.

Wissenschaft drove a wedge between the stories of Jewish tradition and accounts that survived rational analysis of a new cadre of Jewish historians, archeologists, and geographers. Historical understanding was the fruit of a painstaking process of locating events in temporal contexts, and trying to reconstruct the assumptions, beliefs, and worldviews of past actors living at particular moments. The discipline of history progressed haltingly but steadily. Scientific history drew inspiration from the precision and exactitude of the natural sciences rather than the humanistic traditions of literature, poetry, and art. It was said of von Ranke that he would "cross an ocean to verify a comma."

Wissenschaft was on a collision course with traditional conceptions of the Jewish past. The rift was irreparable. Yosef Hayim Yerushalmi, the esteemed Columbia University historian, mournfully wrote that there was no way to pick up the pieces: "Jewish historiography [is] divorced from Jewish collective memory and, in crucial respects, thoroughly at odds with it."[11] The historian, and perhaps especially the Jewish historian, can be no sentimentalist whose job it is to "replenish gaps of memory."[12] If they are to have integrity as scholars, historians must play by the rules of the academy. Without malice or ill intent, they must follow the scent of inquiry wherever it led. The responsible

---

9   "L.A. Rabbi Blasted for Fifth Question: Was There Really a Passover Exodus?" *Jewish Telegraphic Service*, April 27, 2001, http://www.jta.org/2001/04/27/jewish-holidays/passover/l-a-rabbi-blasted-for-fifth-question-was-there-really-a-passover-exodus.
10 Watanabe, "Doubting the Story of Exodus."
11 Yosef Hayim Yerushalmi, *Zakhor: Jewish History and Jewish Memory* (New York: Schocken, 1989), 94.
12 Ibid.

historian, wrote Yerushalmi, "challenges even those memories that have survived intact."[13]

Which brings us back to Raphael's question. Across the denominational divide, parents send their children to Jewish schools with certain hopes and dreams. They want their children to emerge from Jewish schooling with strong Jewish identities. They want their children to understand that against all odds, the Jewish people have endured throughout the ages, and thrived. They hope that their children will come to see the stories of the Jewish people as their own. They hope their children will learn that they are part of a chain that binds them to their ancestors and prepares them for the future. If Yerushalmi is right and history destroys without malice, what role is left for it the curriculum of the Jewish school?

One explicit answer comes from Robert Chazan, the Scheuer Professor of Hebrew and Judaic Studies at New York University, who put forth his vision in a 2010 article in *HaYidion*, the practitioner-oriented journal of "community" (i.e., non-denominational) Jewish day school movement.[14] Like Wolpe, Chazan distinguishes between two ways of thinking about the past: "critical history" and what he termed "traditional thinking about the past." But whereas Wolpe dismantled the Exodus, Chazan takes a hatchet to Hanukkah. The story widely taught, of the wicked Antiochus, who defiled the Temple and forced the Jews to worship Greek gods, turns out to be an admixture of myth, half-truth, and distortion. Modern scholarship yields "no evidence whatsoever for such a Seleucid policy in any sector of the far-flung empire or at any time." Immortalized in songs, rituals, and insertions in the Siddur, Hanukkah is actually a bundle of twisted fictions. Critical history has "radically altered the traditional story," Chazan writes, "to the dismay of many Jews." And this is just the start.

Chazan is playing with dynamite and he knows it. He titles his article "Faith and Critical Jewish History: A Complex Relationship." He is aware that many parents see critical history as "corrosive," a threat to Jewish identity and thus a "disservice to young children enrolled in Jewish schools." He admits that such a charge—that critical history will *weaken* Jewish commitment—makes "prima facie" sense.

Prima facie. From the Latin, "on its face," or as we might say, "on the surface." In other words, when we examine the situation more closely, the charges

---

13 Yerushalmi, 94.
14 Robert Chazan, "Faith and Critical Jewish History: A Complex Relationship," *HaYidion* (2010), 50–53.

against critical history are baseless. The deeper threat, Chazan warns, comes not when the Jewish school teaches critical history, but when it doesn't. Our students are born into a modern world. They will go off to college and be exposed to the tools of critical scholarship. Is it not preferable, Chazan asks, for students to be exposed to critical history "within the confines of Jewish education" rather than in a "less supportive environment"?

Notice, then, that the "complex relationship" referred to in Chazan's title has little to do with the history part of the equation, its epistemological assumptions, or how the discipline has responded to the challenges from an entourage of post-modernists, post-structuralists, anti-foundationalists, as well as from quarters within the discipline: social and micro-historians, feminist scholars and scholars of color, historians who study gay, lesbian, and transgender issues.[15] For Chazan, critical history itself—its methodology, its claims to truth—is not at issue. Rather, the source of complexity is pedagogic.

How should educators reconcile critical history's blinding light with the tender minds and open hearts of young children? At what age should critical history be introduced? How do we ease the transition from "traditional thinking about the past" to an analytic approach that prepares students for the next stages of their education, as middle class American kids, at Brown or Wesleyan or Ohio State? Should critical history be dished out in small portions or should we tell children the truth right off the bat? Such questions, according to Chazan, demand "more nuanced and thoughtful deliberation."

Although Chazan does not invoke notions of psychological development, its timbre echoes between the lines. One is reminded of Ernst Haeckel's claim that "ontogeny recapitulates phylogeny," the idea that the development of the individual roughly parallels the evolution of the species.[16] Our ancestors

---

15 It is beyond my scope to review all of the challenges to critical history, as Chazan portrays it. For an overview see Peter Novick, *That Noble Dream: The "Objectivity Question" and the American Historical Profession* (New York: Cambridge University Press, 1988). Perhaps the most powerful critique comes from Michel Foucault; an excellent introduction is Paul Rabinow's opening essay to *The Foucault Reader*. See Michael Foucault, et al., *The Foucault Reader* (New York: Pantheon Books, 1984). Evenhanded treatments of the epistemological challenges to history as "normal science" come from Richard Evans, *In Defense of History* (New York: W. W. Norton and Company, 1999), and Thomas Haskell, *Objectivity is Not Neutrality: Explanatory Schemes in History* (Baltimore, MD: Johns Hopkins, 1998). Finally, David N. Myers's brilliant *Resisting History: Historicism and its Discontents in German-Jewish Thought* (Princeton, NJ: Princeton University Press, 2003) is indispensable to anyone examining these issues from a Jewish perspective.
16 Ernst Haeckel, *Generelle morphologie der organismen* [*General Morphology of the Organisms*] (Berlin: G. Reimer, 1866). Haeckel is typically credited with the phrase, but it is unclear

credulously accepted leaping frogs, manna dropping from Heaven, and a God who delivered his people from slavery. Successive generations believed these stories because their ancestors believed them and their ancestors' ancestors believed them. As science progressed, warranted knowledge displaced old stories. We can still cherish those stories because our forefathers cherished them—but we should not be confused. Whether we call such stories "spiritual history," "Midrash," or "traditional ways of thinking about the past," they are no substitute for the real thing.[17] We must, according to Chazan, "communicate to the young student that the tradition puts a premium on mature reflection and valorizes intellectual engagement." In contrast to the assumptions of those who believe that critical history subverts traditional commitments, Chazan seems to propose that critical history is not just a necessary evil but in fact an important element of the process of development and maturation. In other words, if we want our children to grow up, they need the bone-strengthening sustenance of critical history.

What, then, are we to tell our students as they delve into the Jewish past in search of understanding the Jewish experience throughout the ages? Go ahead and light your Hanukah candles, but remember that Antiochus's downfall resulted from military miscalculations, overstretched forces, tactical errors, economic considerations, misplaced priorities, or any variety of causes—except the one recited during morning prayers during Hanukah: *amade'ta la-hem ba'et tzaratam*, "You stood by them in their hour of need"?[18]

What happens when one of our students, searching for a way to make sense of the sweep of Jewish history, stumbles across Mark Twain's 1899 essay, *Concerning the Jews*:

> [The Jew] has made a marvelous fight in this world, in all the ages; and has done it with his hands tied behind him.... The Egyptian, the Babylonian, and the Persian rose, filled the planet with sound and splendor, then faded ... the Greek and the Roman followed, and made a vast noise, and they

---

whether it actually originated with him. Regardless, as is well known, the theory of "recapitulation" is not in fact true. See, for example, Stephen Jay Gould, *Ontogeny and Phylogeny* (Cambridge, MA: Belknap Press of Harvard University Press, 1977).

17 On *midrash* as an alternative to either critical history or memory, see Michael A. Meyer, "Reflections on the Educated Jew from the Perspective of Reform Judaism," in *Visions of Jewish Education*, ed. Seymour Fox et al. (New York: Cambridge University Press, 2003), 149–77.

18 See Michael L. Satlow, *How the Bible Became Holy* (New Haven, CT: Yale University Press, 2014), 124–35.

are gone.... The Jew saw them all.... All things are mortal but the Jew; all other forces pass, but he remains. What is the secret of his immortality?[19]

Twain ends with a question—but the work has already been done. We can supply our own answers to the secret of the immortality of the Jewish people, but in fact, the power of his argument lies in how he explains the survival of the Jews as extraordinary, even implicitly miraculous.

Critical history retorts: there are no "secrets" of history, only unsolved problems. There can be no legitimate claims of immortality, and no appeals to the miraculous. History progresses in bits and pieces, each datum a piece of an endlessly complex puzzle. All historical events have precedents. Everything comes from something else. Everything evolves. Even the Jews and their supposed immortality is easily deconstructed: the Jews at any particular historical moment evolved from preceding civilizations and cultures, as did the Egyptians and the Babylonians and the Persians, and at any particular historical moment, gave rise to succeeding civilizations and cultures. Only in retrospect do we impose a narrative coherence on the story of the Jews. Unlike Mark Twain's puzzle, critical history has no corner pieces. For corner pieces would betray a belief in an overall pattern, a framework into which pieces, scattered hither and yon, would be slotted.

Such beliefs catapult us back to pre-modern thinking in which Jewish history, often inscrutable and impossible to predict, was marching zigzaggedly but inexorably toward *ge'ulah*, Redemption, guided by the invisible but unmistakable hand of HaShem.

To this critical history hoists a red card. The past can be no more and no less than the sum of its parts; meaning imposed rather than discerned as part of a Divine plan. Overarching schemes, teleological endpoints, frameworks of ultimate value, puzzle pieces forming an outline, shards casting a shadow whose outline points to something larger than so many bits of broken clay: such thinking violates critical history's ground rules. These rules scorn the pronouncement of grand schemes. They enjoin the practitioners to lower their sights. Yet, we might wonder, with the historian David N. Myers, whether the "obsessive demand to situate every historical datum in a discrete local context precludes the possibility of enduring meaning."[20] Local contexts do not a coherent story make.

---

19 Mark Twain, "Concerning the Jews," *Harper's Magazine*, March 1898, http://legacy.fordham.edu/halsall/mod/1898twain-jews.asp.
20 Myers, *Resisting History*, 5.

To the student who connects *Shoah* to *T'kumah*, echoing Soloveitchik's belief that the founding of the State of Israel was a "point along the eschatological pathway of Jewish history," we should answer that the words "eschatology" and "history" are incompatible in the same sentence.[21] Eschatology implies the very framework of meaning that critical history abjures. There can be no foundational assumptions in critical history other than a Lockean commitment to empiricism and Popperian commitment to falsification.[22] If the student persists, we may tell him that the jury's out on whether God exists, noting that such a question is not for the history class, anyway. What we *can* say, however, is that even if God does exist, He plays no role in history. In the Jewish history classroom, God is dead.

In this regard, Jewish history has a status no different than the study of Irish history, Hindu history, or the history of the New Orleans bayou. Critical history must play by the metaphysical rules of the natural sciences. And here, we move from the more general point about the absence of overarching meaning to a more specific point about theological assumptions. In other words, if it is true that Mark Twain's question about the secret of the immortality of the Jew is out of order, then it is even more true that a theistic answer to the question—that God is the answer to the immortality of the Jew—is beyond the pale. Brad Gregory, a Catholic historian at Notre Dame, observes that any appeal to God-in-History or God-as-Prime Mover must be regarded as "social, political, anthropological, psychological, economic, or natural because by definition there is nothing more for it to be."[23] Or as Dipesh Chakrabarty puts it, critical history—indeed the entire edifice of Western science—pivots on the assumption "the human is ontologically singular, that gods and spirits are 'social facts,' that the social somehow exists prior to them."[24] People invent their gods. Or as we might say in Hebrew, *Bereishit bara ha'adam et ha-elohim*, "In the beginning, man created God."

---

21 "Destruction" and "Rebirth" are typically used in tying the events of the Holocaust to the birth of the State of Israel; see David Myers's summary of the position of Rabbi Joseph B. Soloveitchik (1903–1993) in Myers, *Resisting History*, 159.

22 Postmodernism has done a real number on this position, but the challenges from hermeneutics are also powerful. See Hans-Georg Gadamer, "The Problem of Historical Consciousness" in *Interpretative Social Science: A Second Look*, ed. Paul Rabinow and William M. Sullivan (Berkeley: University of California Press, 2001).

23 Brad Gregory, "The Other Confessional History: The Secular Bias in the Study of Religion," *History and Theory* 45, no. 4 (2006): 137.

24 Dipesh Chakrabarty, *Provincializing Europe: Postcolonial Thought and Historical Difference* (Princeton: Princeton University Press, 2000), 16.

At this juncture, we must ask whether critical history is really as value-free as it claims. Gregory thinks not. He asserts that critical history carries its own "undemonstrable metaphysical beliefs" that can neither be affirmed nor denied using the empirical tools of modern social science.[25] Indeed, he likens the absolutism of critical history, one that *a priori* denies truth to all religious claims, to the practice of church history, where the terminus of every historical investigation was known in advance. Just as church history embraced unassailable first principles, Gregory argues, so does modern science. In the academy, a commitment to "metaphysical naturalis[m] and cultural relativis[m] . . . contend that religion is *and can only be* a human construction."[26]

A God-less narrative is taken for granted in historical writing. Chazan, for example, writes 1,500 words on teaching history in Jewish schools without mentioning God.[27] Richard White, the esteemed Stanford historian, dismisses his late mother's devout faith in short order: "I am a historian. I don't believe in transcendence. There is only the everyday."[28] White plainly admits his assumptions. In most historical writing, the same assumptions go without saying. There are exceptions, to be sure; the eminent Columbia University historian Richard Bushman, a Mormon and scholar of Mormonism, comes to mind. But in the main, a historian who embraced God in any causal scheme would be laughed out of the American Historical Association (AHA).

As Jewish educators, we are faced with a conundrum. Many of us have encountered students who see God behind every waving blade of grass, a stance that blocks the path of serious intellectual engagement with the past. Why even bother probing the causes of historical events, or the decisions of historical actors, if the answer is always God? But the alternative—banishing God from the history or allowing Him a cameo role and only then with the asterisk of "spiritual history"—seems equally unpalatable. Can there be a course that steers between dogmatic belief and absolutist disbelief?

Gregory thinks so. He proposes a way of thinking about religious claims—what he calls "metaphysical neutralism"—which neither affirms them as first principles nor dismisses them out of hand:

---

25 Gregory, "The Other Confessional History," 137.
26 Ibid., italics in the original.
27 Chazan, "Faith and Critical Jewish History," 50–53.
28 Richard White, *Remembering Ahanagram: Storytelling in a Family's Past* (New York: Hill and Wang, 1998), 40; quoted in Gregory, "The Other Confessional History," 136.

> To reject the partisan religious convictions of traditional confessional history does not force one to adopt the metaphysical naturalism of secular confessional history. Instead, an approach that is metaphysically neutral neither privileges a particular tradition or specific religious claims, nor does it imply that scholars of religion must conduct research as if no religious claims could be true.[29]

A variation of metaphysical neutralism was examined in a symposium organized by the journal *Historically Speaking* in 2008.[30] Under the title of "abundant history," Robert Orsi reviewed the events in Lourdes, France, when in 1858 the fourteen-year-old Bernadette Soubirous allegedly witnessed the appearance of the Virgin Mary. Historians have since explained away Marian apparitions using any variety of reasons: as a calculated attempt by the Papacy to centralize power; as a pretext by the secular state to justify the expansion of its transportation system (increasing taxes and using the excuse of transporting pilgrims to a far-flung village in the foothills of the Pyrenees); or by employing a Freudian framework that attributes the phenomenon to women's need to "experience vicariously the fulfillment of their desire for sexual contact with, and a baby from, their fathers."[31]

What would happen, asks Orsi, if historians considered the possibility of Marian apparitions as examples of the "transcendent breaking into time," not unlike a burning bush that was not consumed or a divine voice endorsing the *halakhic* interpretation of Rabbi Eliezer rather than his opponent Rabbi Yehoshua? "Any claim that natural laws are necessarily exceptionless," notes Gregory, "is a dogma beyond the possibility of empirical confirmation."[32]

Gregory cites the philosophical critiques of Hume's dismissal of miracles to justify his position.[33] I, however, understand metaphysical neutralism in a

---

29 Gregory, "The Other Confessional History," 147.
30 See Robert Orsi, "Abundant History: Marian Apparitions as Alternative Modernity," *Historically Speaking* (September-October 2008), 12–16.
31 Michael P. Carroll, *The Cult of the Virgin Mary: Psychological Origins* (Princeton: Princeton University Press, 1986).
32 Brad Gregory, "Back to the Future: A Response to Robert Orsi," *Historically Speaking* (September–October, 2008), 21.
33 Gregory cites among other works, J. Houston, *Reported Miracles: A Critique of Hume* (New York: Cambridge University Press, 1994); David Johnson, *Hume, Holism, and Miracles* (Ithaca: Cornell University Press, 1999); and John Earman, *Hume's Abject Failure: The Argument Against Miracles* (Oxford: Oxford University Press, 2000). I am relying on Gregory's reading here, not my own.

slightly different way. I see it as an act of humility that has a place in the Jewish school.

To reiterate, I am explicitly not addressing the students who, on the first day of class, dogmatically assert that all events in Jewish history can be explained as the will and design of HaShem. Such students may believe that they are providing an answer to historiographical questions, but they are making a category error. *Hashgacha peratit,* divine intervention in the details of life, is a theological principle, rather than an historical explanation. Students who do not understand this have not fully grappled with discipline of history as its unique way of thinking.[34]

Rather, I take up the case of the student who has gotten As during the year, who is able to corroborate documents and pinpoint where the evidence stops and speculation begins. This student is able to explain how the Jews survived the Babylonian exile by regrouping at Sura and Pumbedita; how they outlived the Romans by fleeing to Yavneh; how they weathered the Arab invasions by adjusting to Dhimmi status; how they survived the Crusades and the Inquisition by converting to Christianity and secretly keeping their Judaism in the basement; how they responded to the pogroms by turning to Zionism; and how the *sh'erit ha-pletah,* the escaped remnant of the people, proved that even the modern technology of genocide has limits. This student's sure hand and quick mind can explain every affliction and every act of resilience of the Jewish people by weaving together local contexts and situating circumstances in a defined temporal framework. But at the end of the year the student is filled with disquiet. It is this student who on the last day of class brings up the quotation by Mark Twain and asks, "What should I think about this?" Is there nothing more to our history than the concatenation of isolated events? Is *that* the secret to the Jews' "immortality"? Are we forbidden to suggest that there might be some force beyond what reason can comprehend that motivates the course of Jewish history?

What would happen if we were to respond that critical history can do many things but that it, too, has limits? Can there be no discussion in the Jewish school, in the Jewish school's *history* class, about what we might call "points along the eschatological pathway of Jewish history"? Must the Jewish history classroom embrace one of secularism's deepest and least reflected upon assumptions? If so, then what makes learning Jewish history in a Jewish school different from learning American history in a public school? Is there not room for a small dose of humility in the face of the limits of knowledge,

---

34 I am indebted to Jonah Hassenfeld for helping me think about this issue. I admit, however, only to a partial understanding of what he was trying to teach me.

as that enterprise is constituted and verified in the academy? Indeed, the Biblical minimalism of Israel Finkelstein and Neil Asher Silberman, on which Wolpe based his *drash*, has not fared well of late.[35] As science repeatedly teaches us, we cannot affirm the null hypothesis. The absence of evidence is not evidence of absence. What is historical revisionism if not the admission that our cocksureness would have benefitted from a moment of silence?

What are the aims of learning history in the Jewish school and who gets to set them?[36] From the vantage point of critical history, the answer of how to learn history differs only topically from approaches in a secular context. In the public school, we dissect different accounts of the Battle of Lexington, how myth has shrouded this event, how invented tradition makes its way into American lore, its zenith coming in the form of a postage stamp depicting a battlefield scene that contradicts all available evidence.[37] From such investigations, students learn evidence-based reasoning, how historical argument is crafted and evaluated, and how to be more critical readers and evaluators of historical events. I have spent a good part of my career trying to understand how learning this kind of history—as opposed to rote memorization of names and dates—can be applied in a wide variety of contexts and sustained by teachers who work under the most difficult conditions.[38]

I have long argued that history, well taught, sharpens the mind. But surely this aim does not exhaust the justifications for history's place in the curriculum. An earlier rationale, one prominent among the framers of the American Constitution, is that engagement with the past offers moral tutelage.[39] History exposes us to acts of courage and heroism. We meet figures who inspire us to lead better, bolder, and more meaningful lives.

---

35 Israel Finkelstein and Neil Asher Silberman, *The Bible Unearthed* (New York: Free Press, 2001). For an update, see Robert Draper, "Kings of Controversy: Was the Kingdom of David and Solomon a Glorious Empire—or Just a Little Cow Town? It Depends on which Archaeologist You Ask," *National Geographic*, January 8, 2015, http://ngm.nationalgeographic.com/2010/12/david-and-solomon/draper-text.

36 I am indebted to Daniel Marom for gently but persistently imploring me to address this issue over the many years of our friendship.

37 See Sam Wineburg, *Historical Thinking and Other Unnatural Acts: Charting the Future of Teaching the Past* (Philadelphia: Temple University Press, 2001); Sam Wineburg et al., *Reading Like a Historian* (New York: Teachers College Press, 2001).

38 Teresa Watanabe, "L.A. Unified Adopts Free History Curriculum from Stanford University," *Los Angeles Times*, November 27, 2014, http://www.latimes.com/local/education/la-me-history-stanford-20141126-story.html#page=1.

39 See David Tyack, "Ways of Seeing, An Essay on the History of Compulsory Schooling," *Harvard Educational Review* (Fall 1976).

Such aims crashed and burned during the tumultuous years of the 1960s, when America convulsed with race riots, the Feminist and Antiwar movements, and the profound social changes that rocked every area of American life. Hero debunking became a national pastime. Thomas Jefferson was a slave owner and probably a rapist; Woodrow Wilson, who tirelessly fought to create the League of Nations, an unrepentant racist; FDR, a philanderer.

Like so many other sacred cows, the idea that history could provide moral instruction fell victim to a hermeneutic of suspicion, reaching its apex in Howard Zinn's *A People's History of the United States*, a relentless unmasking of the hypocrisy of practically any figure who had ever been praised in a traditional textbook. Zinn did not abandon moral judgment but gave it a new meaning. More than anything else, the study of history demanded an accusing finger to mete out moral judgments. *J'accuse* became the order of the day.[40]

Moral judgment, however, fertilizes the hubris of posterity. Robert Tracy McKenzie, chair of the history department at Wheaton College, "the Evangelical Harvard," takes up the question of moral judgment in his book, *The First Thanksgiving*, a work that overturns much of what we have grown up thinking about what happened between Pilgrim settlers and the indigenous people they encountered on their arrival in the "new world."[41]

While teaching about Pilgrims at Wheaton, McKenzie found his Christian students as ready to condemn the hypocrisy of Pilgrims as their secular counterparts were to vilify President Truman for his decision to drop the bomb. His students were quick to indict the Pilgrims for their grim and unyielding notions of right and wrong, and their sacred rush to pillory, literally, anyone who thought otherwise.

I recently encountered similar moral outrage among a group of Jewish students at Stanford, with whom I had a conversation about Ari Shavit's book, *My Promised Land*. We were discussing his chapter on Ein Harod, and how members of the kibbutz resorted to trickery, dishonesty, subterfuge and every means possible to remove their Arab neighbors from adjoining property—one of the first acts, if you will, of Palestinian displacement. Shavit's book allowed these college students, many of whom but a semester away from positions at Google, Twitter, Booz Allen and McKinsey, to affirm twenty-first century values of fairness, anti-racism, and a commitment to social justice for all. They flexed their accusing finger at the pioneers of Ein Harod. "We

---

40 See Sam Wineburg, "Undue Certainty: Where Howard Zinn's *A People's History* Falls Short," *American Educator* 37 (2012–13): 27–34.
41 Robert Tracy McKenzie, *The First Thanksgiving: What the Real Story Tells Us about Loving God and Learning from History* (Downers Grove, IL: InterVarsity Press, 2013).

would've known better, felt deeper, and acted more righteously than our ancestors," they seemed to say.

Moral judgment makes for lousy history. It's an even lousier tool for *tikkun ha-middot*, the never-ending process of human perfection and growth toward decency. Moral judgment, writes McKenzie, "renders a verdict but requires nothing of the knowing heart."[42] McKenzie proposes *moral reflection* as an alternative, in which our meeting with those who come before us is an attempt to understand who *we* are. This meeting requires that we "make ourselves vulnerable to the past."[43] It obliges us, in the words of David Harlan, to engage in a "conversation with the dead about what we should value and how we should live."[44] At stake in this encounter is not the judgment of our predecessors' blemishes, but an attempt to hold a mirror to our own faces. This mirror does not whisper that we are the fairest of them all but calls on us to examine our foibles and reflect on what we consider to be the source of ultimate meaning. Moral reflection for these Stanford careerists would have had them consider not just the failings of their great-grandparents, but to consider what their ancestors gave up. What did it mean for young people their own age, armed with degrees from the finest European universities, to sacrifice their own personal ambitions and bind themselves to a collective mission of the Jewish people? And not just for ten days on an air-conditioned bus?

My son's question launched me on this quest but I end with more questions than when I started. I remain uncertain about what to say to Raphael, now twenty-four, working in Iowa as an AmeriCorps team leader. But recently, I was cheered to learn that in responding to difficult questions from youngsters at a Passover table, I am not alone.

The novelist and Hebraist, Jonathan Safran Foer, recently explained what motivated him to undertake a new translation of the *Haggadah*. He recounts a story from his own family Seder, when at the end of the night he was asked by his six-year-old son if Moses was a "real person." Foer, too, was taken aback. But his response hints at the humility that should be our aim.

"I don't know," he told his son, "but we're related to him."[45]

---

42 Ibid., 182.
43 McKenzie, *The First Thanksgiving*, 182.
44 David Harlan, *The Degradation of American History* (Chicago: University of Chicago Press, 1997), 206. On a related point, see the important statement coming from hermeneutics, Deborah Kerdeman, "Pulled Up Short: Challenging Self-Understanding as a Focus of Teaching and Learning," *Journal of Philosophy of Education* 37: 293-308 (2003).
45 Jonathan Safran Foer, "Why a *Haggadah*?" *New York Times*, March 31, 2012, http://www.nytimes.com/2012/04/01/opinion/sunday/why-a-haggadah.html?pagewanted=all&_r=0.

Bibliography

Carroll, Michael P. *The Cult of the Virgin Mary: Psychological Origins*. Princeton: Princeton University Press, 1986.

Chakrabarty, Dipesh. *Provincializing Europe: Postcolonial Thought and Historical Difference*. Princeton: Princeton University Press, 2000.

Chazan, Robert. "Faith and Critical Jewish History: A Complex Relationship." *HaYidion* Nurturing Faith (2010), 50–53.

Derrida, Jacques. *Limited Inc*. Evanston, IL: Northwestern University Press, 1988.

Draper, Robert. "Kings of Controversy: Was the Kingdom of David and Solomon a Glorious Empire—or Just a Little Cow Town? It Depends on which Archaeologist You Ask." *National Geographic*, January 8, 2015. http://ngm.nationalgeographic.com/2010/12/david-and-solomon/draper-text.

Earman, John. *Hume's Abject Failure: The Argument Against Miracles*. Oxford: Oxford University Press, 2000.

Evans, Richard. *In Defense of History*. New York: W. W. Norton and Company, 1999.

Finkelstein, Israel, and Neil Asher Silberman. *The Bible Unearthed* (New York: Free Press, 2001).

Foucault, Michel. "Nietzsche, Genealogy, History [1971]." In *The Foucault Reader*. Edited by Paul Rabinow. 76–100. New York: Pantheon, 1984.

Gadamer, Hans-Georg. "The Problem of Historical Consciousness." In *Interpretative Social Science: A Second Look*. Edited by Paul Rabinow and William M. Sullivan. 103–60. Berkeley: University of California Press, 2001.

Gregory, Brad. "Back to the Future: A Response to Robert Orsi." *Historically Speaking* (September–October, 2008), 20–22.

———. "The Other Confessional History: The Secular Bias in the Study of Religion." *History and Theory* 45, no. 4 (2006): 132–49.

Haeckel, Ernst. *Generelle morphologie der organismen* [*General Morphology of the Organisms*]. Berlin: G. Reimer, 1866.

Harlan, David. *The Degradation of American History*. Chicago: University of Chicago Press, 1997.

Haskell, Thomas. *Objectivity is Not Neutrality: Explanatory Schemes in History*. Baltimore: Johns Hopkins, 1998.

Houston, J. *Reported Miracles: A Critique of Hume*. New York: Cambridge University Press, 1994.

Johnson, David. *Hume, Holism, and Miracles*. Ithaca: Cornell University Press, 1999.

Kerdeman, Deborah. "Pulled Up Short: Challenging Self-Understanding as a Focus of Teaching and Learning." *Journal of Philosophy of Education* 37 (2003): 293–308.

"L.A. Rabbi Blasted for Fifth Question: Was There Really a Passover Exodus?" *Jewish Telegraphic Service*, April 27, 2001. http://www.jta.org/2001/04/27/jewish-holidays/passover/l-a-rabbi-blasted-for-fifth-question-was-there-really-a-passover-exodus.

McKenzie, Robert Tracy. *The First Thanksgiving: What the Real Story Tells Us about Loving God and Learning from History*. Downers Grove, IL: InterVarsity Press, 2013.

Meyer, Michael A. "Reflections on the Educated Jew from the Perspective of Reform Judaism." In *Visions of Jewish Education*. Edited by Seymour Fox, Israel Scheffler, and Daniel Marom, 149–77. New York: Cambridge University Press, 2003.

Myers, David N. *Resisting History: Historicism and its Discontents in German-Jewish Thought*. Princeton: Princeton University Press, 2003.

Niebuhr, Gustav. "Religion Journal; A Rabbi's Look at Archaeology Touches a Nerve." *New York Times*, June 2, 2001.

Novick, Peter. *That Noble Dream: The "Objectivity Question" and the American Historical Profession*. New York: Cambridge University Press, 1988.

Orsi, Robert. "Abundant History: Marian Apparitions as Alternative Modernity." *Historically Speaking* (September–October 2008): 12–16.

Rabinow, Paul. "Introduction." In *The Foucault Reader*. Edited by Paul Rabinow, 3–30. New York: Pantheon, 1984.

Safran Foer, Jonathan. "Why a *Haggadah*?" *New York Times*, March 31, 2012. http://www.nytimes.com/2012/04/01/opinion/sunday/why-a-haggadah.html?pagewanted=all&_r=0.

Satlow, Michael L. *How the Bible Became Holy*. New Haven: Yale University Press, 2014.

Twain, Mark. "Concerning the Jews." *Harper's Magazine*, March, 1898. http://legacy.fordham.edu/halsall/mod/1898twain-jews.asp.

Tyack, David. "Ways of Seeing, An Essay on the History of Compulsory Schooling." *Harvard Educational Review* 46: 3 (Fall 1976): 355–89.

von Ranke, Leopold. *Geschichten der romanischen und germanischen Völker von 1494 bis 1535 (History of the Latin and Teutonic nations, 1494–1535)*. Leipzig: Reimer, 1824.

Watanabe, Teresa. "Doubting the Story of Exodus." *Los Angeles Times*, April 13, 2001.

———. "L.A. Unified Adopts Free History Curriculum from Stanford University," *Los Angeles Times*, November 27, 2014. http://www.latimes.com/local/education/la-me-history-stanford-20141126-story.html#page=1.

White, Hayden. *Metahistory: The Historical Imagination in 19th-century Europe*. Baltimore, MD: Johns Hopkins University, 1973.

White, Richard. *Remembering Ahanagram: Storytelling in a Family's Past*. New York: Hill and Wang, 1998.

Wineburg, Sam. *Historical Thinking and Other Unnatural Acts: Charting the Future of Teaching the Past*. Philadelphia: Temple University Press, 2001.

———. "Undue Certainty: Where Howard Zinn's *A People's History* Falls Short." *American Educator* 37 (2012–13): 27–34.

Wineburg, Sam, Daisy Martin, and Chauncey Monte-Sano. *Reading Like a Historian*. New York: Teachers College Press, 2001.

Yerushalmi, Yosef Hayim. *Zakhor: Jewish History and Jewish Memory*. New York: Schocken, 1989.

Learning to be Jewish

Eli Gottlieb

Jewish education is, among other things, a form of religious education. But what does it mean to learn religion, or to learn a particular religion? We can learn facts about a particular religion or theories about religions in general—but that seems more like social studies, history, or the study of comparative religion. In this chapter, Gottlieb addresses three aspects of this question. First, he focuses on children's religious thinking, reporting on his discovery that the existing theories about developmental stages fit poorly with the Israeli Jewish children that he studies. In some instances, and on some topics, these children exhibit more sophistication in their religious thinking than the theories would have predicted. He then turns to examining more closely the affects of different schools on their students' religious thinking. Whereas the psychological literature tends to assume that religious thinking is a function of psychological development, he documents that, in fact, "these ways of believing are embedded in distinctive ways of talking about belief that are characteristic of particular Jewish-Israeli communities." Finally, Gottlieb describes his study of the "epistemic switching" that occurs even among sophisticated readers, as they move between academic and religious modes in understanding and talking about religious texts. This observation raises intriguing questions about precisely what learning outcomes we aspire for our students to achieve.

Meet Sophie. Sophie is an eighth-grader in a North American Jewish day school. It's Tuesday morning, 10:55 a.m. Sophie sits quietly, two rows from the front, second desk to the right, half-listening to Rabbi David review the material from last week's class, half-watching a fly buzzing in and out of the open window. In Sophie's schedule, the class appears as "Jewish Studies." It comes after Mathematics and before English. What does Sophie do in this class that is different from what she does in the classes before and after it? What, if anything, does Rabbi David (or the principal or the board of governors or Sophie's parents) *want* to be different?

Sophie, her desk, her schedule, Rabbi David, and the fly are all figments of my imagination. But the scene is familiar. In some day schools, Sophie would be Devorah, Jenny, or Stav. Rabbi David might be Rabbi Sarah or Dr. Jacobson or Ha-Morah Avital. Instead of "Jewish Studies," it might be "Judaic Studies" or *"Limmudei Kodesh"* or, less generically, *"Tanakh"* or *"Machshevet."* The question, however, remains the same: *Mah nishtanah hakitah hazo mikol hakitot*? How is this class different from all other classes? And how *ought* it to be different?

I am tempted to answer that in other classes the goal is for Sophie to know particular things, whereas in this class the goal is for Sophie to become a particular kind of person. Immediately, however, this distinction begins to look like an overstatement, if not an outright false dichotomy. Researchers have been aware that knowing and being are intertwined since at least as far back as the 1990s, when the study of cognition took a cultural turn,[1] if not a good deal earlier, when L. S. Vygotsky[2] first suggested that all higher-order thinking is social. Indeed, some of the most interesting research in the learning sciences in recent years has been about the ways that knowing and being are connected. Researchers like Donna LeCourt,[3] Stanton Wortham,[4] and Paul Cobb and colleagues,[5] for example, have shown how students become particular kinds of person while learning school subjects like literature or mathematics.

Nevertheless, learning to be Jewish does seem to be different. As conventionally conceived, the educator's primary goals in teaching secular school subjects like mathematics and English are to increase learners' knowledge and practical competence. That students' identities are entangled in this process is a significant by-product that researchers and theorists, like those cited above, ask us acknowledge and to address responsibly. In Jewish education, however, the priorities are reversed. The acquisition of knowledge is a by-product or a necessary precondition. But the ultimate goal is to encourage learners to

---

1 For example, Jerome Bruner, *The Culture of Education* (Cambridge, MA: Harvard University Press, 1996); Michael Cole, *Cultural Psychology: A Once and Future Discipline* (Cambridge, MA: Harvard University Press, 1998); Barbara Rogoff, *Apprenticeship in Thinking: Cognitive Development in Social Context* (Oxford: Oxford University Press, 1990).
2 L. S. Vygotsky, *Mind and Society: The Development of Higher Mental Processes* (Cambridge, MA: Harvard University Press, 1978).
3 Donna LeCourt, *Identity Matters: Schooling the Student Body in Academic Discourse* (New York: SUNY Press, 2004).
4 Stanton Wortham, *Learning Identity: The Joint Emergence of Social Identification and Academic Learning* (Cambridge: Cambridge University Press, 2006).
5 Paul Cobb et al., "An Interpretive Scheme for Analyzing the Identities that Students Develop in Mathematics Classrooms," *Journal for Research in Mathematics Education* 40, no. 1 (2009), 40–68.

be particular kinds of person. Learning to be Jewish is the focus of the entire enterprise. Learning the laws of *kashrut* or what to do in a synagogue or how to read a page of Talmud are a means to this end. Abraham Joshua Heschel[6] makes a similar point:

> It is not only important what a person does; it is equally and even more important what a person is. Spiritually speaking, what he does is a minimum of what he is. Deeds are outpourings, they are not the essence of the self. Deeds reflect or refine but they remain functions. They are not the substance of the inner life. Hence it is the inner life that is the problem for us, Jewish educators, and particularly the inner life of the Jewish child.

My research over the last two decades has sought to characterize more precisely the ways in which learning to be Jewish differs from other kinds of learning. In this chapter, I focus on three kinds of difference: differences in content, differences in context, and differences in goals. The order in which I discuss these three differences is not accidental. It recapitulates my own professional journey as an educational practitioner and cognitive psychologist. I began by studying differences in how children think about religious and non-religious content. I then investigated how the development of these differences varies across cultural contexts. Finally, and most recently, I have studied models of mature religious thinking that Jewish education might seek to cultivate.

What each of these phases of my research have in common is their empirical focus. My research examines what people do—not what they say they do or what someone else thinks they ought to do.[7] Herein, I believe, lies its value to Jewish educators. To the extent that my findings are credible, they provide us with the beginnings of an empirical foundation on which to base instructional design, one that takes into account how Jewish education is different to other kinds of education.

Different Contents

It is surprising how little thought we give to theology in contemporary Jewish education. It is true that, compared with other Western religions, Judaism is

---

6 Abraham Joshua Heschel, "The Spirit of Jewish Education," *Journal of Jewish Education* 24, no. 2 (1953), 16.
7 Eli Gottlieb, "On the Corruption of Jewish Education by Philosophy," in *Educational Deliberations: Studies in Education Dedicated to Shlomo (Seymour) Fox*, ed. Mordecai Nisan and Oded Schremer (Jerusalem: Keter, 2005), 404–29.

more practice-oriented than belief-oriented. Indeed, only five out the 613 commandments in Maimonides' *Sefer Hamitzvot* refer to things that we are commanded to believe. Nevertheless, belief is far from irrelevant to Jewish life and practice. For example, belief in one God—as opposed to none or many—was for much of Jewish history a necessary condition for participation in Jewish community. As Baruch Spinoza and others learned the hard way, transgress that one and you were out.[8]

In educational practice, however, belief in God tends to feature as an unexamined background assumption. In educational theory and research, it is generally ignored. As a result, our knowledge about Jewish children's religious beliefs, and our articulation of the goals of Jewish education in relation to such beliefs, is partial and informal, to say the least.

Several years ago, I embarked on a program of empirical research aimed at understanding how children's religious thinking develops. Initially, my interest in these questions was practical. As a Jewish educator, I noticed that my colleagues and I were working on the basis of all kinds of assumptions about what children can and cannot understand at different ages. Based on these assumptions, we derived all sorts of practical rules of thumb about which issues to raise when. But I began to wonder whether these assumptions were justified. Perhaps children were more sophisticated than we assumed. I presumed that this kind of thing had been thoroughly studied by cognitive and developmental psychologists and that all I needed to do was to read the relevant literature and derive the appropriate practical conclusions.

As I began to acquaint myself with the existing research, however, I realized that my expectations were misplaced. First, very few studies had been conducted in this area. Second, those that had been conducted were generally not very rigorous, and I therefore needed to take their conclusions with a pinch or two of salt. Third, studies differed substantially in their conceptual frameworks, methods, and conclusions, making it difficult to determine the overall implications of their findings for educational practice.[9]

My most troubling discovery, however, was the extent to which the existing research on children's religious thinking rested on broadly Protestant

---

[8] Asa Kasher and Shlomo Biderman, "Why Was Baruch de Spinoza Excommunicated?," in *Spinoza: Context, Sources, and the Early Writings*, ed. Genevieve Lloyd (London: Taylor & Francis, 2001); Yirmiyahu Yovel, *Spinoza and Other Heretics: The Marrano of Reason* (Princeton, NJ: Princeton University Press, 1991).

[9] See Eli Gottlieb, "Development of Religious Thinking," *Religious Education* 101, no. 2 (2006), 242–60.

conceptions of mature faith. Interestingly, this was true even of studies conducted by Jews.[10] The reasons for this theological bias are unclear. I suspect that it has something to do with the fact that many of the studies were conducted in the United States and countries in Western Europe where Protestantism is deeply ingrained in the culture. I also suspect that it has something—perhaps even more—to do with the influence of Jean Piaget on developmental psychology. The tendency to view abstract thought as by definition more advanced than concrete thought is one that, applied to religious thinking, can have the unintended effect of classifying characteristically Protestant tendencies (e.g., valuing faith over deeds; interpreting religious language as allegorical) as more mature or sophisticated than tendencies characteristic of other faith traditions.

In short, my search for off-the-shelf answers to my practical questions ended in disappointment. Rigorous and relevant research was scarce and the assumptions that Jewish educators were making about children's religious thinking lacked empirical support. I realized that if reliable empirical data about the religious thinking of Jewish children and adolescents wasn't available off the shelf, I should collect it myself.

And that is what I did. Over a number of years, I conducted empirical studies that compared how children think about religious and non-religious content.[11] My initial research examined within-subject differences with respect to analogical reasoning, that is, differences that appear in data gathered from the same person engaged in two different domains. I compared the scores of a sample of British elementary school children on a battery of written reasoning tasks. Some of the items were excerpted from intelligence tests and contained no religious content; other items were excerpted from Ronald Goldman's[12] test of religious thinking. Contrary to the claims of previous studies,[13] I found no significant correlation

---

10 For example, David Elkind, "The Child's Conception of His Religious Domination: (1) The Jewish Child," *Journal of Genetic Psychology* 99, no. 2 (1961), 209–25; David Elkind, "The Child's Conception of His Religious Domination: (2) The Catholic Child," *Journal of Genetic Psychology* 101, no. 1 (1962), 185–93; David Elkind, "The Child's Conception of His Religious Domination: (3) The Protestant Child," *Journal of Genetic Psychology* 103, no. 2 (1963), 291–304.
11 Eli Gottlieb, "The Role of Analogical Reasoning in the Development of Religious Thinking" (master's thesis, Cambridge University, 1994); Eli Gottlieb, "Religious Thinking in Childhood and Adolescence: Argumentative Reasoning and the Justification of Religious Belief" (PhD thesis, Hebrew University of Jerusalem, 2002).
12 Ronald Goldman, "Religious Thinking from Childhood to Adolescence" (London: Routledge and Kegan Paul, 1964).
13 For example, James W. Fowler, *Stages of Faith: The Psychology of Human Development and the Quest for Meaning* (San Francisco, CA: Harper and Row, 1981); Goldman, "Religious

between children's understanding of Biblical texts and their general ability to reason by analogy. Indeed, contrary to Goldman's claim that children who cannot reason analogically are incapable of mature religious thinking, my study found that children's ability to reason analogically was neither a necessary nor a sufficient condition for mature religious thinking, as measured by Goldman's own test!

Next, I investigated how religious thinking develops among Jewish-Israeli children and adolescents. The study included individual, semi-structured interviews with two hundred fifth, eighth, and twelfth graders about two controversies (i.e., situations in which interviewees are asked to imagine two interlocutors arguing about a contentious topic)[14]—one about belief in God and the other about punishment of children. My sample was stratified by age, gender, and school type.[15] The interviews took place, for the most part, on school premises, so I spent time in both state (secular) schools and state-religious (modern orthodox) schools in Israel's largest school district.

Prior to analyzing the data, and based on the claims of previous research into children's religious thinking,[16] I predicted that the interviewees' thinking about the religious controversy would lag behind their thinking about the non-religious controversy, since these earlier studies indicated that religious thinking involves cognitive abilities that are sophisticated and late-developing. What I found was almost exactly the opposite. Sophisticated forms of argumentation previously associated with late adolescence and early adulthood appeared *earlier* in the religious controversy than the non-religious controversy. In other words, children exhibited sophisticated reasoning in relation to religious content at younger ages than they did with respect to non-religious content.

To sum up this first phase of my research, I found that the picture painted by earlier studies of children's religious thinking needed redrawing. Instructional design in Jewish education based on early studies of religious thinking rested on shaky empirical foundations. Yet, at the same time, differences between the pace and direction of cognitive development in the religious domain versus other domains were sufficiently well-documented to give us pause before

---

Thinking"; Fritz Oser and Paul Gmünder, *Religious Judgment: A Developmental Perspective* (Birmingham, AL: Religious Education Press, 1991).

14 Anne Colby and Lawrence Kohlber, *The Measurement of Moral Judgment: Theoretical Foundations and Research Validation* (New York: Cambridge University Press, 1987).

15 See Eli Gottlieb, "Religious Thinking in Childhood and Adolescence"; Eli Gottlieb, "Learning How to Believe: Epistemic Development in Cultural Context," *Journal of the Learning Sciences* 16, no. 1 (2007), 5–35.

16 For example, Fowler, *Stages of Faith*; Goldman, "Religious Thinking"; Oser and Gmünder, *Religious Judgment*.

basing our instructional designs on generic assumptions about children's cognitive development. We needed more specific and detailed research.

Different Contexts

In addition to the differences that I found between how individuals reasoned about religious and non-religious content, my study also yielded intriguing findings related to context, namely, differences between schools. Most notably, over two-thirds of pupils in state schools considered their belief in God to be fallible (i.e., they were willing to entertain the possibility that their belief in God might be mistaken), compared with less than a third of pupils in state-religious schools. This difference was preserved even when removing non-believers from the analysis (thirty-seven out of the two hundred participants, or about 19 percent of the sample), or when controlling for age and family religiosity. In other words, even when subscribing to ostensibly the same belief, participants from state-religious schools believed it "differently" to their peers at state schools. Specifically, whereas state-religious pupils considered belief in God to be something akin to a demonstrable and incontrovertible fact, state pupils considered it to be more like an opinion or a personal preference.

To understand better these differences and their possible sources, I attended very carefully to how participants in the study described the kinds of theological discourse they encountered at school. In state-religious schools, pupils reported encountering theological discourse within the context of official classes in which teachers or rabbis set out to prove God's existence and to rebut conclusively any potential counterarguments. As Hannah, a state-religious eighth-grader, commented, "Every seminar they bring up the whole thing; that God exists, proving to us that God exists."

In contrast, when pupils in state schools referred to previous occasions on which they had discussed the question of God's existence, they tended to cite informal conversations with peers that ended with the opposing sides agreeing to disagree. The following comment by Ron, a state twelfth-grader, is typical: "To tell you the truth, I had exactly the same argument with my friend. We sometimes go hiking and speak about this kind of stuff. And I didn't succeed. I'm always saying stuff to him and he's always saying stuff to me, but neither of us is ever persuaded."

Further insight into these differences was provided by two instances of "pre-interview coaching" at two of the state-religious elementary schools in which I conducted interviews.[17] In each of these schools, my suspicions of prior coaching were first aroused after encountering almost identical lines of argumentation in my interviews with pupils from one particular class. These suspicions were later confirmed by pupils' explicit admissions later in the interview that they had indeed been "prepared" for my visit. In one school, pupils had been told a story about Rabbi Akiva (though in one version, Akiva had mutated into Maimonides), who convinces a skeptic (in some versions a gentile, in others a heretic) by showing him a beautiful painting and telling him that his cat (in almost all versions: "Mitzi") had painted it by accident by upsetting a box of paints on a canvas. When the skeptic objects that a cat could not have produced such a magnificent work of art, the rabbi points out the much greater complexity and beauty of the natural world, showing that it too must be the result of design. In the second school, pupils were told a story about a school inspector who challenges the pupils by insisting that, since he can't see God, He must not exist. One of the pupils in the story then responds that the inspector must have no intelligence, since he can't see that either.[18]

These snippets of unsought evidence provide an intriguing glimpse of how the discourse to which children and adolescents are exposed in school relates not only to what they believe, but to *how* they believe. By exposing pupils to models of theological discourse in which all questions can be answered clearly and conclusively in the affirmative, state-religious schools appear to foster an absolutist religious epistemology, within which believers are so confident in the truth of their position that they consider it effectively infallible. Conversely, by

---

17 See Eli Gottlieb, "Arguments as Venues for Cultural Education: A Comparison of Epistemic Practices at General and Religious Schools in Israel," in *Cultural Education—Cultural Sustainability*, ed. Zvi Bekerman and Ezra Kopelowitz (Mahwah, NJ: Erlbaum, 2008), 404–29.

18 My initial reaction to discovering these instances of coaching was to consider excluding the transcripts from the study, due to their being "contaminated" by the explicit instruction that preceded the interview. However, on reflection, I realized that this would be a mistake, for at least three reasons. First, it would exclude precisely those data most pertinent to my research questions. It would be paradoxical indeed to exclude data from a study of the effects of cultural practices on the grounds that they were "contaminated" by cultural practices. Second, it would distinguish arbitrarily between instances of prior instruction of which I was aware and those of which I was not. Each participant entered the interview with his or her own unique epistemological baggage, accumulated over the course of his or her entire life prior to that moment, and from an indefinite variety of sources. Who is to say, and on what grounds, which of that person's epistemological statements were "real" and which "merely parroted"? Third, viewing these instances as "contaminated" makes sense only if one assumes that "genuine" epistemological beliefs are things that one constructs in one's head without outside assistance.

implicitly consigning religious beliefs to the private domain, state schools seem to promote a view of theological matters as questions of personal preference that lie beyond the pale of rational debate.

These between-school differences are striking enough in their own right. They are even more striking when considered in comparative context. In addition to asking each of the two hundred participants a series of questions about his or her belief in God, I asked them a parallel series of questions about their beliefs regarding a non-religious belief, namely, whether or not children should be punished when they misbehave. My analyses of their responses to this latter series of questions indicated no significant between-school differences whatsoever. This suggests that the differences observed in relation to belief in God were not due to some general difference in epistemological practices in state-religious schools versus state schools, but rather to divergent practices with respect to religious belief in particular.

When I first published these findings, my intended audience was learning scientists. The ideas I wanted to emphasize were that not all learning is the same; that children and adolescents learn to treat religious beliefs differently to how they treat other kinds of belief; and that the nature and extent of these differences is affected by the kinds of discourse to which they are exposed in school. However, I believe the study has implications for Jewish education that are both more general and more specific.

The study showed that state-religious and state pupils had different ways of believing. But it showed something else too. These ways of believing are embedded in distinctive ways of talking about belief that are characteristic of particular Jewish-Israeli communities. To be a contemporary secular Jew in Israel is, among other things, to talk about belief in God as if it were a private matter of personal preference. Similarly, to be a contemporary religious Jew in Israel is, among other things, to talk about belief in God as if it were a public matter of provable fact. There are of course exceptions and variations to these patterns. But these are the patterns. In both state-religious and state schools, pupils are learning to be Jews of particular kinds.

Though, as I noted at the start of this chapter, there is a good deal more to Jewishness than theology, God is still a pretty prominent character in many Jewish texts and traditions. If pupils in state-religious and state schools understand God-talk differently to one another, then the ways they interpret Jewish texts, ideas, and traditions may also diverge in significant ways. In other words, even when studying the same texts as one another, pupils at state-religious and state schools may be engaged in encounters of quite different kinds with the material. The implications of these differences have yet to be comprehensively addressed by educators.

Different Goals

No Jew today lives within just one community. We all participate in multiple communities. I am not talking only about the expanding number of groups to which each of us subscribes on WhatsApp or Twitter. I mean the different social, professional, ideological, and recreational groupings through and around which we organize our lives. I don't know if any human has ever lived his life entirely within a single community. Perhaps. But even in eras when tribes, castes, religious orders, and professional guilds provided more rigid boundaries, I suspect that crossing, mixing, and switching between groups was the norm rather than the exception. Today, the number of groups in which an average Jew participates, and the rate at which this number is increasing, is probably higher than ever before in history. From the *yeshiva bocher* in Bnei Brak checking the NBA results on his iPhone to the secular *kibbutz* retiree posting a comment on YNET's *parshat ha-shavua* page—each of us moves between communities, sometimes without blinking, often without thinking, several times per day.

(It is worth noting—for now, parenthetically and midrashically—that the idea of boundary-crossing and belonging to more than one place or community has been at the heart of the Jewish experience since antiquity. The term, "Hebrews," means, quite literally, "those who cross over." Jews have wandered, and been defined by wandering, throughout history—from the wilderness of Sinai to the mass migrations of the nineteenth century.)

One of the many challenges this poses for Jewish education is that of defining goals in relation to multiplicity. Toward what kind of a person do we wish to educate? Is the ideal graduate of a Jewish education someone who prioritizes participation in Jewish community over participation in other communities? Is it someone who crosses or alternates between communities in a particular way?

These rather abstract questions have very practical corollaries. For the present purposes, I will focus on one that relates specifically to reading Jewish texts. This focus is not arbitrary, but neither should it be taken for granted. I appreciate that there are ways of participating in Jewish community that are text-lite. The Maccabiah athlete, J-Date user, and nostalgic bagel eater are all participants in recognizable forms of Jewish community. The "people of the book" are not defined by books alone. Nevertheless, Judaism is a profoundly textual tradition.

Scholars and practitioners of Jewish education (of each and every stripe) have given much thought to general questions about how to teach Jewish texts, and how to combine Jewish and secular school subjects in day schools. However, we have devoted little attention to characterizing how, ultimately, we would like graduates of a good Jewish education to read. We know more about what we don't want than what we do want. We don't want our graduates to read Jewish texts in ways that are either uncritically loyal or disloyally critical. On one hand, we want them to read in ways that show the texts are *theirs*; that the texts belong to them and they to the text. On the other hand, we want them to read in ways that take into account other perspectives; that are awake and alive to criticisms and alternatives and modern challenges. We lack not only a clear characterization of what such reading looks like but also of the kinds of learning that are likely to lead students to read this way.

One thing that might help here is to collect and study exemplars of expert performance. Just as researchers have studied how expert chess players and historians read chessboards and historical documents,[19] so might we study expert readers of Jewish texts to understand better what it means to "read like an educated Jew."

In a recent study,[20] Sam Wineburg and I collected and analyzed several such exemplars. This was not the initial goal of our research. When we began the study, we wanted more generally to examine how people's religious commitments and historical expertise influence their readings of historical texts. We compared how eight religious believers (historians and clergy) and eight skeptics (historians and scientists) read a series of documents on two topics: the Biblical Exodus and the origins of the First (American) Thanksgiving. We found that readings by religiously committed historians differed from those of their non-religious peers. Navigating between the competing commitments of their faith communities on one hand, and an academic guild on the other, religious historians engaged in *epistemic switching*, varying epistemological criteria to align with the allegiances triggered by the document under review. To explain these findings, we proposed that historical understanding be conceived not as a unitary

---

19 William G. Chase and K. Anders Ericsson, "Exceptional Memory," *American Scientist* 70, no. 6 (1982), 607–15; Sam Wineburg, "Reading Abraham Lincoln: An Expert/Expert Study in the Interpretation of Historical Texts," *Cognitive Science* 22, no. 3 (1998), 319–46.
20 Eli Gottlieb and Sam Wineburg, "Between Veritas and Communitas: Epistemic Switching in the Reading of Academic and Sacred History," *Journal of the Learning Sciences* 21, no. 1 (2012), 84–129.

construct, but as a form of coordination between multiple axes: a vertical axis of increasing intellectual sophistication as defined by the discipline; and a horizontal axis of identification and commitment, along which individuals move between a variety of allegiances and affiliations as they engage the epistemological criteria of sacred history.

Only a few of the participants in our study were Jewish. Most of the religious participants identified themselves as Christians. However, the ways in which religiously committed historians—from whichever tradition—combined and alternated between different ways of reading provide (in our view) fascinating insights into how readings of religiously significant texts can be both loyal and critical.

The religiously committed historians in our study felt the competing pulls of their professional guild, on one hand, and the religious communities with which they affiliated, on the other. These dual commitments sometimes led to visible tensions. We coined the term *epistemic switching* to describe how participants dealt with the multiple memberships evoked by these texts. This term denotes a participant's use of multiple frameworks of epistemological assumptions (e.g., historical, theological, scientific) for interpreting documentary evidence. Some employed multiple epistemologies serially; others employed them simultaneously. Some granted equal weight to distinct epistemologies; others privileged one epistemology over another.

One of our interviewees, Professor C, was a religiously observant Jewish professor of history at a public university in the Pacific Northwest. When we asked him which Exodus document best represented his own views, he looked puzzled and asked, "On what day of the week? When I'm teaching my class or when I'm in the synagogue?" He elaborated:

> When I'm teaching my courses I'm bound by the rules of historical research and I have an obligation to explain to my students what the tradition of historical scholarship has to say about this material . . . . Now when I'm in a synagogue, I'm not going to be talking about the historical evidence of the Exodus, I'm going to be doing pretty much actually what the guy I laughed at [in Document 7, at an opinion expressed about the contemporary relevance of the Exodus in an article from the *LA Times*] does—contemporizing, metaphorizing, allegorizing—because essentially my task there is to make the traditional come alive and address people where they live. To do that, as I said, the historical veracity of the business is hardly relevant at all.

Relevant exemplars in our study include not only religious historians but also members of the clergy. Rabbi K taught Talmud at a local Jewish high school. He had studied for many years at elite *yeshivot* in Britain and Israel, but had not attended college. Like Professor C, Rabbi K switched between religious and historical epistemologies. But whereas Professor C granted each of these epistemologies equal weight, Rabbi K maintained a clear hierarchy. Rabbi K's antipathy for critical history blazed from the first sentence of Israel Finkelstein and Neil Asher Silberman's *The Bible Unearthed*[21] (Document 5 in our Exodus set): "This person has a problem with religion and that's why he's saying this." To the archeologists' claim that the Israelites are nowhere to be found in Egyptian court records, Rabbi K shot back, "Why should they be? The Egyptians were massacred."

This comment is puzzling. The Hebrew Bible makes no mention of wholesale destruction of the Egyptian monarchy, only the crushing defeat of the brigades that tried to overtake the Hebrews (Exodus 15: 1-18). Rabbi K's comment, as well as others he fired off in rapid succession—that Egyptian bondage lasted 210 years instead of the Bible's reckoning of 400, that the Hebrews enjoyed a bountiful water supply during their wanderings, that the manna was so pure that it was digested whole—comes not from the Biblical account but are drawn instead from over two thousand years of rabbinic commentary. Indeed, Rabbi K's protocol on Document 5 was the most densely contextual reading in our entire data corpus, with fourteen separate intertextual references, or one per every eighteen words of the text reviewed. Yet none of these references, each claiming authority to an unbroken oral tradition delivered to Moses at Sinai along with the Ten Commandments, would be considered legitimate sources for establishing the Exodus as a documentable historical event.

Based on his ahistorical approach thus far, we might have assumed that Rabbi K would reject the archeologists' assertions wholesale. It is precisely this expectation that makes his final comments on Document 5 so intriguing. As he reads the excerpt, he begins to wonder what happened to the bones of the Israelites who perished in the desert:

> I wonder what [the archeologists] would expect to be there, for a nation that was only there for a short amount of time. . . . The longest place that they camped in was a year. . . . Maybe there are places where they stayed

---

21 Israel Finkelstein and Neil Asher Silberman, *The Bible Unearthed: Archeology's New Vision of Ancient Israel and the Origin of Its Sacred Texts* (New York: Free Press, 2001), 59–63.

for more than a year. Even still. Now, they did bury their dead in the wilderness. So I suppose there should be . . . some bones. But I wonder if they didn't look and didn't find any bones of people. That's a good point. There should be bones there. That's interesting. There are no bones there. Interesting. I don't know.

This transcription only approximates the puzzlement in Rabbi K's voice, his fits and starts as he paused with genuine uncertainty, a stance quite different from his earlier dismissal of Silberman and Finkelstein as heretics with an axe to grind. Confronted in the next document with the apologetics of Rabbi David Gottlieb,[22] who asserts that one must adopt the Biblical account as whole cloth rather than picking and choosing among its threads, Rabbi K refused to abate:

> You have to also look for bodies. . . . The *Gemara* [Talmud] does say that they went out and dug their own graves . . . so there was definitely a period of time when people were dying in the wilderness. I wonder what they did with those bodies. It doesn't necessarily say they buried them there. Maybe they took those bodies back to Israel, in which case that would explain why there's no bodies. Or maybe they just haven't looked for bodies. Or maybe they did find bodies, but didn't think that was such a tremendous thing, finding dead bodies in a desert, because you'd expect to find dead bodies in a desert. Okay. Okay. Okay, but I think that's a good point.

The "good point" that stumps Rabbi K is the nagging question of why no bones have been found. Never does he question the Torah's account, a fact that reflects his unwavering commitment to revelation. However, as he wrestles with the question of the bones, steadily working through possibilities and laying out options, he seems less the theologian falling back on stock answers from the rabbinic tradition than a genuine historical inquirer, critically reasoning about hypotheses, thinking about evidence, and resisting premature closure.

Whether we prefer Professor C's approach to Rabbi K's, or vice versa, each of them provides a model of educated reading that it is worth considering in our efforts to formulate goals for Jewish education. And these are just two of the models we encountered in our study. I am confident that additional studies, with different kinds of readers and different kinds of text, would reveal additional

---

22 David Gottlieb, *Living Up to the Truth*, 2nd rev. ed. (Jerusalem: Ohr Sameach International, 1997).

models we have not yet considered. As has been done in the field of history,[23] curriculum designers could draw on such analyses to develop curricula and assessments that focus explicitly on teaching students to read in the desired ways.

At the very least, data of the kinds we collected provide a concrete background against which to define educational goals. We might ask ourselves, for example, whether the strategies our readers used to coordinate epistemologies are ones that we would like to see emulated by students in Jewish day schools. If not, what alternative strategies for addressing multiplicity do we want to promote in their place? If epistemic switching and navigation between multiple commitments are indeed features of real-life engagement with sacred texts, then what are the responsibilities of Jewish educators in preparing students to think critically on one hand, without frustrating possibilities for belonging and participation on the other?

Sophie's World

What does all this have to do with Sophie and her Jewish Studies class? What do these studies teach us about differences between the learning she does in this class and the learning she does in other classes? And what practical difference does any of this make to what Sophie's teachers do or ought to do?

Unfortunately for those who seek simple solutions, these studies raise more questions than they answer. They do not provide us with a cheat sheet of ages and stages of religious thinking, which educators can use as a basis for curricular design. Nor do they provide us with easy generalizations about differences between religious and non-religious thinking that would allow us to apply our general knowledge of developmental psychology straightforwardly to the particular case of Jewish content.

What they do offer, however, is a set of lenses with which to view learning in Jewish educational contexts, and some empirical beacons by which to steer. Rather than making broad assumptions about what Sophie is capable and incapable of understanding in eighth grade, her teachers might attend more carefully to the kinds of questions she asks. In designing their Jewish Studies

---

23 See, for example, Joel Breakstone et al., "Beyond the Bubble in History/Social Studies Assessments," *Phi Delta Kappan* 94, no. 5 (2013), 53–57; Avishag Reisman, "Reading Like a Historian: A Document-Based History Curriculum Intervention in Urban High Schools," *Cognition and Instruction* 30, no. 1 (2012), 86–112; Sam Wineburg and Abby Reisman, "Disciplinary Literacy in History," *Journal of Adolescent & Adult Literacy* 58, no. 8 (2015), 636–39.

classes, Sophie's teachers might give more thought to the ways in which they would like Sophie and her classmates to talk about Jewish content and how these are similar and different to the ways they would like them to talk in other classes and about other school subjects. Finally, Sophie's teachers might consider the models of educated Jewish practice toward which their instructional efforts are directed. Defining how the ideal graduate of a Jewish education ought to read Jewish texts is just one aspect of this. Perhaps, given the centrality of text to Jewish culture, it is a good place to start. But our work to define goals cannot stop there. In an age in which people increasingly participate in multiple communities simultaneously, decisions about which kinds of "switching" to encourage and discourage are of great moment. Jewish educators cannot afford to bury their heads in the sand and pretend that we live in a simpler age. The question is not, "to switch or not to switch?" Instead, given that we switch, it is "how can we (and our students) learn to switch in ways that balance loyalty and openness?"

These are big questions. They are not of a grain size that Sophie's teachers can answer on their own or in a single classroom. But they set an agenda. Not just of things for Jewish educators to consider in planning and implementing specific interventions, but also for future research and deliberation about how people learn to be Jewish.

Bibliography

Breakstone, Joel, Mark Smith, and Sam Wineburg. "Beyond the Bubble in History/Social Studies Assessments." *Phi Delta Kappan* 94, no. 5 (2013), 53–57.

Bruner, Jerome. *The Culture of Education*. Cambridge, MA: Harvard University Press, 1996.

Chase, William G., and K. Anders Ericsson. "Exceptional Memory." *American Scientist* 70, no. 6 (1982), 607–15.

Cobb, Paul, Melissa Gresalfi, and Lynn Liao Hodge. "An Interpretive Scheme for Analyzing the Identities that Students Develop in Mathematics Classrooms." *Journal for Research in Mathematics Education* 40, no. 1 (2009), 40–68.

Colby, Anne, and Lawrence Kohlber. *The Measurement of Moral Judgment: Theoretical Foundations and Research Validation*. New York: Cambridge University Press, 1987.

Cole, Michael. *Cultural Psychology: A Once and Future Discipline*. Cambridge, MA: Harvard University Press, 1998.

Elkind, David. "The Child's Conception of His Religious Domination: (1) The Jewish Child." *Journal of Genetic Psychology* 99, no. 2 (1961), 209–25.

———. "The Child's Conception of His Religious Domination: (2) The Catholic Child." *Journal of Genetic Psychology* 101, no. 1 (1962), 185–93.

———. "The Child's Conception of His Religious Domination: (3) The Protestant Child." *Journal of Genetic Psychology* 103, no. 2 (1963), 291–304.

Finkelstein, Israel and Neil Asher Silberman. *The Bible Unearthed: Archeology's New Vision of Ancient Israel and the Origin of Its Sacred Texts*. New York: Free Press, 2001.

Fowler, James W. *Stages of Faith: The Psychology of Human Development and the Quest for Meaning*. San Francisco, CA: Harper and Row, 1981.

Goldman, Ronald. *Religious Thinking from Childhood to Adolescence*. London: Routledge and Kegan Paul, 1964.

Gottlieb, David. *Living Up to the Truth*. 2nd Revised Edition. Jerusalem: Ohr Sameach International, 1997.

Gottlieb, Eli. "Arguments as Venues for Cultural Education: A Comparison of Epistemic Practices at General and Religious Schools in Israel." In *Cultural Education - Cultural Sustainability*. Edited by Zvi Bekerman and Ezra Kopelowitz, 404–29. Mahwah, NJ: Erlbaum, 2008.

———. "Development of Religious Thinking." *Religious Education* 101, no. 2 (2006), 242–60.

———. "Learning How to Believe: Epistemic Development in Cultural Context." *Journal of the Learning Sciences* 16, no. 1 (2007), 5–35.

———. "On the Corruption of Jewish Education by Philosophy." In *Educational Deliberations: Studies in Education Dedicated to Shlomo (Seymour) Fox*. Edited by Mordecai Nisan and Oded Schremer, 404–29. Jerusalem: Keter, 2005.

———. "Religious Thinking in Childhood and Adolescence: Argumentation and the Justification of Religious Belief." PhD diss., Hebrew University of Jerusalem, 2002.

———. "The role of analogical reasoning in the development of religious thinking." Master's thesis, Cambridge University, 1994.

Gottlieb, Eli, and Sam Wineburg. "Between Veritas and Communitas: Epistemic Switching in the Reading of Academic and Sacred History." *Journal of the Learning Sciences* 21, no. 1 (2012), 84–129.

Heschel, Abraham Joshua. "The Spirit of Jewish Education." *Journal of Jewish Education* 24, no. 2 (1953), 9–62.

Kasher, Asa, and Shlomo Biderman. "Why Was Baruch de Spinoza Excommunicated?" In *Spinoza: Context, Sources, and the Early Writings*. Edited by Genevieve Lloyd. London: Taylor & Francis, 2001.

LeCourt, Donna. *Identity Matters: Schooling the Student Body in Academic Discourse*. New York: SUNY Press, 2004.

Oser, Fritz, and Paul Gmünder. *Religious Judgment: A Developmental Perspective*. Birmingham, AL: Religious Education Press, 1991.

Reisman, Avishag. "Reading Like a Historian: A Document-Based History Curriculum Intervention in Urban High Schools." *Cognition and Instruction* 30, no. 1 (2012), 86–112.

Rogoff, Barbara. *Apprenticeship in Thinking: Cognitive Development in Social Context*. Oxford: Oxford University Press, 1990.

Vygotsky, L. S. *Mind and Society: The Development of Higher Mental Processes*. Cambridge, MA: Harvard University Press, 1978.

Wineburg, Sam. "Reading Abraham Lincoln: An Expert/Expert Study in the Interpretation of Historical Texts." *Cognitive Science* 22, no. 3 (1998), 319–46.

Wineburg, Sam, and Abby Reisman. "Disciplinary Literacy in History." *Journal of Adolescent & Adult Literacy* 58, no. 8 (2015), 636–39.

Wortham, Stanton. *Learning Identity: The Joint Emergence of Social Identification and Academic Learning*. Cambridge: Cambridge University Press, 2006.

Yovel, Yirmiyahu. *Spinoza and Other Heretics: The Marrano of Reason*. Princeton, NJ: Princeton University Press, 1991.

The Holistic Goals of Jewish Education

Gil G. Noam and Jeffrey S. Kress

In this chapter, Noam and Kress bring to the fore a theme that has been present in many of the previous chapters, namely, the need to expand our horizons beyond the cognitive. The goals of Jewish education are holistic, encompassing behavioral and affective learning outcomes, as well as cognitive. The authors begin by articulating a rationale for the importance of a holistic approach, and then discuss affordances provided by Jewish education for addressing outcomes in multiple domains. They then discuss the applicability of social and emotional learning theory and practice, with particular focus on a Developmental Domain Theory, which posits four intersecting areas of development (action, assertiveness, belonging, and reflection). They recommend that Jewish educators employ a more systematic and intentional approach to promoting and assessing outcomes in this area, and conclude by discussing the possibilities and challenge in doing so.

Discourse about schooling and its outcomes tends naturally toward mastery of academic, discipline-related, or subject matter- oriented, skills and competencies. Why can't Johnny read? Where does the United States rank among other nations in terms of math and science scores? What are the key historical events a student should know, and how can they evaluate evidence related to these? Academic achievement is tested repeatedly and on multiple levels, within classes, by state tests, and through exams that help determine college admissions.

At the same time, there is a line of discussion about the goals of education in terms of social, cultural, and affective outcomes such as preparation for citizenship, promotion of democratic ideals, and the fostering of valued virtues, dispositions, and behaviors. A variety of approaches to promoting socio-affective outcomes—such as moral education, character education, and social and emotional learning—strongly intersect, though there are details that distinguish each from the others.[1] We will use the term *whole child education* (WCE) as a shorthand for an approach in which academic, social, and emotional growth are not only seen as interconnected but are also addressed with intentionality across the curriculum.

WCE manifests, broadly speaking, in two interconnected ways. "From at least the time of the Bible and Aristotle, people have wondered about humankind's potential to learn more effective ways of managing emotional experiences and social relationships."[2] Whole child educators embrace their role in helping to develop that potential through actively addressing core intra- and inter-personal competencies (e.g., emotional awareness, self-control, and problem-solving) in their work.

A second thrust of WCE focuses on the conditions under which learning (in the academic, discipline- or content-specific sense of the word) takes place. For example, the Association for Supervision and Curriculum Development[3] suggests that we

> redefine what a successful learner is and how we measure success. A child who enters school healthy and feels safe is ready to learn. A student who feels connected to school is more likely to stay in school. All students who have access to challenging and engaging academic programs are better prepared for further education, work, and civic life. These components must work together, not in isolation. That is the goal of whole child education.

This second focus speaks to the intersection of the socio-affective and "academic" elements of learning. The *whole* in WCE does not imply a rejection of academic rigor, but rather a *yes, and* approach with multiple goals. Friction emerges, however, when it comes to the use of the limited time and resources available to educators, what outcomes to assess and how to do so, and the articulation of those values and dispositions that are shared by members of a diverse community. As the push for accountability under No Child Left Behind has led to a focus on test-scores, educators and parents have fought to protect children from a one-dimensional focus on academic achievement that they see taking away time

---

[1] Maurice J. Elias et al., "Socioemotional Learning and Character and Moral Education in Children: Synergy or Fundamental Divergence in Our Schools?," *Journal of Research in Character Education* 5, no. 2 (2007), 167–82.

[2] Ibid., 263.

[3] Association for Supervision and Curriculum Development, *Making the Case for Whole Child Education* (Alexandria, VA: ASCD, 2012), 2.

from time for interpersonal interactions, exploration, experimentation, the arts, physical education, and civic education—all of which are associated with WCE.

Whole Child Jewish Education

A religious and cultural tradition such as Judaism can be seen as engaging the "whole person," and the goals of Jewish education are framed accordingly. Far from being solely a set of beliefs or behaviors, Judaism is often conceptualized as an encompassing "mode of life."[4] This idea can be traced back to the Bible. Deuteronomy 6 alone, portions of which are included in the daily Jewish liturgy as the *Shema*, paints Judaism as a whole-person experience. Judaism is a religion of action and behavioral expectations (though these will differ in different Jewish communities) in which we "teach in order to do" (Deut. 6:1). Emotions are central as well; we are instructed to "love the Lord your God" (Deut. 6:5) as well as to "fear" God (Deut. 6:2). Being a Jew also means knowing *about* Judaism—its laws, history, etc. For example, Deuteronomy 6: 20–25, included as part of the Passover *seder*, suggests providing a lesson in Jewish history ("We were slaves to Pharaoh in Egypt. . .") as a response to a child's broad question about Judaism ("What are the laws. . ."). Finally, we can even see an interpersonal element in this chapter, with the exhortation to "speak about" (Deut. 6:7) the commandments—presumably with an interlocutor.

A whole-person approach resonates, as well, with Martin Buber's emphasis on relationship and community, and the importance of education in facilitating entry into these. Both self-awareness and empathy are gateways into the sort of I-Thou relationships that, to Buber, contain elements of the divine. To Buber: "Every man's foremost task is the actualization of his unique, unprecedented and never-recurring potentialities, and not the repetition of something that another, and be it even the greatest, has already achieved."[5]

With these Jewish thinkers and texts as a backdrop, it is not surprising that many contemporary theorists envision a multidimensional set of outcomes or goals for Jewish education—bridging the cognitive, social, affective, and behavioral. Michael Rosenak, for example, in his contribution to *Visions of Jewish Education*[6] frames the desired outcome of Jewish education as:

---

4 Mordecai M. Kaplan, *Judaism as a Civilization: Toward a Reconstruction of American-Jewish Life*, 2nd ed. (Philadelphia: Jewish Publication Society, 2010), 411.
5 Martin Buber, *The Way of Man According to the Teaching of Hasidism* (New York: Citadel Press, 1964), 16.
6 Seymour Fox et al., *Visions of Jewish Education* (Cambridge: Cambridge University Press, 2003), 23.

a Jew who is animated by love of his language yet open to others, loyal to his community yet critical of its shortcomings, involved with its problems yet sensitive to ultimate concerns and responsive to the universal, proud of his identity yet secure enough not to trumpet his pride.

Likewise, the goals of Jewish education articulated elsewhere in the same volume repeatedly reference a broad range of outcomes that span developmental realms. Moshe Greenberg, for example, refers to "acceptance of the Torah as a moral guide; a way of life that creates a community; [and] a relationship to the Jewish people in all the lands of their dispersion."[7]

Seymour Fox discusses the importance of educating "the entire child—including his or her mind" which includes paying "equal attention to emotional and spiritual issues, and to the articulation and living out of Jewish values."[8] To Fox, "[k]nowing is not the only precondition for doing. Man's feelings can and should be educated. Joy and happiness must somehow be correlated with appropriate behavior."[9]

Finally, educational theorist Lee Shulman frames the goals of Jewish education "along three dimensions—habits of mind, habits of practice, and habits of the heart."[10] The first entails a (cognitive) understanding of Jewish texts, ideas, literature, and liturgy. Habits of practice involve mastery and comfort with a variety of ritual and Hebrew language skills. Habits of the heart include the development of values, beliefs, and dispositions appropriate to a member of the Jewish community.[11]

Yet, even with such a strong theoretical connection to WCE, Jewish educational contexts, like those in secular education, often struggle to attend to socio-affective elements with the same intentionality and rigor with which they attend to academic outcomes. Jewish day schools, for example, must navigate a dual curriculum and powerful parent expectations for academic attainment.

---

7 Seymour Fox et al., "Six Visions: An Overview," in Fox, *Visions of Jewish Education*, 26.
8 Seymour Fox and William Novak, *Vision at the Heart: Lessons from Camp Ramah on the Power of Ideas in Shaping Educational Institutions* (Jerusalem and New York: The Mandel Institute and The Council for Initiatives in Jewish Education, 1997), 11.
9 Seymour Fox, "Ramah: A Setting for Jewish Education," in *The Ramah Experience: Community and Commitment*, ed. Sylvia C. Ettenberg and Geraldine Rosenfield (New York: Jewish Theological Seminary and National Ramah Commission, 1989), 36.
10 Lee S. Shulman, "Pedagogies of Interpretation, Argumentation, and Formation: From Understanding to Identity in Jewish Education," *Journal of Jewish Education* 74, sup. 1 (2008), 8.
11 Ibid., 8.

Congregational schools struggle with time constraints. Informal settings such as camps or youth groups are often staffed primarily by part-time employees with little or no training; while they may be relatively free of typical academic expectations, they usually lack a robust conception of the kinds of learning that they aspire for their participants to achieve. Here we draw from our experiences in both general and Jewish educational settings to propose suggestions for how WCE efforts can become tightly integrated into the learning agenda of Jewish Education.

Opportunities for Whole Child Jewish Education

There are many opportunities within Jewish education to address whole child outcomes in ways that are both rooted in Jewish text and tradition and are validated by research.[12] Consider the following six examples:

1. Exploration of the social and emotional elements of Jewish (classic and contemporary) texts and within Jewish history: Biblical narratives provide one of the most basic entry points to WCE in Jewish education. Study of the weekly Torah portion, a common activity, brings learners into dialogue with characters in emotion-laden situations. The family dynamics in the book of Genesis, for example, let us encounter a range of emotions (e.g., jealousy in the stories of Cain and Abel and of Joseph and his brothers). The array of material is as wide as the definition of "Jewish text," including Rabbinic stories as well as contemporary literature. Historical events, too, provide opportunity to develop cause-and-effect thinking, empathy, and perspective taking, all firmly rooted within academic Jewish studies.
2. Participation in *tikkun olam* ("repairing the world") activities: Research suggests that participation in social action or service learning projects can build a variety of social and emotional competencies.[13] Many Jewish schools involve students in social action or service, under the banner of *tikkun olam*, throughout their

---

12 Maurice J. Elias et al., *Promoting Social and Emotional Learning: Guidelines for Educators* (Alexandria, VA: Association for Supervision and Curriculum Development, 1997); Joseph E. Zins et al., *Building Academic Success on Social and Emotional Learning* (New York: Teachers College Press, 2004).
13 Shelley Billig, "Research on K-12 School-Based Service Learning: The Evidence Builds," *Phi Delta Kappan* 81 (2000), 658–64.

educational experience. These activities can take many forms, from fundraising for a local shelter to a group trip to help build houses in communities that have suffered a natural disaster. Some schools have a requirement that students volunteer for such activities on their own for a certain number of hours. The bar/bat mitzvah "project"—framed as *tikkun olam*, or sometimes as a *tzedakah* (charity/justice), or *mitzvah* (commandment) project—has become commonplace. When service becomes service learning, the learning that takes place is not merely cognitive (e.g., learning about the causes of homelessness or about resources available to the mentally ill) but potentially encompasses the full range of social and emotional competencies.

3. Prayer: Though prayer is a central element of Judaism, prayer education poses multiple challenges to educators. Learners struggle to parse the complex liturgy and to master the choreography of formal prayer. Prayer, however, presents wonderful opportunities to address emotional and spiritual developmental elements.[14] It can allow participants moments of individual reflection as well as shared emotional experiences.

4. Education in informal settings: To this point, we have been focusing on the school as the primary setting of Jewish education. It is also important to recognize non-school venues. Summer camps, particularly overnight camps, provide opportunities to grow skills in communal living and for self-exploration in a safe environment. The power of such settings emerges in large part in their providing an "encompassing"[15] Jewish experience interwoven with day-to-day "secular" activities.

5. *Mussar*, a Jewish approach to character development that emerged in Eastern Europe in the nineteenth century, is having a contemporary resurgence. This approach is notable in its overlap with core components of whole child education. *Mussar* involves (1) a focus on well-articulated core *middot* (often translated as values or character traits, such as humility and patience); (2) reflective self-evaluation of one's strengths and needs with regard to these values; (3) action planning for behavioral change; and (4) tracking progress with the help of a group and through journaling. The *middot* are drawn from Jewish (primarily

---

14 Amy Walk Katz, "Teaching Tefillah," in *What We Now Know about Jewish Education: Perspectives on Research for Practice*, ed. Roberta Louis Goodman et al. (Los Angeles: Torah Aura Productions, 2008), 299–309.

15 Jeffrey S. Kress and Maurice J. Elias, "Distancing in Encompassing Education Settings: Lessons from Jewish Education," *Journal of Applied Developmental Psychology* 29, no. 4 (2008), 337–44.

rabbinic) sources that often draw out nuances that are easy to overlook. Humility (*anavah*), for example, may be framed in terms of how much space one occupies in a situation. In this light, humility is not expressed only in terms of self-effacement and stepping back humbly, but also by stepping up and asserting one's self as needed. Perhaps because of the contemporary, self-help spin often given to the process, *mussar* study has taken root among diverse segments of the Jewish community. For example, adult *mussar* study groups have sprung up across the country[16] and school-based approaches, such as that developed by Rabbi David Jaffe[17] brings *mussar*-based learning to educators and students.

6. *Hevrutah* learning is a traditional format of Jewish study in which pairs of students grapple with the meaning of texts. In contemporary Jewish education, *hevrutah* has been discussed as a venue in which learners can practice interpersonal communication – often taking the form of argumentation or debate—in the context of Jewish learning.[18]

Developmental Process Theory as an Organizing Idea

While these potential entry points exist, and creative whole-child work occurs regularly in Jewish schools, it has been our observation that there is seldom a structured, school-wide developmental plan for education in the socio-affective sphere. As such, the development-promoting experiences in schools often happen in isolation, as "one-offs," or as chance "teachable moments."[19] While these experiences can be impactful, they may not integrate deeply into the every-day life of the school, and they may fail to capitalize on the synergy that can emerge from a coordinated whole child approach.[20]

---

16   For example, Arielle Levites and Ira Stone, "Carrying the Burden of the Other: Musar and Adult Development," in *Growing Jewish Minds, Growing Jewish Souls*, ed. Jeffrey S. Kress (New York: URJ Press, 2013).

17   As described in Jeffrey S. Kress, "Learning from a Mussar-Based Initiative in a Jewish Community Day School," *Journal of Jewish Education* 83 no. 2 (2017), 133–50.

18   Elie Holzer, "What Connects 'Good' Teaching, Text Study and Hevruta Learning? A Conceptual Argument," *Journal of Jewish Education* 72, no. 3 (2006), 183–204; Orit Kent, "Interactive Text Study: A Case of Hevruta Learning," *Journal of Jewish Education* 72, no. 3 (2006), 205–32.

19   Jeffrey S. Kress, *Development, Learning, and Community: Educating for Identity in Pluralistic Jewish High Schools* (Brighton, MA: Academic Studies Press, 2012).

20   Stephanie M. Jones and Suzanne M. Bouffard, "Social and Emotional Learning in Schools: From Programs to Strategies," *SRCD Social Policy Report* 26, no. 4 (2012), 3–22.

As with any educational endeavor, developmental guideposts can help create a comprehensive longitudinal focus. There is a reason we do not introduce calculus to a second-grader or provide an adolescent with a children's book. Similarly, socio-emotional content has to be introduced with sensitivity to development, and skills have to be tied to a larger, whole-child emphasis that understands what children at different ages tend to be working on naturally. A new model, developed by the first author and colleagues, organizes the goals of WCE into four domains and has been used to help educators structure their efforts.[21]

Developmental Process Theory, also known as the Clover Model, uses the image of a clover to describe whole person development from childhood through adolescence. Each of the clover's four leaves reflect a particular kind and domain of development.[22] The four leaves of the clover are (1) active engagement, (2) assertiveness, (3) belonging, and (4) reflection. These four dimensions and their interactions do not follow each other sequentially, but are each present at all points of development. Furthermore, the leaves are not orthogonal; rather they overlap like in a Venn diagram.

Each domain will be explained in further detail below, but first it is important to state that the purpose of this theory is to create the most simple and efficient set of constructs, basic frames, and needs that are present from the beginning of life and continue throughout. It is not hard to make out of the four dimensions eight, ten, or even forty as, for example, the asset model of Peter Benson[23] and his colleagues have shown. The goal of the developers of this construct was not to divide and subdivide, but to seek the very minimum dimensions necessary to provide heuristic guidance to the efforts of those working with WCE.

Every individual employs all four of these developmental processes. At the same time, each domain takes prominence for specific age groups. People move along a continuum, prioritizing the task of one domain before another,

---

21 Gil G. Noam and Tina Malti, "Responding to the Crisis: RALLY's Developmental and Relational Approach," *New Directions for Youth Development* 2008, no. 120 (2008), 31–55; Gil G. Noam and Tina Malti, "Future Systemic Transformations," *New Directions for Youth Development*, 179–88; Gil G. Noam et al., "Social Cognition, Psychological Symptoms, and Mental Health: The Model, Evidence, and Contribution of Ego Development," in *Developmental Psychopathology*, 2nd ed., ed. Dante Cicchetti and Donald J. Cohen (Hoboken, NJ: John Wiley & Sons, 2006).

22 Noam and Malti, "Responding to the Crisis," 31–55; Noam and Malti, "Future Systemic Transformations," 179–88.

23 Peter L. Benson, "Developmental Assets and Asset-Building Community: Conceptual and Empirical Foundations," in *Developmental Assets and Asset-Building Communities: Implications for Research, Policy, and Practice*, ed. Richard M. Lerner and Peter L. Benson (New York: Kluwer, 2003), 19–46.

but that priority does not mean that the other dimensions are not applicable. In early adolescence, for example, the belonging dimension becomes essential. But the physical needs of the active engagement leaf, the issues of assertion (e.g., of will and trying to make an impact), and reflection about self and the world also are active. These establish a new balance with belonging as the preeminent developmental tension. This model preserves a developmental point of view while broadening the scope from a stage-wise progression of sense-making (Jean Piaget) or life tasks (Erik Erikson) or a singular focus on relationships (John Bowlby). Body, will, attachment, and cognition are in continuous exchange. They evolve together and apart, maintaining a tension between progression and regression.

Understanding this can help educators assess the strengths and risks posed by the particular developmental process facing youth of their students' age. The model's utility lies in its understanding of the balancing act among these four essential elements throughout development and can provide the underpinning of a whole child perspective.

Having explained the purpose in developing the theory, and how the developers understand what the theory does and does not represent, we can now turn to defining each of the leaves or domains (See Figure 1).

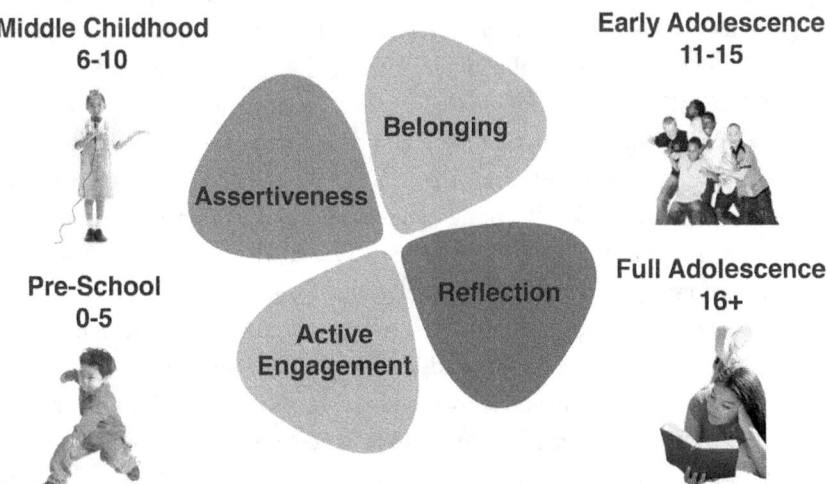

Figure 1: The Clover Model.

Active Engagement. The child in early childhood is often all about action, though this tends to be slightly more so for boys than girls. They need to be active, they think better when active, and they view the world in terms of concrete consequences of behavior. They are aware of and concerned with their own perspective, primarily, and with actively engaging in the world. Their goal is to learn about the world, experience mastery of different activities, and in doing so satisfy immediate needs. But time spent in action also helps youth learn about who they are and whom and what they like.

<u>Assertiveness</u>. Exploring their world is paramount for children, and to do this, they assert themselves, their wants and needs, and interests (now more verbally than via action). They can appear oblivious to the needs of others because they don't yet have the capacity to fully coordinate multiple perspectives. Learning to do so will require asserting themselves and dealing with the reactions of others. Of course, what they anticipate the reactions of others may be will be shaped—for better or worse—by attachment history as well as by their expectations for hostility or support from others, and their cognitive abilities. Knowing a youth may be expecting hostility from others and understanding aggressiveness in terms of striving for assertion may help a mentor normalize a mentee's aggressiveness[24] and help the mentor provide a corrective emotional experience.

<u>Belonging</u>. With a secure attachment, a youth will explore the world with ease, and if the youth has successfully achieved mastery during his or her industrious explorations of talents, interests, and skills, both of these experiences will dovetail with the emergence of the mutual-inclusive perspective-taking skills that typically appear during the shift from middle to high school (sometimes earlier for girls). The result is a concern for belonging and a sense of allegiance with like-minded and affirming peers. A sense of belonging becomes all-important, such that peers take on magnified importance, sometimes trumping family connectedness as the youth's primary source of social-affirmation. Of course, too much concern with belonging can result in an overly conforming approach to peer relationships that limits self-exploration and can even handicap a youth whose potential could catapult him or her beyond the reaches of her peers academically or professionally.

<u>Reflection.</u> The teen who is able to take a perspective on his or her friendships, cultural group, or family, can begin to reflect on ways in which he or she differs from others, in values, potential, interests, and needs. A deeper degree of identity exploration can ensure with the full force of mutual-inclusive

---

24 Tina Malti and Gil G. Noam, "A Developmental Approach to the Prevention of Adolescent's Aggressive Behavior and the Promotion of Resilience," *International Journal of Developmental Science* 3, no. 3 (2009), 235–46.

perspective taking being applied to self-discovery. Reflection, which is hampered by anxious attachment but helped by the security of solid attachment style, results in exploration beyond the comfortable boundaries of the collective views of peers, families, and other familiar people. Knowing this, a mentor can help the youth who wants (and now is able) to engage in deeper reflection to consider opportunities the youth has never considered.

As should be clear from this brief overview, children are not located within a particular domain to the exclusion of the other three. At each position on the clover, other leaves can take prominence for a brief or extended period, or in specific relationships or contexts. And the process of one leaf may be needed to bridge two others. For example, the transition from the belonging to reflection position may require an altogether new type of assertion to chart new educational territories or career terrain. Normative changes that occur from middle childhood to late adolescence mean that adolescents typically have different needs for belonging, assertion, action, and reflection than children. From a developmental perspective, it also means that significant relationships need to foster child and adolescent needs and thereby fill a unique function in the youth's life.

When educators talk about the whole child, or about socio-emotional learning, they typically list skills such as perseverance, teamwork, and critical thinking, the kind of twenty-first century tools that everyone needs to succeed. The Clover Model can provide a developmental frame within which to address core socio-affective skills (Figure 2).

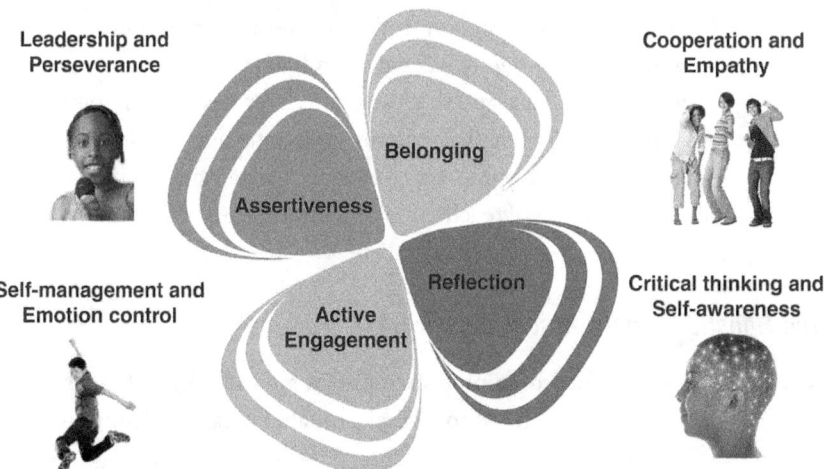

Figure 2: The Clover Model and Socio-emotional Skills.

This model is used in educational settings as a translational language for teachers, mental health professionals, and afterschool providers to simplify communication. Notably, the use of the clover can help educators and others avoid falling into the prevalent language of psychopathology (e.g., this is an ADD, oppositional, depressed student).

Assessment for Fostering WCE

In a climate in which there is debate about the amount of "testing" to which students are subject, it may seem strange to bring assessment into the conversation about WCE. However, a structured approach to WCE assessment can help educators be proactive in addressing the socio-affecting needs of their students, and can provide the data needed to track the evolution of those needs over time. Because rigorous assessment can be done quickly via self-report, logistical challenges are minimized.

Numerous approaches and instruments have been developed to assess elements of socio-affective elements of development.[25] Here, we discuss one of these, the Holistic Student Assessment (HSA), developed by the first author based on the Clover Model described above.

It might seem like a stretch to bring assessment into play; but it is not if we embrace a few premises:

- That student voice matters and that self-report is a short and fast way to ask for student feedback and self-evaluation.
- That the data are collected early in the school year so that it can inform teacher strategy and student support interventions.
- That the data are tied to strengths, so that they can be enlarged and brought to good use and that they also cover risk so socio-emotional support can be put in place to prevent mental health disorders.
- That results are only one way of collecting data, with the intuitive and relational aspects of teacher-student connection being at the fore.

The Holistic Student Assessment (HSA)

The HSA is a self-report containing sixty-one items and takes fifteen minutes to administer. It is administered to groups and always taken voluntarily with

---

25 Joseph Ciarrochi et al., "Measuring Emotional Intelligence," in *Emotional Intelligence in Everyday Life: A Scientific Inquiry,* ed. Joseph Ciarrochi et al. (New York: Psychology Press, 2001), 25–45.

parental agreement. The results are confidential and schools and afterschool programs have the results back within a week. Typically, the assessment is administered at the beginning of the school year to "know every child" and to be able to build on the strengths and to reduce the vulnerabilities before a whole school year is lost. Typically a post assessment is administered to review changes (again, from the perspective of the students) at the individual, classroom, school, and even district levels. A short teacher version has been developed and a parent version is being piloted. Most of the HSA's scales (Table 1) are organized around the Clover Model. These scales fit into three domains: resiliencies, relationships to adults and with peers, and learning orientation.

HSA results are reported through the HSA Dashboard, an interactive visual interface that summarizes data for individual students and for groups. It is possible to go from individual students to whole classrooms to support the teacher in understanding patterns of an entire class. One can also aggregate up to the whole school with a possibility to create a school-wide dashboard for planning and evaluation. Results can be discussed with individual students and learning plans developed accordingly.

Table 1: HSA Subscales

- <u>Action Orientation:</u> Assesses the respondent's level of activeness, physical activity, and physical engagement.
- <u>Emotional Control:</u> Measures the respondent's emotional control, self-discipline, and self-control. These two scales make up the Active Engagement Clover.
- <u>Perseverance:</u> Evaluates one's willingness to work hard and solve problems despite obstacles and challenges.
- <u>Assertiveness:</u> Examines the participant's level of comfort in advancing their own personality, beliefs, wishes, or thoughts, and whether one has the confidence to stand up for what one believes is fair. These two scales make up the Assertive Clover.
- <u>Trust:</u> Considers one's level of trust and vulnerability to the actions of others and one's confidence that others will support them when called upon.
- <u>Empathy:</u> Assesses the ability to recognize and share in the feelings of others, and one's initiative to help others and improve surroundings.

> - Relationship with Peers: Assesses the respondent's relationships with friends and feelings of connection with her classmates.
> - Relationship with Adults: Measures perceived level of support from adults and positive engagement with adults. These four scales are part of the Belonging Clover.
> - Reflection: Assesses the participant's sense of self, level of internal monologue, and feeling of social responsibility.
> - Critical Thinking: Critical thinking is the ability to analyze and evaluate information on a deeper level than simply the surface with which you are presented. This can involve evaluating, questioning, forming arguments, debating, and comparing and contrasting. These two scales make up the Reflection Clover domain.
>
> ***Additional scales that are not directly related to the Clover Model but are relevant to the school and life experience are listed below:***
>
> - Learning Interest: Measures the respondent's interest in education and learning, in general, especially learning outside the classroom.
> - Academic Motivation: Assesses interest and motivation in academic success, without necessarily including interest in learning in general.
> - School Bonding: Examines one's feeling of connection to school or program one's sense of belonging in relation to that school or program.
> - Optimism: Measures one's level of positivity in their perspective about the world and the future.

A Case Example

We will describe a fifth-grade girl and her assessment to further illustrate the utility of the instrument and the potential use in a Jewish education context. When looking at her HSA results, shown in Figure 3, we can see that this student has a balance of five strengths and five challenges. In the learning and school engagement section, this girl scores above the norm on every scale, with strengths in Learning Interest and Academic Motivation. Based on her self-reported strengths in academics, this student most likely is a successful student in the classroom. But when we look at the Resiliencies and Relationships scales, we see that she has some challenges that may not be apparent to the teacher, specifically in Assertiveness, Trust, Optimism, and Relationships with Peers. These challenges, when found together particularly with her high Reflection and academic strengths, speak of a student who is internalizing her challenges and struggling in her relationships with others. This struggle leads to a lack of Optimism and Trust. The good news is that this girl does not need a clinical intervention, but reorganization in the classroom structure to give her a peer leadership role to strengthen her assertiveness. She could benefit from a summer or afterschool program that allows and encourages students to have a voice. These kinds of preventative measures could help to address some of the internal struggles of an otherwise strong and successful student.

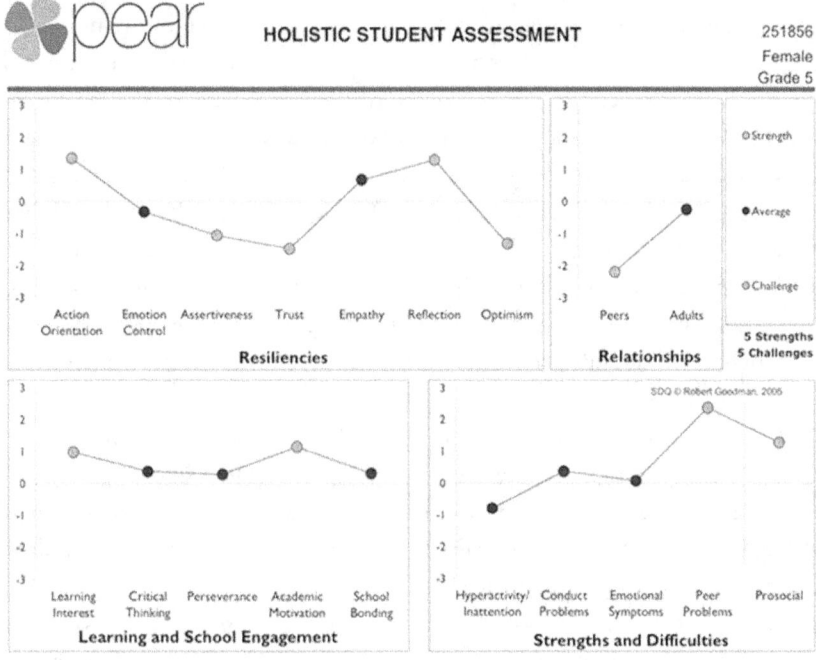

Figure 3: Sample HSA Individual Portrait.

Jewish schools can benefit greatly from this type of information. It is not very expensive to set up this system and to provide information and coaching to educators. This approach also allows for developing and adding scales that are important to specific educational goals without losing one of the main benefits: That at all times it is possible to compare one classroom to another and to always review data compared to a national normative sample.

We have discussed the HSA in relationship to schools and classrooms, but it can also be used in Jewish afterschool and summer settings, where limited contact hours and staff educators with less training often make it difficult to assess students' strengths and needs. The fact that the HSA is easily administered and gets scored centrally and inexpensively with individual and group results clearly graphed makes use in supplemental and informal settings very possible.

Whole Child Assessment in Jewish Education

As discussed above, the idea of whole person education is deeply ingrained within the project of Jewish education. Outcomes in the socio-affective realm should be approached with at least the same degree of intentionality as other outcomes. We see this as part of a trend in Jewish education toward taking outcomes seriously and "backward planning" toward their achievement. Accountability and assessment have increasingly taken the spotlight in communal discussions of Jewish educational policy.[26] The "Standards and Benchmarks" project undertaken by the Davidson Graduate School of Jewish Education with funding from the AVI CHAI and Legacy Heritage Foundations and others, is an example of this planful intentionality. Specific goals and outcomes have been articulated for Bible education, and are currently being developed for Rabbinics education. Importantly, socio-affective elements are interwoven throughout.

Assessment in the WCE sphere can and should be done in the spirit of deepening our knowledge of each learner as an individual, allowing our education and engagement efforts to be best targeted to better leverage their strengths, and address their needs.[27] While this deep knowledge would be important to any educator, it could be particularly useful as an efficient way of gathering information in those settings with limited contact hours. Knowing the social and emotional profiles of learners would allow time and resources to be targeted appropriately. One can imagine a social and emotionally based differentiated instruction in which, for example, "action-oriented" learners are provided with hands-on activities while those high on "reflection" are offered additional opportunities for making personal connections. Educators working in informal settings, particularly immersive ones, could benefit from information

---

26 For example, Chip Edelsberg, "Are You High Performance? Leap of Reason Can Help You Answer 'Yes!'" Jim Joseph Foundation, published March 11, 2015. https://jimjosephfoundation.org/high-performance-leap-reason-can-help-answer-yes/.

27 Jim Joseph Foundation, "Effective Strategies for Educating and Engaging Jewish Teens," Jim Joseph Foundation, BTW Informing Change, Rosov Consulting, March 2013, http://jimjosephfoundation.org/wp-content/uploads/2013/03/Report_and_Appendix_Effective_Strategies_for_Educating_and_Engaging_Jewish_Teens.pdf.

that allows them to proactively address the social and emotional competencies needed by participants to navigate these complex environments.

While Jewish educational settings often have whole child growth at the core of their missions, there are notable challenges to implementing our recommendations with regard to structured assessment. We do not present our ideas as a "how-to manual," but rather a call to the field for creative approaches, even given challenges of logistics, funding, etc. A first step involves being willing to grapple with these challenges. The application of these ideas to different Jewish educational settings should be explored. For example, on the surface, the idea of structured assessment may seem counter to the culture of informal settings such as camps and youth groups. However, if such an assessment can help these settings achieve their whole-person developmental goals, then they ought to consider how it might be incorporated into practice. This is not impossible; even a broad survey of these issues can provide a camp with a profile of programmatic strengths and needs.[28]

One may also wonder if assessment can really capture the complex intra- and inter-personal outcomes of Jewish education. Of course, any measure will fall short of capturing the richness of the human experience for which it is a proxy. We recommend taking such approaches for what they are—tools to help concretize a complex set of outcomes in order to enhance practice—and not to reify the outcomes.

Inroads have been made in this regard within Jewish educational settings, illustrating the potential for a more structured approach to assessment. For example, Melissa Werbow and Yael Silk challenge us to "Imagine a world in which religious schools don't just work toward goals like inspiring a love of Jewish learning, but also assess their classrooms to determine if they are achieving their goals."[29] These educators take concrete steps toward achieving this vision by developing a rubric by which to analyze Jewish learning. Notably, this rubric encompasses the sort of socio-affective elements at the core of whole child education. For example, they capture the notion of seeking wisdom through observing the questions asked by students.

---

28 For example, Jeffrey S. Kress and Michael Ben-Avie, "Social Climate at Ramah: Relationships and Motivation," in *Ramah at 60: Impact and Innovation*, ed. Mitchell Cohen and Jeffrey S. Kress (New York: National Ramah Commission, 2010), 143–58.

29 Melissa Werbow and Yael Silk, "All You Need is Love ... And A Rubric." eJewish Philanthropy, Published November 24, 2013, http://ejewishphilanthropy.com/all-you-need-is-love-and-a-rubric/.

A behavioral-criterion approach was also used by second author in his work with a *mussar*-based character education program developed by Rabbi David Jaffe, with support from the Covenant and AVI CHAI Foundations, for use at the Gann Academy in Waltham, Massachusetts.[30] Participants in this program focused on monthly *middot*, perhaps best translated here as character traits. As part of the assessment of the initiative, we linked focal *middot* with behavioral indices related to the work of the school administrators (our pilot group for this self-rating). With *savlanut* (patience) for example, participants were asked to self-rate whether "I tend to respond to stressors without fully thinking things through." One can imagine a sort of 360-degree *middah* indicator assessment.

We also call for further work linking WCE concepts with Jewish texts and ideas, so that whole child efforts can permeate Jewish educational settings. Existing examples include Jonathan Cohen's work linking each of the Search Institute's 40 Developmental Assets with a Jewish value or ideal[31] and the Open Circle Program's initiative to link social and emotional competencies with Jewish texts.[32] Further work in this area will help create an infusion of authentic Jewish concepts with research-validated whole person learning approaches.

Finally, as we noted previously, WCE focuses on both socio-affective competencies and also the climate in which education takes place. While this chapter has focused on the former, it is worth noting that class and school climate have been measured in various ways in Jewish educational contexts. For example, Ian Cohen, Jeffrey Kress, and Maurice Elias[33] used student self-report to assess class climate and Michael Ben-Avie and Kress assessed school climate as reported by teachers[34] and camper climate as reported by campers.[35]

---

30 Kress, "Learning from a Mussar-Based Initiative," 133–50.
31 These had been previously posted on the Search Institute's website and can now be found reported to http://www.chabadpw.org/templates/articlecco_cdo/aid/444694/jewish/40-Developmental-Assets.htm.
32 Shoshana Simons and Ruth Gafni, "Fine-Tuning the Listening Heart: Weaving Together the Teaching of Jewish Ethics and Socio-Emotional Learning through the Open Circle Program," in Kress, *Growing Jewish Minds*, 85–100.
33 Ian J. Cohen et al., "Classroom Climate in an Orthodox Day School: The Contribution of Emotional Intelligence, Demographics, and Classroom Context," *Journal of Jewish Education* 68, no. 1 (2002), 21–33.
34 Michael Ben-Avie and Jeffrey S. Kress, *A North American Study of Educators in Jewish Day and Congregational Schools: Technical Report of the Educators in Jewish Schools Study* (Jewish Educational Change, N.d.).
35 Kress and Ben-Avie, "Social Climate at Ramah," 143–58.

Conclusion

This chapter addresses a number of interconnected issues. First, we wanted to call attention to a shift occurring in this country toward a more holistic approach in education with such diverse constituencies as community education, character and moral development, and social-emotional learning. Second, it was our goal to show that there is a great deal of foundational thinking about these topics in Jewish education supporting a whole child view. Third, we introduced the Clover Model as one way to simplify this wide variety of theories and concepts and ideas so that teachers, parents, and students can make sense of the psychological and developmental mission and goals relating to whole child education. Next, we wanted to show that assessment can be used to improve the quality of whole child learning in a school or other educational setting, to help adults support the healthy development of children and youth, and to prevent negative outcomes educationally, psychologically, and socially. As a final step, we discussed the use of these systems in Jewish schools and how we believe that these schools should open themselves to more data guidance.

The most important point underlying all of our ideas is this: socio-emotional life is an essential part of Jewish identity and ought to be central to the articulated and pursued learning outcomes in Jewish education. Jewish pride, suffering, survival under hugely adverse conditions, the role of stories and humor, family celebrations, and the study of the Bible with all its deep wisdom about living a whole life embedded in the community—all of this is socio-emotional development and learning. We have research to support these ideas in secular forms. As Jewish educators, we ought to broaden our perspectives and hone our skills to educate children and youth to be sensitive, empathic, ethical, and intellectually skilled and curious people—that is, to be whole people and whole Jews.

Bibliography

Association for Supervision and Curriculum Development. *Making the Case for Whole Child Education*. Alexandria, VA: ASCD, 2012.

Ben-Avie, Michael, and Jeffrey Kress. *A North American Study of Educators in Jewish Day and Congregational Schools: Technical Report of the Educators in Jewish Schools Study*. Jewish Educational Change. Accessed (November 12, 2017). www.jewishdatabank.org/studies/downloadFile.cfm?FileID=2708.

Benson, Peter L. "Developmental Assets and Asset-Building Community: Conceptual and Empirical Foundations." In *Developmental Assets and Asset-Building Communities: Implications for Research, Policy, and Practice*. Edited by Richard M. Lerner and Peter L. Benson, 19–46. New York: Kluwer, 2003.

Billig, Shelley. "Research on K-12 School-Based Service Learning: The Evidence Builds." *Phi Delta Kappan* 81 (2000), 658–64.

Buber, Martin. *The Way of Man According to the Teaching of Hasidism*. New York: Citadel Press, 1964.

Ciarrochi, Joseph, Amy Chan, Peter Caputi, and Richard Roberts. "Measuring Emotional Intelligence." In *Emotional Intelligence in Everyday Life: A Scientific Inquiry*. Edited by Joseph Ciarrochi, Joseph P. Forgas, and John D. Mayer, 25–45. New York: Psychology Press, 2001.

Cohen, Ian J., Jeffrey S. Kress, and Maurice J. Elias. "Classroom Climate in an Orthodox Day School: The Contribution of Emotional Intelligence, Demographics, and Classroom Context." *Journal of Jewish Education* 68, no. 1 (2002), 21–33.

Edelsberg, Chip. "Are You High Performance? Leap of Reason Can Help You Answer 'Yes!'" Jim Joseph Foundation, published March 11, 2015. https://jimjosephfoundation.org/high-performance-leap-reason-can-help-answer-yes/.

Elias, Maurice J., Sarah J. Parker, V. Megan Kash, and Ed Dunkeblau. "Socioemotional Learning and Character and Moral Education in Children: Synergy or Fundamental Divergence in Our Schools?" *Journal of Research in Character Education* 5, no. 2 (2007), 167–182.

Elias, Maurice J., Joseph E. Zins, Roger P. Weissberg, Karin S. Frey, Mark T. Greenberg, Norris M. Haynes, Rachael Kessler, Mary E. Schwab-Stone, and Timothy P. Shriver. *Promoting Social and Emotional Learning: Guidelines for Educators*. Alexandria, VA: Association for Supervision and Curriculum Development, 1997.

Fox, Seymour. "Ramah: A Setting for Jewish Education." In *The Ramah Experience: Community and Commitment*. Edited by Sylvia C. Ettenberg and Geraldine Rosenfield, 19–37. New York: Jewish Theological Seminary and National Ramah Commission, 1989.

Fox, Seymour, and William Novak. *Vision at the Heart: Lessons from Camp Ramah on the Power of Ideas in Shaping Educational Institutions*. Jerusalem and New York: The Mandel Institute and The Council for Initiatives in Jewish Education, 1997.

Fox, Seymour, Israel Scheffler, and Daniel Marom. "Six Visions: An Overview." In *Visions of Jewish Education*. Edited by Seymour Fox, Israel Scheffler, and Daniel Marom, 19–43. Cambridge: Cambridge University Press, 2003.

Fox, Seymour, Israel Scheffler, and Daniel Marom. *Visions of Jewish Education*. Cambridge: Cambridge University Press, 2003.

Holzer, Elie. "What Connects 'Good' Teaching, Text Study and Hevruta Learning? A Conceptual Argument." *Journal of Jewish Education* 72, no. 3 (2006), 183–204.

Jim Joseph Foundation. "Effective Strategies for Educating and Engaging Jewish Teens: What Jewish Communities Can Learn from Programs that Work." Jim Joseph Foundation, BTW Informing Change, Rosov Consulting. March 2013. http://jimjosephfoundation.org/wp-content/uploads/2013/03/Report_and_Appendix_Effective_Strategies_for_Educating_and_Engaging_Jewish_Teens.pdf.

Jones, Stephanie M., and Suzanne M. Bouffard. "Social and Emotional Learning in Schools: From Programs to Strategies." *SRCD Social Policy Report* 26, no. 4 (2012), 3–22.

Kaplan, Mordecai M. *Judaism as a Civilization: Toward a Reconstruction of American-Jewish Life*. 2nd ed. Philadelphia: Jewish Publication Society, 2010.

Katz, Amy Walk. "Teaching Tefillah." In *What We Now Know about Jewish Education: Perspectives on Research for Practice*. Edited by Roberta Louis Goodman, Paul A. Flexner, and Linda Dale Bloomberg, 299–309. Los Angeles: Torah Aura Productions, 2008.

Kent, Orit. "Interactive Text Study: A Case of Hevruta Learning." *Journal of Jewish Education* 72, no. 3 (2006), 205–32.

Kress, Jeffrey S. *Development, Learning, and Community: Educating for Identity in Pluralistic Jewish High Schools*. Brighton, MA: Academic Studies Press, 2012.

———. "Learning from a Mussar-Based Initiative in a Jewish Community Day School." *Journal of Jewish Education* 83 no. 2 (2017): 133–50.

Kress, Jeffrey S., and Michael Ben-Avie. "Social Climate at Ramah: Relationships and Motivation." In *Ramah at 60: Impact and Innovation*. Edited by Mitchell Cohen and Jeffrey S. Kress, 143–58. New York: National Ramah Commission, 2010.

Kress, Jeffrey S., and Maurice J. Elias. "Distancing in Encompassing Education Settings: Lessons from Jewish Education." *Journal of Applied Developmental Psychology* 29, no. 4 (2008), 337–44.

Levites, Arielle, and Ira Stone. "Carrying the Burden of the Other: Musar and Adult Development." In *Growing Jewish Minds, Growing Jewish Souls*. Edited by Jeffrey S. Kress. New York: URJ Press, 2013.

Malti, Tina, and Gil G. Noam. "A Developmental Approach to the Prevention of Adolescent's Aggressive Behavior and the Promotion of Resilience." *International Journal of Developmental Science* 3, no. 3 (2009), 235–46.

Noam, Gil G., and Tina Malti. "Future Systemic Transformations." *New Directions for Youth Development*, no. 120 (2008), 179–88.

Noam, Gil G., and Tina Malti. "Responding to the Crisis: RALLY's Developmental and Relational Approach." *New Directions for Youth Development*, no. 120 (2008), 31–55.

Noam, Gil G., Copeland H. Young, and Janna Jilnina. "Social Cognition, Psychological Symptoms, and Mental Health: The Model, Evidence, and Contribution of Ego Development." In *Developmental Psychopathology*, 2nd Edition. Edited by Dante Cicchetti and Donald J. Cohen. Hoboken, NJ: John Wiley & Sons, 2006.

Shulman, Lee S. "Pedagogies of Interpretation, Argumentation, and Formation: From Understanding to Identity in Jewish Education." *Journal of Jewish Education* 74, sup. 1 (2008), 5–15.

Simons, Shoshana, and Ruth Gafni. "Fine-Tuning the Listening Heart: Weaving Together the Teaching of Jewish Ethics and Socio-Emotional Learning through the Open Circle Program." In *Growing Jewish Minds, Growing Jewish Souls*. Edited by Jeffrey S. Kress, 85–100. New York: URJ Press, 2013.

Werbow, Melissa, and Yael Silk. "All You Need is Love . . . And A Rubric." eJewish Philanthropy. Published November 24, 2013. http://ejewishphilanthropy.com/all-you-need-is-love-and-a-rubric/.

Zins, Joseph E., Roger P. Weissberg, Margaret C. Wang, and Herbert J. Wallberg. *Building Academic Success on Social and Emotional Learning*. New York: Teachers College Press, 2004.

Subject-Specific Learning Versus Jewish-Developmental Outcomes in Jewish Education: What Should We Aim For?

Jeffrey S. Kress and Jon A. Levisohn

How should we think about the desired learning outcomes in Jewish educational settings? Should we frame them primarily in terms of specific subjects, such as Talmud or Hebrew or Jewish history, or even in terms of specific domains of practice like reading Torah or Israeli dance? Or should we instead prioritize broader developmental goals, in the spirit of what is sometimes called "Whole Child" education? The two sides of this debate are presented in this chapter by two fictional characters, Abraham and Sarah, to make it clear that neither of the actual authors of the chapter would endorse the strong version of the positions that are presented here. Nevertheless, the discussion will illuminate a question about goals that is centrally important to advancing the learning agenda in Jewish education.

Abraham: Let's start this conversation by picturing a real setting: A local day school, which is holding an event for prospective parents. In terms of its Jewish approach, the school is situated in what Arnie Eisen might call Judaism's "vital center." It could be a denominationally affiliated school, like a Schechter school, or a "community" school unaffiliated with a denomination. But enrollment is an issue, with the school needing to keep its numbers steady or growing. So tonight, the leaders and faculty have gone all out. Kids' art is up on the walls and their projects are displayed in the foyer. There's a new brochure, full of big, glossy photos of bright, shiny faces. The facility is spotless.

Sarah: I can picture it. In fact, I think I've been in that very school!

Abraham: Right! Me too. So now, picture the head of school taking the microphone, as prospective parents settle into their seats. She's been readying her pitch for a week, writing and rewriting. "Welcome, parents!" she starts. "You've seen our modern facilities. You've seen the kids' art and their creative projects. Now let me tell you about our school's true strengths. If you send your kids here, I can guarantee you that they will learn a *ton* of Talmud. They'll be able to tell their *amoraim* from their elbows and their *tannaim* from their tucheses. They'll become Talmud readers extraordinaires." With this, the parents start to look at each other anxiously.

"But wait," the head continues, "I'm just getting going. They will also know so much Tanach you'll be completely blown away. We even teach Sefer Vayikra! And you should see how they score on our Jewish history exams!" By this point, if you and I are imagining similar parents and schools, you can hear the crickets chirping as the attendees start inching toward the door.

Why do parents send their kids to day school? Setting aside excellent general studies and wonderful college acceptance rates, they want things like "the development of personal Jewish meaning in the context of interaction with the secular world."[1] Or they want their kids to make Jewish friends, or to build Jewish pride, or to instill whatever it is that makes it more likely that they will date and marry Jews.[2] Or they want their children to develop lenses rooted in positive values—framed in a Jewish context—through which to view the worlds and themselves. Or they want their kids to develop parameters for making decisions, particularly those with ethical components (which covers a lot of ground, not limited to a sense of responsibility for others and *tikkun olam,* repairing the world); to come to see themselves within the flow of Jewish history; and to be prepared for "citizenship" within the current and emerging Jewish community. To use a term that has unreasonably fallen into disfavor, they may well want them to develop their identities, in general and specifically as Jews. Perhaps the most long-lived and wide-spread of all desired Jewish educational outcomes is for a child to become a *mensch.*

I just tossed out a lot of different ideas, each of which deserves serious consideration and critical development. Let me use the admittedly bulky term

---

[1] Naava Frank, "A Judaic Curriculum for Jewish Day Schools: The Time is NOW," *Contact: The Journal of the Jewish Life Network* 4, no. 2 (2002), 12.

[2] Steven M. Cohen and Shaul Kelner, "Why Jewish Parents Send Their Children to Day Schools," in *Family Matters: Jewish Education in an Age of Choice,* ed. Jack Wertheimer (Waltham, MA: Brandeis University Press, 2007), 80–100.

"Jewish developmental outcomes" to refer to these and related outcomes. Perhaps not all of them are worthy. But my point is to highlight how different they sound from the kind of subject-specific outcomes that our imagined Head of School was talking about. And there's no reason to downplay these outcomes. These are the outcomes that most parents want, and these are the outcomes that Jewish educational institutions ought to focus on. Furthermore, if we really care about these Jewish developmental outcomes, we should make sure to assess our progress in promoting them among our students, and we should plan to intentionally and specifically address these outcomes in our education and not just assume that they will be a byproduct of learning.

Sarah: Thanks for painting that picture for us, Abraham. I agree that parents would not be excited by the pitch about how much Talmud the kids will learn. But I'm not sure that I draw the same conclusions from it that you do. In other words, I'm sure that a lot of parents would get turned off by excessive attention to academic subjects, especially if they're presented in dry and unexciting ways, just as you described. But that may tell us more about them—and their sophistication as educational consumers—than it tells us about our desired outcomes.

Let me put my cards on the table. First, I believe that domain-neutral outcomes—the kind of "Jewish developmental outcomes" that you are talking about—are bogus, artificial constructions. We invent them, and then we turn around and we believe in them as if they're really real. And second, not only are they bogus, they're actually harmful.

What do I mean when I say that domain-neutral outcomes are bogus and artificial? I mean that they are invented for particular purposes. Psychologists and sociologists invent them because they want a quick-and-dirty way of capturing a whole set of phenomena. So, for example, rather than talking about a set of Jewish practices—ritual practices like candle-lighting on Shabbat and fasting on Yom Kippur, communal practices like giving to Federation, social network robustness like how many Jewish friends you have—the researchers can assemble an index of these various phenomena, and call it "Jewish identity." Some people do better on the index and some do less well. Before you know it, we're talking about Jewish identity as something that can be measured, that some people have more of than others. That's not a bad thing in itself. But there's no justification for turning the idea of "strengthening Jewish identity" into a goal of Jewish education.

The other purpose for inventing domain-neutral outcomes is more instrumental: some folks, namely philanthropists, want a way of comparing one domain to another. They are desperate to figure out some way to decide where to invest their money. Talmud classes teach Talmud. Israeli dance classes teach dance. How can you decide which one is better, more effective, a better use of resources? There has to be a domain-neutral metric that we can affirm, and that each domain tries to advance in its own way, right? That way, we can measure how well intervention A does, in advancing toward metric X, and how well intervention B does. By contrast, if A is advancing metric X and B is advancing metric Y, then we cannot measure them against each other. It's not surprising that Israeli dance classes teach more dance than Talmud classes do, and Talmud classes teach more Talmud than Israeli dance classes do. So there has to be *something* that we can point to, as the basis of comparison.

But that, I suggest, is a terrible argument. The fact that philanthropists need that domain-neutral metric to help them make their investment decisions is not good evidence that such a domain-neutral metric exists. Of course, it is often useful to look at a set of data and aggregate them in some way, to explain what they represent at a higher level of abstraction. But we have to remember that this is not a real thing. There is no "Jewish identity" muscle in the body, which then controls our candle-lighting and Federation-giving. And since there's no "Jewish identity" muscle, we shouldn't expect that Jewish education is going to strengthen it!

You know, thirty years ago, our teacher Lee Shulman developed a research project around domain-specificity with regard to teaching.[3] To that point, teaching was mostly just considered a generic activity: you might be teaching math or history or home economics, but it was all basically the same. Shulman's argument, and his research, forced the field to recognize how absurd that was. He demanded that we pay attention to teachers' knowledge of specific subject areas and the particular ways they held that knowledge, proposing a new construct he called Pedagogical Content Knowledge. That was enormously important for how we think about the work of teaching, and especially, for how we think about the education of educators.

Subsequently, one of his leading students, Sam Wineburg, extended Shulman's inclination toward domain-specificity and focused on students, paying much more attention to what students know and are able to do within the specific domain of history. And once he did that, he grew increasingly impatient with our tendency to focus on domain-neutral capacities.

---

3   For example, Lee S. Shulman, "Those Who Understand: Knowledge Growth in Teaching," *Educational Researcher* 15, no. 2 (1986), 4–14.

Consider his discussion of what's usually called "critical thinking," a topic that is notable mostly for how outlandish its claims are. Seriously—can you imagine that some folks believe that the way to promote critical thinking is to make students take Introduction to Logic? Although I suppose that's no more ridiculous than the belief that people will become better critical thinkers by studying art or poetry or other humanities.

Here's how Wineburg expresses his skepticism. "I really don't believe," he says, "that there are generic, domain-general, free-floating cognitive capacities that hover above a person's ability to read a poem, to solve a physics problem, to interpret historical documents, or to figure out infelicities of grammar in an essay."[4] Poetry, physics, history, and grammar are substantively different from each other. They each have their characteristic challenges and puzzles, their characteristic intellectual moves, the traditions on which they call implicitly or explicitly. Engaging in the work of any of these fields does not entail the application of a generic disposition called "critical thinking." Rather, what students need is to develop sensitivity to these challenges, familiarity with these moves, and appreciation of these traditions.

Proponents of domain-neutrality often sound like they believe or imagine that there's a muscle called "critical thinking," or "Jewish identity," or "looking at the world through a Jewish lens," or something else, that operates across domains. Proponents of domain-specificity like me, on the other hand, think about domains like languages. We don't learn "language," we learn a specific language—first our native tongue, and then sometimes another one, and then another. You have to get good at each one, individually. Is it sometimes possible to transfer vocabulary or grammatical forms from one to another? Sure. But that's not domain-neutral learning. That's just drawing on one specific idea to help us understand another. So, fundamentally, we learn within specific domains rather than developing domain-neutral capacities.

Abraham: Wow, that's a rather sweeping dismissal of a whole body of literature in psychological development. You're using a pretty broad brush there, along with a rather narrow focus on cognitive abilities. Trust me, Sarah, I've got some things to say about this. But before I do, you also said that domain-neutrality is not just bogus but harmful. Can you explain what you meant by that?

---

4 Sam Wineburg, "Online Faculty Seminar Conversations On: A Conversation with Sam Wineburg," Virtual Knowledge Project, 2001, accessed November 7, 2008, http://crossroads.georgetown.edu/vkp/conversations/2001webcast/interview.html.

Sarah: Of course. It's harmful because there's an unintended consequence that sometimes follows from a focus on domain-neutral outcomes and assessment of those outcomes. I think about that unintended consequence as the *instrumentalization of Jewish education*. Let me explain what I mean.

Once upon a time, in the 1980s and 90s, when "the Israel Experience" became a thing, we thought that sending kids to Israel was a good thing to do because we cared about Israel and we thought that kids should have a first-hand experience of Israel rather than just learning *about* Israel. To make the point a little more conceptually, we believed in that kind of knowledge and experience of Israel as part of our conception, our vision, of a robust and healthy Jewish life. First-hand experience of Israel was a Good Thing, with a capital G and a capital T. It had intrinsic value—not absolute value, of course, but still, relatively intrinsic.

But then Birthright came along. Not just the initiative itself, but also the research on it. I'm not criticizing the research, which is excellent methodologically. I'm pointing to an unintended consequence. Now that we have good research on what happens as a result of the trip, the whole way that we think and talk about the Israel experience has shifted. A decade into the Birthright research, a trip to Israel is good not for itself, not because first-hand experience of Israel is part of what it means to live a robust and healthy Jewish life, but rather because of what it produces ten or twenty years down the road—a Birthright bump of Jewish babies. For a lot of us, especially in the philanthropic community, the Israel trip is a means to that end.

That's part of what I mean by the instrumentalization of Jewish education. Once a Jewish educational mode or domain is conceptualized as a means to a domain-neutral end, then we stop assessing its merits and instead simply assess whether it is producing that other thing.

But that's not yet the harmful part. The harmful part is this: When we focus on domain-neutral outcomes, we disrupt the connection between the outcomes and the pedagogic practices that produce them. In the case of Birthright, when we focus on the domain-neutral outcome of more Jewish babies, we disrupt any connection between the outcome and the pedagogy of the Birthright trip—the careful sequencing of sites, the creation of spaces for reflection and group processing, the *mifgash* with Israeli peers, etc. All of that educational work by excellent and thoughtful practitioners is now devalued. So education becomes even more of a black box than it already is, and our research on outcomes cannot help to improve the quality of the education.

Abraham: I'm with you on the concern about instrumentalization, but I think you're barking up the wrong tree. The problem of instrumentalization isn't necessarily linked to Jewish developmental outcomes. We can focus on the latter without falling into the former! But before I say more about that, your arguments have all been negative ones. It's time you said something about how subject-specificity avoids these problems.

Sarah: You're right! So let's talk about Talmud. Remember how you started this conversation by wondering who would possibly want to prioritize outcomes specific to the domain of Talmud? I readily accept that many parents in the kinds of schools that you were depicting are not going to get excited by a pitch about how much Talmud their kids are going to know. But there are other ways of thinking about this.

Let's imagine a teacher of Talmud who has a well-developed conception of the field, clearly articulated goals, and a very specific set of skills that she wants her students to learn. She teaches toward those goals, and she has developed a sophisticated assessment instrument, to find out whether her students have actually learned those subject-specific skills. This assessment is not like most superficial assessments: it's not about whether the students can repeat what they think she wants to hear, and it's not measuring whether they have learned in English class how to write a research paper (a skill that they are now expected to reproduce in Talmud class, with the result that it is mis-assessed as a Talmud-specific skill), and it's not about whether they have learned one of those fuzzy humanities skills like, say, "an openness to the diversity of the human experience." Those outcomes are all very nice but none of them are specific to this domain. Instead, this teacher is after something that really is domain-specific, like how the students read a passage in Talmud.

This might not seem so exciting to kids, or to parents. But here's the thing: The more she is focused on the subject-specific capacity, the better and sharper her planning will be, and the more focused and constructive her assessment will be. She will actually find out whether the students have learned what she wanted them to learn, and if they haven't, she will have to adjust her pedagogy accordingly. Moreover, she'll be able to articulate to the students what it is that they are actually learning, and if they work at it, what they'll be able to do—and she'll be able to do that in a way that provides the kids with a sense of actual accomplishment within the domain. They will feel like they're making real progress toward clear, articulated goals. All of this is driven by *specificity*, by a refusal to resort to generic, domain-neutral goals that are disconnected from her pedagogy and difficult to assess responsibly.

When we're thinking about this issue of domain-specificity or –neutrality, we might think about a non-academic domain like karate. When my kids were taking karate, it was crystal clear what they were supposed to be learning, and crystal clear, too, when they had learned it. There was a long, intense exam in which they had to actually perform the moves, and do them correctly. Not a lot of wiggle room: Can they do it or not? The outcome is domain-specific, and the assessment is too. That doesn't mean that karate is only about learning moves. It's a form of physical and mental training. It also teaches a certain mental and physical discipline. No one could or should deny this. As John Dewey[5] wrote, there's always a lot of "collateral learning" that goes on, in any educational environment; we're never just learning one thing. At the same time, it's clear that there's a particular practice, with a particular focus. Nobody walks out of a karate class saying, "I don't know how to do any of the moves but I made a lot of progress this year in honoring the sensei." Honoring the sensei is valued—but that's not considered a success in the domain.

My claim is that domain-specificity can provide us with precise, concrete measures of accomplishment that are satisfying to learners and educators alike. I have in mind examples like testing for karate belts, or performing in the high school musical, or taking apart a *sugya,* or *leyning* a *parashah*. When we develop clear articulations of particular domains as domains of practice, we—as educators—are then able to plan learning experiences that help students to learn that practice, to get better at it, to find satisfaction in that growth, to demonstrate their learning in ways that feel authentic rather than contrived, and to move forward on the basis of those demonstrations to higher levels of the practice. And those kinds of assessments also tell us—as educators—how we're doing, too, in ways that enable us to improve *our* practice.

No Birthright educator will ever change her spiel on Masada because of the data on inmarriage among Birthright alumni. But domain-specific data? If that educator were to have access to those students' understanding of Jewish history and its significance? Well, that could make a difference to her spiel. In the end, that's why I believe that we should resist the siren song of domain-neutrality, and instead, we should focus on domain-specificity in our educational practice and our scholarship.

Abraham: Got it. I think your point about a sense of accomplishment is particularly important; I think a lot about motivation for learning, and it seems clear to me that we need to do a better job of fostering intrinsic motivation of

---

5   John Dewey, *Experience and Education* (New York: Kappa Delta Pi, 1938), 48.

the kind that flows from a sense of accomplishment. So I think you're on to something there. But, Sarah, I'm not sure that your karate example really proves your point that you want to make about domain-specificity. Perhaps increased "respect for the sensei" really *is* a valued outcome of karate class! If it is, then it should be an intentional part of instruction. And come to think of it, in a lot of dojos, it probably is. Moreover, it's not too hard to imagine that the karate teachers want this respect-for-teachers to persist beyond the dojo. They want those kids to learn something in karate that they will carry with them into their relationships with other teachers. In other words, it's a desired outcome, but it's what I would call a "developmental" outcome, not a domain-specific outcome.

Now, I certainly agree with you that that kind of transfer won't happen automatically. Some kids are totally respectful to their senseis, but somewhat less respectful to their rabbis. But that doesn't mean it *can't* happen. It needs to be reinforced and promoted—and, if it's really the desired outcome, assessed—outside of the dojo, beyond the karate domain. The point is, we can think about that respect as a cross-domain outcome that is probably much more important than the ability to break wooden boards with your forehead! We should not underestimate parents' wisdom about this.

There is a saying that I have heard attributed to both James Comer and Seymour Sarason, either of whom would be a worthy source. We can adapt it for our purposes. The saying goes: We don't teach math (or Talmud, or Bible), we teach children (or adolescents, or adults). The key "domain" of Jewish education is the developing learner, his or her set of dispositions, his or her ways of engaging with Judaism and the world at large, or whatever stand-in term for "identity" you want to use. When we teach math or Talmud or Bible, we are seeking to create learning opportunities for that developing person. We care about the specific subjects, sure, and we want to treat them with intellectual integrity, but in the end, they are all means to an end—not, as in the Birthright example, the goal of more Jewish babies, but the goal of a healthy Jewish life.

In that sense, Jewish education *is* instrumental. But this is not a criticism, because there's no reason to think any particular domain is inherently valuable—at least not when compared to the bigger, loftier goal of a healthy, flourishing life. This is what Maimonides proposed when, in the twelfth century, he declared that the purpose of the entire Torah is the improvement of the body and the improvement of the soul. If Talmud is a good thing, it's good because of how it helps people make sense of their lives, or fixes their moral compass, or grounds them in the literature of their civilization, or something like that. Those are the things we really care about, and they transcend particular domains.

Furthermore, Sarah, what do you even mean, when you talk about domains? You seem to be proposing a surprisingly sharp differentiation between the various academic disciplines. Sure, the way one studies Talmud is different than the way one studies other subjects, in certain respects, but students of Talmud are also, inevitably, students of Hebrew and Aramaic language, and students of Bible and biblical interpretation, and students of Jewish history, and students of law, and students of folklore, and on and on—all at the same time. You can't avoid crossing domains. How could Jewish history, for example, be irrelevant? For that matter, how can Sassanian Persian history—the history of the period when the Talmud was composed in the Persian Empire—be irrelevant to the study of Talmud? I'm not arguing that every Jewish day school class in Talmud should also include Sassanian history. I'm just wondering how you can be so confident about the boundaries around these domains.

In fact, in many schools, these boundaries are collapsing because thoughtful practitioners are re-examining their assumptions about Jewish studies disciplines, or just under the weight of time constraints, so that a single integrated "Judaics" course is becoming the norm.

But even putting that aside, do these distinctions mean anything to the students? And, isn't there more than a little arbitrariness? Don't we want students to walk away not only with knowledge of these fragmented subjects, but also with a big picture of how they are related to each other? That what we call Rabbinics, for example, is deeply related to Tanakh and takes place at a particular moment (or moments) of Jewish history? Or that there is a value system woven throughout the tradition? Don't we want students to find relevance and meaning in this tradition as it plays out outside of the classroom? And, don't forget that a lot of learning in schools happens outside of formal domain-based settings. Where in a domain-specific approach do we account for what students take-away from Shabbatonim, for example? In what domain do we file the feelings that accompany the celebration of Shabbat with their friends?

Imagine if a school worked as a cohesive whole to articulate these developmental outcomes, and to achieve them. It would mean mapping the curricular and co-curricular activities against social and emotional Jewish outcomes that cross domains. The result would be a way into seeing one's self and the world through a Jewishly informed lens. How much did their Talmud class contribute to such an outcome? Their Bible class? Their participation in a Shabbaton? These may be interesting questions to study, but they are all secondary to the basic question of whether students are developing a Jewishly informed way of thinking of themselves and the world, a set of outcomes that cannot be pegged to a domain. If students are intentional about their eating habits because they remember the theme of *bal tashchit,* the biblical prohibition against wasting resources, does it really matter if they learned it mostly in Talmud class, or on a field trip to a food pantry? Or, if they feel a sense of empowerment or agency in Jewish spaces, does it matter if that happens because they learned how to lead Tefillah or because they organized the senior Shabbaton?

Reifying these domain divisions may actually work against our goal of an integrated understanding of Judaism, and create a disconnect between the classroom and the real world. Research in general education suggests that students generally do not automatically weave disparate subject matters into a common narrative; and research in Jewish schools suggests that there are rarely efforts to connect discussion of "content" with Jewish developmental outcomes. Now *that* can be harmful!

Sarah: But doesn't domain-specific learning result in the sort of outcomes you are describing?

Abraham: Domain-based learning can have a role to play, for sure, but it's only part of the story. Jewish developmental outcomes transcend individual subject areas, and deep subject matter proficiency is certainly not sufficient for the achievement of these outcomes. We all know that there are plenty of disaffected day school graduates who learned a lot of Bible and Rabbinics. And, even if someone develops a sense of connectedness to a subject area, such as Jewish history or Tanakh, there is no reason to think that this would generalize to anything beyond their relationship with that subject area. In fact, I believe you argued that there is every reason to be suspicious of such generalizations!

Sarah: Alright, maybe specific subject matter knowledge is not sufficient. You are certainly correct that there's no guarantee that doing well in Talmud class will lead to a thriving Jewish life—although maybe that's always going to be the case, because education is not the kind of thing where we should look for guarantees. But in any case, perhaps we can say that specific subject matter knowledge is a necessary prerequisite?

Abraham: I'm not so sure. Can one develop a Jewishly informed framework for understanding one's self and the world without deep content knowledge? I certainly know people who know enough to have Judaism inform their decisions and lives, but are far from what we might consider content experts. What they "know" is more about a way of being in the world. They know who they are, in deep ways, even if they cannot read Talmud. Actually, I often wonder if our fetishizing of content knowledge results in distancing and barriers, with people being discouraged from Jewish involvement because the knowledge barriers to entry are perceived as too high; they are concerned they will seem stupid or inept. While one might say this is an argument for focusing on subject knowledge, to help people overcome the barriers, there is at least as much argument for lowering the barriers, and finding meaningful pathways into Judaism that match people's strengths and passions. To an extent, this may already be happening—look at the blossoming of niche expressions of Judaism.

Sarah: Interesting. I suspect that if we teased out some examples, we would find that these folks whom you're referring to actually do know a lot, about some specific domains that are important to them. It might be the domain of Jewish holiday cooking or something equally "popular," rather than an elite or intellectual domain. And it may have been learned through osmosis or mimicry, rather than in a classroom. But it's still an important domain.

But let's set that aside for a moment, because I want to press you on the assessment question. Even if we value these domain neutral outcomes, what good is it, pedagogically speaking, if we can't assess them? Anybody can say that they're teaching *menschlichkeit* or moral behavior, or promoting a positive Jewish identity, or something else that sounds vaguely developmental. Aren't you worried that it all becomes smoke and mirrors?

Abraham: Well, look, it's definitely easier to assess cognitive or knowledge-based domain-specific growth that it is to assess outcomes in the Jewish developmental realm. But that hardly seems like a rationale for ignoring the latter. Perhaps you have heard the parable: A person is crawling around at night under a streetlight. A passerby asks if there is a problem, and the crawler responds, "I lost my keys and I am trying to find them." This story must have taken place before the days of ubiquitous cell-phone flashlights! Anyway, the passerby joins in the search, but eventually grows frustrated and asks, "Are you sure you dropped them here?" "No," comes the reply, "I know I dropped them down the block, but I'm looking here because the light is better." That's what happens when we allow assessment to drive goals, rather than determining our goals first and then figuring out how to assess as responsibly as we can. We should definitely be working to develop better assessments, not letting the current limitations drive our pedagogical efforts. But it's not impossible. There are some really interesting assessments that have been developed for related secular outcomes, as well as outcomes in Christian education. Are they perfect? No. But no assessment is.

Here's how I want to wrap up, Sarah. I believe, and I expect that you do too, that a Jewish education should prepare Jews to participate in contemporary Judaism. But what does it take to participate in contemporary Judaism? Being a Jew today means being to some extent countercultural and to some extent multicultural. Take the decision, for example, to celebrate Shabbat—whether it is an unplugged, tech-free day, or going to synagogue, or something else. What kind of Jewish education supports that decision?

If you're thinking primarily about academic Jewish studies subject areas, about those "domains," then you might answer that students need to know the relevant portions of Masechet Shabbat from the sixth century, or Maimonides' Mishnah Torah from the twelfth, or Kagan's Mishnah Berurah from the twentieth. But as lovely as it is when Jews are comfortable exploring those texts on their own, I don't actually think that's what most Jews really need to support Shabbat as a practice in their lives.

Instead, I want to argue for the importance of outcomes that don't sit comfortably within a particular domain. For example, they should understand the intersections of Jewish thought and text to perennial societal problems. They should have practice negotiating the conflict of commitments that emerge from living with multiple identities, between cultural norms, as well as negotiating Judaism's tensions between particularism and universalism, and communalism and individualism. They should have developed a stance on the nature of obligation in an era of choice. They should have experience with the joy and meaning of living within community. Any of these, I propose, are actually more important to how a Jew decides to live, and what she decides to do with her Saturdays, than whether she knows the thirty-nine categories of forbidden work, as delineated in Masechet Shabbat.

These Jewish developmental outcomes are not subject-specific, but they're not exactly subject-neutral either. They transcend subject matter divisions and should be addressed and assessed as such.

Sarah: That's a really compelling argument, Abraham. I appreciate you're keeping your eyes on the prize, which is helping students to live happier, healthier, more robust Jewish lives. And I'm particularly intrigued by your suggestion, at the end, that the kinds of developmental outcomes that would really make a difference to individuals are not, actually, subject-neutral. In other words, even though I've been thinking about a dichotomy between subject-specificity and subject-neutrality, I hear you saying that some of our debate may be resolved by thinking differently about how to characterize specific domains that we really care about, rather than just assuming that they map onto the traditional academic subjects.

But here's my final thought. If you ask me why I really care about the issues that we've been talking about, it's not the case that I want a relentlessly cognitivist education that will end up being meaningless to the students—or worse than meaningless. On the contrary, I want to encourage Jewish educational practitioners to structure their curricula so that they will be deeply meaningful to students. And I believe that the way to do that is to do real, serious work on something of value, in a way that makes sense to students and that leads to a sense of real accomplishment and even mastery. They should learn to enact a practice, or more than one, and to do so well. They should learn a cultural performance, or more than one. They should not just feel that they are marking time or, as Denise Clark Pope[6] put it, "doing school."

I might even be willing to say that that's the non-domain-specific Jewish developmental outcome that I'm after—a sense of accomplishment, of mastery, of ownership of a domain or a practice that is culturally valued and which the student has come to value. If that's where we're headed, I don't actually care whether the domain is Talmud or Tanakh or Hebrew, or reading Torah, or Israeli dance or contemporary Israeli pop music, or Jewish social action, or something else entirely. Surely some students will gravitate to some domains and other students will gravitate to others. That's fine! But at the moment, I worry that, for many of our students, they spend years in a day school or other venues without ever having any sense of accomplishment at all. They've never gotten really good at anything. They've never owned any particular domain. They've never gotten the sense that they are on a trajectory, with compelling role models for mastery in the domain whom they want to emulate.

Our teacher Michael Rosenak wrote frequently about Jewish education as the teaching of Jewish language, through the medium of Jewish literature. I find this a really important metaphor, so long as we remember that there's more than one Jewish language—by which I mean not just Hebrew and Yiddish and Ladino and others, but also, the language of Jewish religious ritual and the language of Jewish philosophy and the language of contemporary Israeli culture. The reason the metaphor of languages-and-literatures is compelling is that it reminds us that, at its best, Jewish education can be a process of learning how to actually do something, to become fluent or adept or capable, to get inside of some domain or practice, and thereby to join a community of other people who also speak that language. That community preceded me, so this practice of

---

6   Denise C. Pope, *Doing School: How We Are Creating a Generation of Stressed-Out, Materialistic, and Miseducated Students* (New Haven, CT: Yale University Press, 2003).

language-speaking is not idiosyncratic to me and I don't just get to make stuff up. And it's also the case that the community will continue after I'm gone, so I feel some sense of responsibility to contribute to the conversation, to keep it going in interesting ways.

So thanks, Abraham, for participating with me in that most Jewish practice, the practice of arguing! But not just any argument. To make it an authentically Jewish practice, it should be what the tradition calls a *mahloket le-shem shamayim,* an "argument for the sake of Heaven," an argument about the things that really matter. Which is really what we've been talking about all along: what really matters in Jewish education.

Bibliography

Cohen, Steven M., and Shaul Kelner. "Why Jewish Parents Send Their Children to Day Schools." In *Family Matters: Jewish Education in an Age of Choice*, edited by Jack Wertheimer, 80–100. Waltham, MA: Brandeis University Press, 2007.

Dewey, John. *Experience and Education*. New York: Kappa Delta Pi, 1938.

Frank, Naava. "A Judaic Curriculum for Jewish Day Schools: The Time is NOW." *Contact: The Journal of the Jewish Life Network* 4, no. 2 (2002), 12–13.

Pope, Denise C. *Doing School: How We Are Creating a Generation of Stressed-Out, Materialistic, and Miseducated Students*. New Haven, CT: Yale University Press, 2003.

Shulman, Lee S. "Those Who Understand: Knowledge Growth in Teaching." *Educational Researcher* 15, no. 2 (1986), 4–14.

Wineburg, Sam. "Online Faculty Seminar Conversations On: A Conversation with Sam Wineburg." Virtual Knowledge Project, 2001. Accessed November 7, 2008. http://crossroads.georgetown.edu/vkp/conversations/2001webcast/interview.html.

Index

A
Absolutism 140, 143, 157
Abstract knowledge 61
Academic motivation 196
Accountability 85
Accountable Talk 84, 86, 88, 90, 112
Action orientation 195
Adapted Primary Literature (APL) texts 109
African American book clubs 81
Aliba de-hilkheta 101
American Education Research Association 85
American Historical Association (AHA) 157
Antiochus 152, 154
Aristotle 148, 184
Assertiveness 192, 195
Association for Supervision and Curriculum Development 184

B
Bar/bat mitzvah 77, 188
Barron, Brigid 62
Barton, Angela Calabrese 35
Beis Medrash 99
Beit Hamidrash 99
The Bible Unearthed 177
Blended learning 163
Blondheim, Menahem 102–103
Blum-Kulka, Shoshana 103
Borderland spaces 38
Bowlby, John 191
Brown, John Seely 61
Buber, Martin 185
Burbules, Nicholas 135

C
Calkins, Lucy 87
Callan, Eamonn 135
Cannady, Matthew A. 20n9
Cazden, Courtney 101
Chakrabarty, Dipesh 156
Chazan, Robert 152–154, 157
Choice 17, 22, 24, 39, 41
Class Experiment 41
Clegg, Tamara, L. 42, 43
Clover Model 190, 191, 193–196, 201
Cobb, Paul 166
Cognition, cultural process 66
Cognitive apprentices 61
Cohen, Jonathan 200
Cohen, Steven 11, 12, 23
Cohn-Eskenazi, Tamara 79
Collateral learning 212, 216
Collins, Allan 61
Comer, James 213
Communities of Practice (CoPs) 29, 34, 120
Competency beliefs 16, 19
Concerning the Jews 154
Congregation 60, 63, 77–79, 82, 89, 187
Congregational prayer 60
Conservative movement 76, 78, 83, 101
Core identities 34, 37, 43, 46, 47
Critical thinking 193, 209
Cultural conservatism 111
Curriculum 39, 40, 54, 75, 79, 152, 160, 184, 186

D
Daf Yomi curriculum 79
Davidson, Richard 141
Decision-making 30, 32, 60, 80, 87, 208, 215
Deliberation 140–142
Democratic citizenship 140
Derrida, Jacques 149
Developmental Domain Theory 189–194
    action 191–192
    assertion 192
    belonging 192
    reflection 192–194
Developmental psychology 169
Dewey, John 212

Dialectic-critical approach 111
Dialogic education 86–89
Dialogic forms of teaching 84
Dialogic learning 86
Dialogism 111, 112
Dispositions 13–15, 17, 18, 25, 30, 46
    development 29–49
Distributed intelligence 65
Dorff, Elliot 79
Dorph, Rena 20n9
Duguid, Paul 61
D'var Torah 77
Dynamics of learning 68

E
Educational frameworks 134
Educational goals 179
Educational philosophy 55
Education, changing face 82–86
Eisen, Arnold 79
Emotional control 195
Emotions 135
Empathy 195
An Empire of their Own 82
Enculturation 61
Epistemic switching 6, 175, 176
Erikson, Erik 33, 191
Eschatology 156
Ethical teachings 80–81
Etz Hayim: Torah and Commentary 76
Evangelical school 140
Evidence-based reasoning 160
Experiential learning 57, 119

F
Fascination 16, 17, 19, 21
Feiman-Nemser, Sharon 2
Finkelstein, Israel 160, 177
Florence Melton Adult Jewish Mini-School program 79
Foer, Jonathan Safran 162
Foucault, Michel 149
Fox, Seymour 186
Friday evening services 116–117

G
Gabler, Neal 82
Galston, William 110
Gee, James Paul 34, 37
Geschmack 107, 108
Girl Scouts 55, 62
Goffman, Erving 99

Goldman, Ronald 169, 170
Gordis, Daniel 79
Gottlieb, David 178
Graffiti-writers 138
Grammar of schooling 54
Grant, Lisa 74
Greenberg, Moshe 186
Gregory, Brad 157, 158

H
Habura 99, 107
Haggadah 148, 150, 162
Halakhah 31, 101
Haredi Jews 4, 5, 97, 99, 101–103, 105, 107
Harlan, David 162
Harut 100
Hashgacha peratit 159
Havdalah ceremony 117, 121
Havruta learning 86, 87, 97–112
    central practice in yeshivas 98–101
    dyads 99
    research 101–105
Havurah 63
HaYidion 152
Hebrew Bible 74, 177
Hebrew language skills 186
Herut 100
Hevrutah learning 189
Holistic goals 183–201
Holistic Student Assessment (HSA) 194–195
    case example 196–198
    subscales 195–196
Holocaust education 5, 133–143
Holzer, Elie 101, 102
Horowitz, Shira 87
Hutchins, Edwin 65, 66

I
Ibn Gabirol 80
Identity development 29–49, *see also* Jewish identity
    Kitchen Science Investigators 38–42
    Science identity 46
Identity refinement 33
Identity, role of 14
Information-delivery model 83
Information transmission 4
Intellectual engagement 154
International Handbook on Jewish Education 55
Interpretive thinking 19, 21
Israel education 1, 2

J

Jaffe, Rabbi David 189, 200
Jefferson, Thomas 161
Jewish book clubs 81, 82, 88
Jewish community 73–90
Jewish day school 3, 152, 165, 179, 186, 214
Jewish-developmental outcomes 205–219
Jewish diaspora 73, 74, 82
Jewish dispositions 46–49
Jewish family life 73–90
Jewish identity 31, 37, 46–49, 207
Jewish-Israeli communities 173
Jewish learning
    activation 11, 13, 18, 19
    analog 17–23
    implications for designing 23–25
    implications for evaluating 25–26
    implications for research 26–27
Jewish social organization 53
Jewish summer camp 5, 25, 46, 53, 56, 62, 67, 89, 116, 117, 129, 188
Jewish text 24, 186, 194
    digitization 63
    interpretation 24, 176
    reading 176, 177
    study 73–90, 173
    teaching 54, 134, 176
Johnson, Lyndon 149–150
Judaic skills 123

K

Kent, Orit 86, 101, 102
King, Martin Luther 149
Kitchen Science Investigators (KSI) 29, 38–42
Kollels 101

L

Lave, Jean 5, 53, 61, 65, 120
Learners
    autonomy and independence 24, 98, 104, 105, 107 111
Learning
    activation 20
    critical history 147–162
    ecologies 62–63
    environment 24
    environments and activities, designing implications 36–38
    expertise 24, 36, 47, 59–60
    interest 24, 36, 40, 196
    learning by wholes 117–120
    outcomes 1–6, 13, 23, 26, 49, 133, 201, 205–219
    process 14, 59, 103
    sciences 3, 29–49, 97–112
    technologies 63–64
Learning by Design (LBD) approach 29–32, 39–41
LeCourt, Donna 166
Legitimate Peripheral Participation (LPP) 5, 34, 120, 121
Lernen 5
Levi, Primo 136
Liberal education 98, 108–112
Lipman, Matthew 85
Literary theory 77
Lithuanian Yeshivas 98
Longitudinal studies 26, 190
Luzzatto, Chaim 80

M

Maimonides 168, 213
McCune, Gardner 42
McKenzie, Robert Tracy 161, 162
Me'ah program 79
Messy lives 137
Metahistory 149
Metaphysical neutralism 157, 158–159
Michaels, Sarah 112
Microaggression 138
Middot 162, 188, 200
Miller, Dianne 38
Minyanim 78
Mir Yeshiva 103
Moral judgment 136, 161, 162
Moral outrage 135, 136, 161
Moral reflection 162
Morinis, Alan 81
Moses 147, 149, 162, 177
Motivation for learning 105–108
Mussar movement 80, 81, 188, 189
Myers, David N. 155
My Promised Land 161

N

Nasir, Na'ilah Suad 35
National Jewish Book Club 88
National-Religious yeshiva 103
A Nation at Risk (1983) 84
Nisan, Mordecai 105, 109
No Child Left Behind 184
Noddings, Nel 141

O

Obedience 100
O'Connor, Catherine 112
Online learning 1, 63, 88
Optimal Jewish experience 124
Optimism 134, 196
Orsi, Robert 158

P

Parker, Walter 140
Pea, Roy 65
Pedagogical Content Knowledge 208
Pentateuch, *see* Torah
A People's History of the United States 161
Perkins, David 5, 117–125, 127, 129, 130
Pharaoh 147, 149
Philosophy for Children 85
Piaget, Jean 54, 148, 169, 191
Plaut, Gunther 79
Pluralism 110–112
Polman, Joseph 36, 38
Pope, Denise Clark 218
Positive feedback loop 16
Prayer 21, 60, 90, 106, 110, 127, 154, 188
Pre-interview coaching 171–172
Presentism 136
Progressive pedagogies 108, 111
Project-Based Inquiry Science (PBIS) 41
Project-based learning 42
Protestantism 169
Psychological development 153

R

Ramah camp in Wisconsin
 theater education 124–126, 126–127
Rashi 102
Rationality 135
Reasonableness 135, 136, 140, 143
Reasoned argumentation 83
Recitation 82–86
Reflection 192–194
Reform movement 46, 73–75, 78, 79, 83, 123
"Reinventing Jewish Education for the 21st Century" 57
Religious education 83, 165
Religious epistemology 172
Religious identities 134
Resnick, Lauren 112
Rogoff, Barbara 61
Rosenak, Michael 185, 218

S

Salanter, Israel 80
Sales, Amy 121
Sarason, Seymour 213
Saxe, Leonard 117, 121
Schindler, Oskar 150
School bonding 196
School ethnographies 62
Schorsch, Ismar 76
Schwarz, Baruch 86
Science education programs 4
Science identity 46
Science learning 24
 activation 4, 11, 13–17, 17n7, 19, 20, 24
 analogy of Jewish learning 13–14
 case of activation 14–17
 desired long-term impact 14
 experiences 15
 goals 16
 identity, role of 14
 learning outcomes 14
 learning process 14
Science Learning Activation Lab 14, 15n4
Science, technology, engineering, and mathematics (STEM) 14, 27
Scientific sensemaking 16
Sefer Hamitzvot 168
Segal, Aliza 103
Self-actualization 106, 108
Sense of the worthy 98, 106, 107, 110, 111
Shabbat 5, 64, 116–130, 207, 214
 at camp as whole game 120–121
 interesting and challenging 127–129
 music and dance 128
 theatre and movement 128–129
Shalif, Yishai 105, 109
Shavit, Ari 161
Shema 185
Shiur 99
Shlihei tzibbur 60
Shulman, Lee 186, 208
Silberman, Neil Asher 160
Situated learning 4, 23, 61
Situational identities 31, 46, 47
Slobodka *kollel* 103
Social affordances 24
Socialization model 118, 121
Social justice 31, 161
Social learning 66–68
Sociocultural learning theory 53
Soloff, David 124
Spinoza, Baruch 151, 168

Spiritual history 154, 157
Spiritual stance 19–21
Spiritual truths 150–151
State of Israel 60, 156
Stein, David 79
Stone, Ira F. 81
Storahtelling 125
Subject-specific learning 205–219
Supplementary education 1, 56, 127

T
Taglit-birthright 67, 210, 212
Talmud 78–80, 97–101, 107, 167, 177, 206–208, 211, 213–215, 218
Tan, Edna 32n3
Teacher education 2
    programs 101
Tedmon, Susan 108n10
Ten Commandments 74, 177
Teutsch, David 80, 90
Tikkun ha-middot 162
Tikkun leil Shavuot/Shavuot eve study 78
Tikkun olam 187, 188
Torah 74–80, 82, 87, 90, 100, 105–108, 111, 123, 129, 150, 151, 186, 187, 213
    Deuteronomy 185
    Exodus 148, 150, 152, 175–177
    Genesis 187
The Torah: A Modern Commentary 79
Transition to pedagogical thinking 2
Twain, Mark 154–156, 159
Tzedakah 188

U
Ultra-orthodox school 139
Union for Reform Judaism (URJ) 123, 128

V
Visions of Jewish Education 185

Von Ranke, Leopold 149
Vygotsky, L. S. 36, 54, 83, 166

W
Wenger, Etienne 5, 34, 37, 65, 120
Wenger's cycle 34
Western psychological theories of motivation 108
What We Know About Jewish Education 55
White, Hayden 149
White, Richard 157
Whole child assessment, Jewish education 198–200
Whole child education (WCE) 184, 188
    assessment for fostering 194
Whole Child Jewish education 185–187
    opportunities for 187–189
Whole games 119
    junior versions of 121–124
Wilson, Woodrow 161
Wineburg, Sam 6, 136, 208, 209
Wissenschaft des Judentums 151
Wolpe, Rabbi David 150–152, 160
Woocher, Jonathan 57, 58
Wortham, Stanton 166
Wright, Travis 137

Y
Yerushalmi, Yosef Hayim 151, 152
Yeshivas 4, 5, 86, 97–101, 104, 139
    bochers 141, 174
    motivation for learning 105–108
Yom Kippur 207

Z
Zinn, Howard 161
Zone of Proximal Identity Development (ZPID) 36
Zone of Proximal Imagination (ZPI) 38

www.ingramcontent.com/pod-product-compliance
Lightning Source LLC
Chambersburg PA
CBHW051116230426
43667CB00014B/2602